366 readings from
ISLAM

Also in the Global Spirit Library

366 readings from Buddhism

366 readings from Christianity

366 readings from Taoism and Confucianism

366 readings from Hinduism

366 readings from Judaism

THE GLOBAL SPIRIT LIBRARY

366 readings from
ISLAM

edited by

ROBERT VAN DE WEYER

THE PILGRIM PRESS
CLEVELAND, OHIO

ARTHUR JAMES
NEW ALRESFORD, UK

First published in USA and Canada by
The Pilgrim Press,
700 Prospect Avenue East, Cleveland, Ohio 44115

First published in English outside North America by
Arthur James Ltd,
46a West Street, New Alresford, UK, SO24 9AU

05 04 03 02 01 00 5 4 3 2 1

North America ISBN 0-8298-1386-1
English language outside North America ISBN 0 85305 452 5

Typeset in Monotype Joanna by
Strathmore Publishing Services, London N7

Printed by
Tien Wah Press, Singapore

CONTENTS

SERIES INTRODUCTION

The Global Spirit Library is the first comprehensive collection of the spiritual literature of the world, presented in accessible form. It is aimed at people who belong to a particular religious community, and wish to broaden their spiritual outlook; and at the much larger group, perhaps the majority of people in the world today, who have little or no attachment to a religious community, but seek spiritual wisdom. Each book contains the major writings of one of the world's spiritual traditions.

Much of the world's spiritual literature was designed to be read or heard in small portions, allowing ample time for personal reflection. Following this custom, the books in *The Global Spirit Library* each consist of an annual cycle of daily readings. Two or more books may be read in parallel at different times of the day; or an entire book may be read straight through. Again following a time-honoured practice, many of the original texts have been condensed.

Spiritual traditions differ from one another in their theological formulations; and the history of humankind is blighted by rivalry between different religious communities. Yet theology is no more than human speculation about truths that are beyond the grasp of the human mind. The writings in these books amply demonstrate that, as men and women actually experience these truths within themselves and others, divisions and rivalries fade, and unity is found. May the third millennium be an era of spiritual unity across the globe.

INTRODUCTION

Islam means 'submission to God'. A Muslim is someone who has submitted to God, recognizing Muhammad as a prophet of God.

In the year 610 CE, on a mountain outside the prosperous Arabian city of Mecca, a few simple words came into Muhammad's mind; this was the first of many messages which Muhammad interpreted as divine revelations. He dictated the messages to scribes, and together the messages form the Quran. Muhammad saw himself as one of numerous messengers, sent by God to every nation in every age; and in his lifetime he sought to convey the Quran to the tribes of the Arabian peninsula. After his death his followers carried it beyond their tribal borders, forming a great empire, and ultimately a global spiritual community.

THE LIFE OF MUHAMMAD

About a century after the death of Muhammad, a historian called Ibn Ishaq collected oral and written accounts of Muhammad's life, and arranged them in chronological order. He appears to have done little editing, so frequently he gives several different accounts of the same incident. This allowed him to be remarkably honest, so he includes not only Muhammad's successes, but also his failures, describing moments of stress and despair.

Although many collections of Muhammad's sayings were made, Ibn Ishaq's great tome is the primary record of his life as a whole, and is the basis of all subsequent biographies.

The Quraysh tribe

Prior to the birth of Muhammad the people of the Quraysh had stopped worshipping God, and had taken to worshipping stones. This began when the population of Mecca grew so large, that the people began to settle in the countryside outside the city. Each man who left the city took a stone from the Grand Mosque, and placed it in the middle of his new settlement. People then walked around these stones, as they had originally walked around the Kaba. And soon they began to regard the stones themselves as divine, especially those which had strange and unusual shapes. Thus they prayed to the stones, as their forefathers had prayed to God.

As the generations passed, the Quraysh people almost entirely forgot the ancient faith of Abraham, which had been passed to them through Ishmael. Instead they put their faith in idols. Yet they retained some of the old practices, such as making pilgrimages to the Kaba at particular times of the year.

51, 52

The birth of Muhammad

When Amina, Muhammad's mother, became pregnant with him, a voice said to her: 'You are pregnant with the future leader of his people. After he is born, many people will envy him and wish him evil. But God will protect him. You should call him Muhammad.' And a light shone from her womb, by which she could see the great castles from which the world was ruled.

Abdullah, Muhammad's father, died while Amina was pregnant.

Muhammad was born in the year of the elephant. Amina sent a message to Muhammad's paternal grandfather to inform him of the birth, inviting him to come and look at the baby. When the grandfather arrived, Amina told him of the voice she had heard while she was pregnant. The grandfather took the baby to the Kaba, the shrine in the centre of Mecca, and gave thanks to God for this gift.

Then he carried the baby back to Amina, and set about finding a foster-mother to suckle him.

102, 103

Grandfather's prophecy

Muhammad lived with his mother and grandfather. God cared for him, so the child was strong and sturdy, like a thriving plant. He was admired by all who saw him. When Muhammad was aged six, his mother Amina died.

His grandfather's sons, Muhammad's uncles, made a bed which they placed in the shade of the Kaba. There the grandfather used to sit or lie during the day, and the uncles used to sit round him. None of the uncles ever sat on the bed itself, out of respect for the grandfather. On one occasion, while still a small boy, Muhammad came to the bed and jumped onto it. His uncles tried to drive him away. But his grandfather said: 'Leave the boy alone, because by God's power he has a great future.' From then onwards his grandfather encouraged Muhammad to sit beside him on the bed; and the old man used to stroke the boy's back with his hand.

When Muhammad was aged eight, his grandfather died. Their family had the honour of providing water to pilgrims coming to the Kaba. Before he died, the old man put his youngest son in charge of this. And he put Muhammad in the care of another of his sons, Abu Talib, since he and Muhammad's father were sons of the same mother. Thus Muhammad became a member of his uncle's family.

107, 108, 114, 115

Khadija's caravan

The people of the Quraysh tribe, who dominated Mecca, were skilled in commerce. Khadija was a widow whose dignity and commercial acumen had earned her great respect. She used to hire men to carry merchandise to distant cities.

As a young man Muhammad gained a reputation for honesty, reliability and fidelity. Khadija heard people speak of him, and she invited him to come and see her. She proposed that he should take her goods to Jerusalem, and trade them there for other goods; and she would give him a higher share of the profit than normal. Muhammad accepted her proposal. She provided him with a young lad, Maysara, to assist him; and the two set off for Jerusalem.

One day during the journey Muhammad stopped in the shade of a tree, near the cell of a Christian monk. The monk came out, and asked Maysara who his master was. Maysara told him, and the monk exclaimed: 'No one except a messenger from God has ever sat beneath this tree.'

Muhammad sold the goods he had bought, and purchased other goods to take back to Mecca. One day at noon on the return journey, when the heat was intense, Maysara saw two angels shading the apostle from the rays of the sun.

When they reached Mecca, Muhammad delivered the goods he had purchased to Khadija; and she sold them at about double the value of the goods she had entrusted to Muhammad.

119, 120

Marriage to Khadija

Maysara reported to Khadija the monk's words, and described to her the angels he had seen. Khadija, who was a determined and intelligent woman, went to Muhammad, and asked him to marry her. Muhammad told his uncle Abu Talib of Khadija's proposal, and Abu Talib arranged the wedding.

After the wedding Khadija went to her cousin, a Christian who was a scholar and had studied the Scriptures deeply, and told him what Maysara had reported to her. 'If this is true,' the cousin replied, 'then truly Muhammad is a messenger of God to his people. I knew that such a messenger would come in the near future – and now he has arrived.' Indeed, the

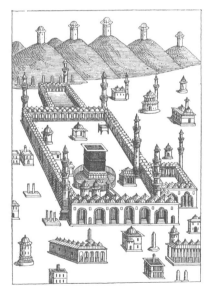

cousin confessed that he had become weary of waiting for God's messenger, and was greatly relieved.

Khadija bore Muhammad three sons, all of whom died in infancy, and four daughters.

121

Rebuilding the Kaba

The Quraysh decided to rebuild the Kaba. Each of the clans belonging to the Quraysh tribe set about gathering stones, and constructing the walls. Eventually the walls were complete, except for the sacred black stone to be placed at the top.

The clans now began to argue amongst themselves, as each clan wanted the honour of lifting the black stone into place. The clans formed alliances, until there were two sides; and they prepared for battle. One clan brought a bowl of blood; and its leaders, along with the leaders of its allied clans, thrust their hands into the blood, pledging to fight to the death. Preparations for battle continued for four days and four nights.

Then the oldest man of the Quraysh summoned the leaders of the clans together, to seek a resolution. He proposed that the first man to enter the Grand Mosque, in which the Kaba stood, should be asked to act as judge in the dispute. At that moment Muhammad entered. All the leaders acknowledged Muhammad as a man of integrity, and agreed to accept his judgement. And Muhammad agreed to be judge.

He asked them to bring a large cloak, and to lay it on the ground. Then he placed the black stone in the middle. He ordered the leaders of all the clans to hold the edge of the cloak. At a signal from Muhammad they lifted up the cloak, with the black stone inside, and laid the stone on the top of the Kaba.

From then onwards the Quraysh people called Muhammad 'the trusted one'.

Accepting God's call

When Muhammad reached the age of forty, God in his compassion appointed him as a messenger to all humanity.

God had made a covenant with all the messengers he had sent before, requiring that they should trust him, testify to his truth, stand up against his enemies, and transmit his message to all who would believe in it. And the previous messengers had fulfilled these duties.

God now said to Muhammad: 'I gave my past messengers many wise words to convey to the people; and these words were written down to guide future generations. Each of these messengers knew that I would send a further messenger to confirm the message I had given them. I want you to be this further messenger. Do you accept this? Will you take up this burden?'

Muhammad answered: 'I accept.'

150

On Mount Hira

Muhammad began to love solitude; he enjoyed nothing better than being alone. He frequently walked out of Mecca to remote hills and valleys, where no one lived. Every stone and tree that he passed seemed to say to him: 'Peace to you, messenger of God.'

At the start of the month of Ramadan he went up Mount Hira; and the angel Gabriel came to visit him there, to give him God's message. Gabriel first arrived at night when Muhammad was asleep. He carried a beautiful brocade, on which some words were written. Gabriel said: 'Read.' 'What shall I read?' Muhammad asked. Gabriel then grasped Muhammad's throat so tightly that he thought he would die. Gabriel let him go, and again said: 'Read.' And again Muhammad asked: 'What shall I read?' Gabriel grasped his throat a second time, and a third time, each time saying to him: 'Read.' And each time Muhammad asked: 'What shall I read?' Muhammad became extremely frightened, fearing that Gabriel would kill him.

Finally Gabriel said: 'Read in the name of your Lord, who created human beings from clots of blood. The Lord is full of compassion. He will give words that are to be written down. These will teach truths which many people have forgotten.' At this Gabriel departed.

151, 152

Gabriel's visit

Muhammad awoke, and felt as though Gabriel's words were written on his heart.

But then he began to reflect on what had occurred. To him none of God's creatures was more hateful than a man possessed by a spirit, or a poet who babbled in a state of ecstasy; he could not bear even to look at such people. He realized that, if he told the Quraysh people in Mecca of his experience, they would regard him as possessed. So he decided to go to the top of the mountain, and throw himself off; he was convinced that only in death would he find peace.

He clambered up towards the summit. When he was halfway there, he heard a voice from the sky saying: 'Muhammad, you are the messenger from God, and I am Gabriel.' He raised his head, and saw Gabriel in the form of a man, with his feet astride the horizon. Again Gabriel said: 'Muhammad, you are the messenger of God, and I am Gabriel.' Muhammad stood gazing at him, moving neither forwards nor backwards. Then after a while he turned his head to look around him. Whichever way he turned, he saw Gabriel standing on the horizon.

Muhammad remained on the mountain for the entire month of Ramadan. During that time he saw no other person. At the end of the month he walked back to Mecca. He went first to the Kaba, walking round it seven times as God had commanded. Then he returned home.

Receiving God's revelations

During the month in which he stayed on the mountain, Muhammad began to receive God's revelations. Muhammad trusted God completely, and accepted without question the truth of what he heard. He knew that in conveying God's revelations to others, he would encounter varying reactions. Some would listen eagerly and treat him well, while others would be angry and hostile. Thus he was aware that God was laying a heavy and troublesome burden upon him. Yet he accepted it willingly, believing that God would give him the courage and determination to face every kind of opposition.

While he had been on the mountain, his wife Khadija had sent her servants in search of him. When he returned home, he sat beside her, drawing her close to him, and recounted what had occurred. She trusted him completely, accepting the truth of the message he had bought from God. And she committed herself to support his work. She was thus the first person to believe in Muhammad as God's messenger.

Through Khadija's support God greatly lightened the burden on Muhammad. Whenever people contradicted him and accused him of falsehood, Khadija encouraged him. And when their opposition made him sad and miserable, she comforted him. She constantly reminded him that those who rejected God's message were mean and small-minded.

155

Month of Ramadan

Every year Muhammad spent the month of Ramadan in seclusion, praying to God and receiving his revelations.

One year the revelations stopped, causing Muhammad to become anxious and distressed. Then Gabriel came to assure him that God had not abandoned him. Gabriel continued: 'Having once loved you, God will never turn against you. On the contrary, God will draw you closer to himself, so the future will be better than the past. You will enjoy great triumph in this world, and even greater triumph in the next. When you return to God, he will bestow honour on you far surpassing anything this world can give.'

Then Gabriel asked Muhammad: 'When you were an orphan, did not God give you shelter? When you were going astray, did he not lead you back to righteousness? When you were poor, did he not make you rich?'

Finally Gabriel gave Muhammad these instructions: 'Do not become proud of your position. Do not become harsh towards those weaker than yourself. And always speak of God's kindness to you.' Muhammad obeyed these instructions diligently throughout his life.

156, 157

Gabriel's teaching on prayer

Gabriel came and spent two days and nights with Muhammad on the mountain, demonstrating how to pray.

Gabriel began by performing the ritual ablution, to show how people should purify themselves for prayer. Muhammad watched, and did the same. Gabriel then taught the words, and when they should be said; Muhammad repeated the words, phrase by phrase. On the first day at noon, just as the sun was starting to decline, Gabriel offered the noon prayer. When his shadow equalled his own height, he offered the evening prayer. When the sun started to set, he offered the sunset prayer. When the twilight had disappeared, he offered the night prayer. And as the dawn rose, he offered the morning prayer.

On the second day he offered the noon prayer when his shadow equalled his height. He offered the evening prayer when his shadow equalled the height of both of them. He offered the sunset prayer just after the sun had disappeared. He offered the night prayer when a third of the night had passed. And he offered the morning prayer when the sun was visible, but not yet shining.

Then Gabriel said to Muhammad: 'Prayers should be said between the times I offered them on the first day, and the times I offered them on the second day.'

Ali's conversion

After Muhammad had been called by God, he used to invite his young cousin Ali into the countryside near Mecca in order to pray. Ali greatly enjoyed praying with Muhammad, and joined him regularly. The two of them would leave home in the morning before dawn, and return home after nightfall, so they could offer all the prayers prescribed by Gabriel.

One day Abu Talib came across them while they were praying. He asked Muhammad what religion they were practising. 'Uncle,' Muhammad replied, 'this is the religion of God and his angels; it is the religion of Abraham and all God's messengers.' Then Muhammad added: 'God has now sent me as his messenger. And you, of all people, deserve to learn the truth from me, and thus receive God's guidance.' Abu Talib said: 'I cannot give up the religion which was handed down to me by my forefathers. But I pray to God that as long as you live, you will not suffer for your faith.'

Abu Talib then turned to Ali, and asked: 'My boy, do you share your cousin's religion?' Ali replied: 'I believe in God, and in Muhammad as God's messenger. I know that Muhammad's words are true. So I pray to God with him, and follow him.' Abu Talib said: 'Muhammad would not ask you to do anything which was not good; so stick with him.' Ali was thus the first male follower of Muhammad.

159, 160

Abu Bakr's conversion

The second male to accept Muhammad as God's messenger, and surrender himself to God, was Zayd, a former slave who had won his freedom.

The third male was Abu Bakr. When he accepted Muhammad as God's messenger, he declared his faith openly, urging others to share it. He was a very popular man, whose courtesy and charm had won him many friends. He was also more knowledgeable about the history of the Quraysh than anyone else: he had studied the genealogy of its clans, and he understood both the tribe's faults and its merits. He was himself a successful and prosperous merchant, renowned for his honesty and generosity. Many people came to seek his advice on both commercial and personal matters, and were invariably satisfied with the insights he offered. After his conversion he always spoke about God to those who visited him, imploring them to surrender themselves to the divine will; and he invited them to meet Muhammad.

Within a short time eight people had accepted Abu Bakr's invitation. All of them, when they had listened to Muhammad, were convinced that he was indeed God's messenger; and Muhammad taught them how to pray. In the following weeks and months Abu Bakr brought many more people to Muhammad, so that soon Muhammad had a substantial body of followers.

160, 161, 162

Silence and bloodshed

As more and more people, both men and women, submitted to God, embracing the religion of Islam, its fame spread throughout Mecca, and it became the main topic of conversation. Initially Muhammad did not speak about Islam publicly, merely talking to those who came to see him. But after three years God commanded him to convey openly the revelations he had received. In particular God ordered Muhammad to preach to those who prayed to idols, warning them in plain language of the dire consequences of such worship.

Muhammad was at first frightened of obeying God's command. So he continued to practise his religion privately, and told his followers to do the same. They never prayed in public places; and from time to time Muhammad led his followers into the countryside around Mecca, where they could worship God in secret.

But on one occasion a group of idol-worshippers came across Muhammad and his followers in a remote valley. The idol-worshippers heard their prayers and were incensed. They shouted out to Muhammad and his followers, ordering them to stop. Muhammad refused, and the idol-worshippers attacked them. One of Muhammad's followers struck an idol-worshipper with the jawbone of a camel, and wounded him. This was the first blood to be shed in the cause of Islam.

Starting to preach

Muhammad now felt compelled to speak openly about the divine revelations he had received. At first people were friendly, listening attentively to what he said; and some were quickly convinced by him. But when he disparaged their ancient gods, most took grave offence; they resolved to regard Muhammad as an enemy, and to treat his followers with contempt. Muhammad was distressed at their reaction, but refused to be deterred from obeying God's command. And Abu Talib, Muhammad's uncle, tried to protect him.

The opponents of Muhammad included most of the leaders of the Quraysh. When they heard that Muhammad continued to insult their gods, they went to Abu Talib, and said: 'Your nephew scoffs at our religion, mocks our way of life, and accuses our forefathers of error. You yourself do not agree with his teaching. So either you must persuade him to desist, or you must allow us to get rid of him.' Abu Talib gave a conciliatory reply, indicating that he would seek a peaceful solution. So they went away.

But Muhammad would not stop preaching. As a result the Quraysh leaders grew steadily more hostile. They spoke about him obsessively, stirring up hatred towards him in each other's breast.

167, 168

Abu Talib's dilemma

The leaders of the Quraysh went to Abu Talib to complain about Muhammad a second time. They said: 'You have a high and respected position amongst us. We asked you to put a stop to your nephew's activities, and you have not done so. We cannot allow our forefathers to be reviled, our customs mocked, and our gods insulted. Until you silence him, we will fight both of you.' With these harsh words they left. Abu Talib was deeply distressed at this breach with his own people, grieving that he too had now incurred their wrath. But he felt unable to betray his nephew.

Abu Talib sent for Muhammad, and told him what the Quraysh leaders had said. He concluded: 'Spare both me and yourself; do not put on me a burden too great for me to bear.' Muhammad was anxious about losing his uncle's help and encouragement, on which he depended. Nonetheless he replied: 'Uncle, if they were to put the sun in my right hand and the moon in my left, I should not give up my task. I shall continue until God has brought me victory, or until I die.'

Muhammad now burst into tears. He got up, and started to leave. His uncle called him back, and said: 'You must preach as you feel guided; I shall never under any circumstances abandon you.'

The start of persecution

The Quraysh leaders now took a young man called Umara to see Abu Talib. The leaders said: 'This is the strongest and most handsome young man in the whole Quraysh tribe. We propose that you adopt him as your son, and thus have the benefit of his intelligence and hard work. In return you must give us your nephew, who opposes the religion of our forefathers, who is destroying the unity of our people, and who mocks our way of life. When you have handed him to us, we shall kill him. Thus the exchange will be a man for a man.'

Abu Talib answered: 'This is an evil proposal that you put to me. Is it really right that you give me your favourite son, for me to feed; and that I give you my brother's son, for you to kill? By God, I will never let this happen.'

One of the Quraysh leaders said: 'We have treated you fairly, and we have been at pains to reach an amicable arrangement with you. Yet you seem completely stubborn.' Abu Talib replied: 'You have not treated me fairly at all. You intend to betray me, and you will strive to turn the common people against me. Do what you like!' At this the quarrel became heated, with many angry words being spoken.

The Quraysh leaders now urged the people to attack Muhammad's followers. By this time there were Muslims in every clan. In some clans they became the objects of vicious insults; in other clans they were physically attacked. But the clan to which Abu Talib belonged continued to treat him and all Muslims with kindness.

169, 170

A single opinion

Shortly before the annual fair was due to be held, one of the Quraysh leaders gathered together all those people who would be organizing the fair. When they had sat down, he spoke to them: 'People from far and wide will be coming to this fair. Many of them will have heard of Muhammad, and will ask you about him. You must agree on a single opinion, so you will not contradict each other.' The organizers replied: 'Tell us your opinion about him.' 'No,' the leader replied; 'you speak, and I shall listen.'

The organizers said: 'He is possessed.' The leader replied: 'No, he is not possessed. He does not have the jerky movements and hoarse voice of someone possessed.' They said: 'He is an ecstatic poet.' He replied: 'No, he does not speak in metre and rhyme.' They said: 'He is a sorcerer.' He replied: 'No, he does not blow and spit like a sorcerer.' They asked: 'Then what are we to say?'

The leader replied: 'His speech is as sweet as the sweetest fruit; and his thoughts have roots that go deep into the soil of wisdom. Thus your statements about him are manifestly false, and would be rejected. Yet we oppose him because his message separates sons from fathers, brothers from brothers, husbands from wives, friends from friends.'

The organizers dispersed, and prepared to greet all the people coming to the fair. They spoke to the people about Muhammad just as the Quraysh leader had instructed.

171, 172

Confronting the Quraysh leaders

When the Quraysh leaders held their regular meetings in the Grand Mosque, they frequently found themselves discussing Muhammad. They cursed him for the success he was enjoying in winning converts.

During one meeting Muhammad himself appeared. He kissed the black stone, and then started to walk round the Kaba. Each time he passed them, he heard insulting words about himself. Finally he stopped, and said to them: 'Will you listen to me? By him who holds my life in his hand, I warn you of eternal torment.' The Quraysh leaders trembled with fear at these words, and remained silent. Then the one who had been most vigorous in his insults broke the silence: 'We know that you do not wish us ill, but want to save us. Yet I ask you to leave us.'

Muhammad left the Grand Mosque. By the following day the Quraysh leaders felt ashamed that Muhammad's words had struck such fear into their hearts; and they were determined to strike fear into his heart. So when they encountered Muhammad, they formed a circle around him, and asked him: 'Do you speak openly against our gods and our religion?' 'Yes, I do,' Muhammad replied. At this one of the Quraysh leaders leapt forward, seized Muhammad; and was about to kill him.

Abu Bakr, who had been watching this encounter, ran forward, and put himself between Muhammad and his attacker. He shouted out: 'Would you kill a man for saying that God is the Lord?' The Quraysh leaders slunk away.

Hamza's conversion

One of the Quraysh leaders, Abu Jahl, had a particular hatred for Muhammad. One day when he saw Muhammad pass, he shouted insults at him. Muhammad remained silent, and continued his journey. Eventually, when Muhammad was out of earshot, Abu Jahl proceeded to the Grand Mosque for a meeting with the other leaders.

A woman had watched this incident from her window. When both men had left, she rushed out into the countryside, in the hope of meeting a man called Hamza as he returned from a hunting trip. Hamza was the strongest man in the whole Quraysh tribe; he also loved justice, and was devoutly religious. After a hunting trip his habit was to go first to the Grand Mosque and walk round it, and then return home.

When the woman told Hamza what Abu Jahl had said and done, and how Muhammad had remained silent, Hamza was outraged. He ran towards the Mosque as fast as his legs would move, not stopping to greet anyone, with the intention of punishing Abu Jahl. When he arrived at the Mosque, he saw Abu Jahl in the middle of the group of leaders, and strode up to him. Hamza was much taller than Abu Jahl, so he found himself looking down on the trembling figure of his enemy.

Hamza boomed out: 'Your religion, which makes you behave in such a way, is useless. So today I commit myself to the religion Muhammad teaches. Will you insult me, as you insulted him? Will you hit me back, if I hit you?' Hamza struck Abu Jahl with all his strength, and then strode away.

An attempt at bribery

Soon after Hamza surrendered himself to God, Muhammad went into the Grand Mosque in order to meditate in silence. A short time later the Quraysh leaders entered the Mosque, and sat down some distance from Muhammad.

Then Utba, one of the leaders, walked over to Muhammad, and said to him: 'Muhammad, if you want money, we shall gather enough property to make you the richest man in the tribe. If you want status, we shall make you our highest chief, so that every decision will require your approval. If you fall ill, we shall find for you the best physician. But our condition is that you must stop your preaching.'

Muhammad replied by explaining at great length the revelations which God had made through him. At the end Muhammad fell on his knees, and prostrated himself to God. And Utba found himself doing the same.

When Utba returned to his companions, they noticed that his expression had changed completely; and they asked him what had happened. He said that the words spoken by Muhammad were entirely new to him, and that they were neither poetry nor witchcraft. He concluded: 'My advice is that we should leave this man entirely alone. The words I have heard will be blazed across the land. If people from other tribes kill him, then we shall be rid of him. But if he is victorious, then his power will be our power, and his prosperity will be our prosperity.'

'He has bewitched your tongue,' the other leaders exclaimed.

186, 187

Demand for a miracle

The faith preached by Muhammad continued to spread throughout Mecca, amongst both men and women. The Quraysh leaders ordered that anyone openly advocating Islam should be arrested and imprisoned. Yet this only encouraged more people to listen to Muhammad.

At a meeting in the Grand Mosque, held after sunset, the Quraysh leaders decided to confront Muhammad publicly, in the hope of destroying his reputation. They invited him to come to the Grand Mosque the following day; and also issued a public invitation.

Muhammad hoped that Utba might have persuaded them to abandon their hostility. But when he arrived, he was gravely disappointed. Again they accused him of insulting the old religion unfairly, and of dividing their tribe; and they demanded that he stop preaching. Muhammad refused, declaring himself to be God's messenger.

The leaders said: 'To prove your claim, we require you to perform miracles. Make these mountains near Mecca move. Straighten out the coast. Cause valleys to appear with mighty rivers flowing through them.' Muhammad replied: 'God has not given me the power to perform miracles; he has simply given me a message. You may either accept it to your own benefit; or reject it and await God's judgement.' At this Muhammad rose up and left them.

Failure to answer

In the city of Medina there was a group of Jewish rabbis, who were renowned for their knowledge of the ancient Hebrew Scriptures. The Quraysh leaders sent one of their own number, a man called Uqba, to visit these rabbis, and ask their advice on how to deal with Muhammad. The rabbis replied: 'Ask him about God's Spirit. If he can give you a good answer, then follow him, because he is truly messenger of God. But if he cannot, he is an impostor who should be treated with contempt.'

Uqba returned to Mecca, and he went to Muhammad, accompanied by other Quraysh leaders, to ask him about God's spirit. Muhammad replied: 'I shall answer your question tomorrow.' But he omitted to add, 'if God wills'.

On the following day Muhammad still had no answer. A further fortnight passed, without any answer coming into his heart. God did not speak to him, and Gabriel did not come to him. The people of Mecca said to one another: 'He promised an answer to Uqba's question within a day; but now fifteen days have gone by, and he is still silent.' Muhammad himself became deeply distressed; and he realized that he had not received an answer because he had not truly trusted God.

Finally Gabriel came to Muhammad. As the angel arrived Muhammad expressed anger: 'You have shut yourself off from me, Gabriel, causing me great distress.' Gabriel replied: 'I can come to you only when God commands' Gabriel then revealed to Muhammad the answer to Uqba's question.

192, 193

Reciting the Book

Muhammad dictated to a scribe the revelations he had received from God; and in this way the sacred Book was composed. His followers then read this book, and learnt it by heart so that they could recite it.

One of Muhammad's followers, called Abdullah, decided that the Quraysh leaders should hear the Book. So he proposed that he should go to the Grand Mosque, and recite it to them in a loud voice, so they could not fail to hear it. The other followers were afraid that he would be attacked, and urged him to take others for protection. Abdullah pronounced: 'I shall go alone, because God will protect me.'

The next morning Abdullah went to the Grand Mosque where the Quraysh leaders were meeting. In a loud voice he began: 'In the name of God who is compassionate and merciful.' He then proceeded to recite the Book, verse by verse. The Quraysh leaders asked one another: 'What on earth is this son of a slave woman saying?' When it became clear that he was proclaiming words Muhammad had given him, they rose up and started hitting him in the face. But Abdullah continued to recite the Book for as long as God willed that he should.

Eventually, when his face was so cut and bruised that he could barely speak, he returned to his companions. 'This is just what we feared would happen,' they exclaimed. Abdullah replied: 'God's enemies were never more contemptible to me than they are now.' Abdullah was the first person to recite God's Book publicly.

Umar's violence

When the Quraysh leaders returned from Ethiopia and re-ported their failure, their fellow leaders were extremely angry. One of them, a man called Umar who was renowned for his physical strength, swore that he personally would kill Muhammad.

The next day Umar took his sword, and set out for the place where he knew Muhammad was staying. On his way he met a friend, who asked him where he was going. Umar replied: 'I am going to kill Muhammad. He has split our tribe, mocked our traditions, and insulted our religion.' The friend replied: 'First go back to your family, and set its affairs in order.' 'What is the matter with my family?' Umar asked. 'Your sister, her husband, and your nephew have all become followers of Muhammad,' the friend said.

Umar rushed back to his house. One of Muhammad's closest helpers was in the house, reciting God's revelations to Umar's sister and her husband. When they recognized Umar's voice outside, the helper hid in a small room. In fact Umar had listened to some of the recitation. So as he entered, he blurted out: 'I accuse you of being followers of Muhammad.' Umar then seized his sister's husband. She rose in her hus-band's defence, and Umar hit her across the face, causing blood to flow. She exclaimed 'Yes, we both believe in God, and we practise Muhammad's religion.'

When Umar saw what he had done to his sister, he was deeply ashamed. He then asked if he could listen fully to God's revelations, and judge them for himself.

224, 225, 226

Umar's conversion

Muhammad's helper came out of the small room in which he had been hiding, and he began reciting God's revelations to Umar. As he continued, Umar's expression gradually softened. Finally Umar declared: 'These words are indeed very fine.'

'Dear Umar,' Muhammad's helper cried out, 'I hope that God has truly spoken to you, and has chosen you for his own. Last night I heard a voice saying that you would give great strength to God's cause. Dear Umar, come to God, come to God!'

Umar took his sword in his hand, and left the house. He went to the place where Muhammad was staying, and knocked on the door. Hamza, the strongest man of the Quraysh tribe who had embraced the faith, was with Muhammad. He looked through a chink in the door, and said: 'Umar is outside, with a sword in his hand. I believe we should let him in. If he comes with peaceful intentions, we shall treat him well. But if he comes with malicious intentions, we shall kill him with his own sword.' Muhammad agreed, and Hamza opened the door.

Muhammad rose as Umar entered. Muhammad seized Umar by the shoulders, saying: 'What has brought you here? I do not believe you will cease your persecution of us, until God brings shame on you.' Umar described how he had struck his own sister for her faith, and then listened to God's revelations. 'Messenger of God,' Umar concluded, 'I have come to declare that I believe in God, and accept his revelations which you have conveyed.'

A rude name

The Quraysh leaders tried to undermine Muhammad's authority by mocking him, and by trying to catch him out with awkward questions.

They started calling him 'Mudhamman', which means 'reprobate'. At first they were very pleased with themselves, believing that this nickname would soon become popular. But Muhammad turned the mockery onto the Quraysh leaders themselves, saying: 'This joke shows how frightened they are of me. They cannot bear to use my real name, which means "praiseworthy", because they know it to be true.'

On one occasion a Quraysh leader called Ubay came to Muhammad in the Grand Mosque, carrying an old bone. A crowd gathered round to watch the encounter. Ubay crumbled the bone into dust in his hands, and held out his hands to Muhammad. 'Do you claim that God can bring this dust back to life?' Ubay asked, and blew the dust into Muhammad's face. 'Yes,' answered Muhammad, 'I do say that. God will raise you back to life, even after you have become dust blowing in the wind.'

The Quraysh leaders also used Muhammad's teachings against his followers. A Quraysh leader owed a Muslim some money. The leader asked the Muslim: 'Does not Muhammad claim that in paradise there is all the gold and silver that his people can desire?' 'Yes, he does,' the Muslim replied. The leader laughed, and said: 'In that case, I shall wait until the day of resurrection — then you will receive the value of my debt in full!'

233, 234, 238

The perils of jeering

The Quraysh leaders also began to jeer at Muhammad's followers. In particular, they pointed to the lowly origins of many Muslims, saying: 'Look at this rabble; look at the scum with which Muhammad surrounds himself. Are we really to believe that God has chosen such wretched creatures to receive his wisdom and guidance? If Muhammad's teaching had truly come from God, then these people would not have been the first to understand it. Educated and cultured people like us would have embraced it long before the lower classes had even heard of it. So the fact that Muhammad's followers are mostly ignorant slaves and peasants proves that his teaching is false.'

One by one the four leaders who made such remarks fell victim to serious injuries and diseases. The first was in the Grand Mosque when a sandstorm erupted; sand blew in his eyes, and he went blind. The second found that his belly started to swell; and few days later he died of dropsy. The third caught his ankle on a thorn bush as he dismounted his donkey; the wound filled with poisonous pus, which quickly killed him. The fourth suffered severe headaches which drove him mad.

260, 272

Mounting Buruq

One night, after visiting his cousin who lived nearby, Muhammad went into the Grand Mosque in order to pray and recite God's revelations. After he had finished, he walked over to an enclosed area within the Mosque, lay down and fell into a deep slumber. While he was asleep, Gabriel came, took Muhammad by the arm, and led him out of the Mosque. At the entrance stood a white animal, half mule and half donkey, with wings on its sides.

Gabriel ordered Muhammad to mount the animal, which was called Buruq. But as Muhammad approached the animal, it shied. Gabriel put his hand on its mane, and exclaimed: 'No one more honourable in the sight of God than Muhammad has ever ridden you before.' The animal was so ashamed that it broke into a sweat; and it stood quite still, so Muhammad could mount.

Gabriel led Buruq, with Muhammad on its back, through the sky until they reached the temple in Jerusalem. Waiting for them at the temple was a great company of God's messengers, including Abraham, Moses and Jesus. Muhammad led them in prayer. Then two large cups were brought in, one containing wine and the other milk. Muhammad took the cup of milk and drank it, but left the wine. Gabriel said: 'You have chosen rightly, and you will guide your people to do the same. Wine is forbidden to all who surrender to God.'

263, 264

The first level of the heavens

A ladder appeared from above, and was lowered into the temple in Jerusalem. The ladder was the most beautiful object Muhammad had ever seen; it was the ladder which comes down to every person as death approaches. Muhammad was led by Gabriel onto the bottom rung, and he climbed up until he reached the gate of the heavens.

Gabriel and Muhammad entered the heavens, and met a man who was watching human spirits go past. At some he said: 'A good spirit from a good body.' At others he said: 'An evil spirit from an evil body.' Muhammad asked who this man was. Gabriel answered: 'It is Adam, reviewing the spirits of his descendants.'

Further on they saw men with lips like those of camels. In their hands were pieces of stone which seemed to be on fire. They thrust the pieces in their mouths, and then immediately excreted them. Gabriel said: 'They are the cheats who devoured the wealth of orphans.'

They passed men with vast bellies, who were being trampled by camels and were unable to move away; and they were gasping with thirst. 'They are the usurers who charged interest on loans,' said Gabriel.

Then they saw men, each of whom was sitting in front of two plates, one with good meat and the other with rotten meat; and they were being forced to eat the rotten meat. 'They are the adulterers who abandoned their wives, and went after the wives of others,' said Gabriel.

268, 269

Higher levels of the heavens

From the first level Gabriel led Muhammad upwards. At the second level they met two maternal cousins of Jesus. At the third level they met Joseph, son of Jacob; his face was as bright as the full moon. At the fourth level they met a man called Idris, who had been a true messenger of God. At the fifth level they met Aaron, a wonderfully handsome man with a long, white beard. At the sixth level Moses stood; he was tall and thin, with curly hair, a ruddy complexion, and a hooked nose.

At the seventh level there was a man sitting on a throne; it was Abraham. Muhammad looked exactly like Abraham, except that Abraham was older. Muhammad greeted Abraham as his father, and Abraham greeted Muhammad as his son. Then Abraham ordered Muhammad to say fifty prayers; and he said that all Muslims should pray fifty times a day.

Then Gabriel took Muhammad back down to the sixth level. Moses asked Muhammad: 'How many prayers has Abraham required you and your people to say each day?' 'Fifty,' replied Muhammad. Moses said: 'Prayer is a weighty matter, and you and your people are weak. Go back to Abraham, and ask him to reduce the number of prayers that you and your people must say to five.' Muhammad returned to Abraham; and after much pleading Abraham agreed.

270, 271

Testing the vision

Gabriel led Muhammad out of the heavens, down the ladder to earth, and back to Mecca. On the following morning the Quraysh leaders assembled for their usual meeting at the Grand Mosque. Muhammad went over to them, and described his journey to Jerusalem and up to the heavens. They replied: 'This is absurd; it is impossible to go to Jerusalem and back in a single night. It takes a caravan a month to reach Jerusalem, and a month to return.'

So Muhammad left them, and went to speak to Abu Bakr and other Muslims about his journey. Some wondered if he had gone mad, and began to doubt whether he was truly God's messenger. That evening a group of these doubters came to see Abu Bakr, to ask his opinion. Abu Bakr replied: 'If Muhammad says he has done something, you can be sure he is telling the truth. Thus you must believe that he made the journey he describes. And what is so surprising about that? All of us accept that God reveals himself to Muhammad at all times of the night and day. So we should have no difficulty in believing that God can lift him to Jerusalem and into the heavens.'

The next day the doubters went to see Muhammad himself. One of them had visited Jerusalem himself, and he asked Muhammad to describe the city. Muhammad described it with complete accuracy. The man exclaimed: 'Everything you say is true. You are indeed a messenger sent by God.'

The year of sadness

Khadija, Muhammad's wife, and Abu Talib, his uncle, died in the same year.

Khadija had supported Muhammad with unswerving loyalty in his religion, from the time that he had begun to receive God's revelations. He always told her of his troubles, and she comforted him.

When Abu Talib fell ill, news quickly spread round Mecca of his condition. The Quraysh leaders met, to decide how to respond. They acknowledged that some of the strongest and finest men of their tribe had embraced the faith which Muhammad preached, and that almost every clan now contained Muslims. Since Abu Talib had not himself become a Muslim, and yet was trusted by Muhammad, the Quraysh leaders saw him as a potential mediator, through whom a treaty could be negotiated between Muhammad and themselves. Thus they decided that four of their number, including Utba and Abu Jahl, should visit Abu Talib before he died.

When they arrived, Utba spoke first: 'Abu Talib, you are highly respected amongst the Quraysh people. And now that you are at the point of death, we are deeply concerned. We believe that you alone can bring peace between us and your nephew. We desire only that he agrees to leave us alone, and we shall leave him alone. Thus we ask you to summon him, and to suggest such an agreement.'

Abu Talib thus sent a message to Muhammad, begging him to come to his deathbed. Muhammad came at once.

Failure to agree

The four Quraysh leaders, who had come to visit Abu Talib on his deathbed, waited there until Muhammad arrived. Abu Talib explained to Muhammad the proposal which the leaders had made, that they would leave him alone to practise his religion, if he agreed to leave them alone to practise theirs.

Muhammad turned to the Quraysh leaders and asked: 'Would it please you if our tribe ruled all the Arabs and the Persians?' They replied that they would be delighted to enjoy such power. Muhammad continued: 'Then I shall tell you how this power can be achieved. You yourselves must simply declare that there is no god but God, and that all other gods must be rejected.'

The Quraysh leaders clapped their hands in anger, and exclaimed: 'Do you really want to make all the gods into one God? That would be an absurd thing to do.' Muhammad remained adamant. The Quraysh leaders said to one another: 'This fellow is not willing to move even a small distance towards us. So let us continue to practise the religion of our forefathers – and let the future decide whether his religion or ours triumphs.' So they departed.

278

Abu Talib's death

After the Quraysh leaders had left, Abu Talib turned to Muhammad. 'Nephew,' he said, 'in urging our tribal leaders to declare that there is no god but God, I do not think you are being absurd.'

On hearing these words Muhammad hoped that Abu Talib might embrace the faith which God had revealed to him. 'Dear uncle,' asked Muhammad, 'will you declare that there is no god but God? Then I shall be able to intercede on your behalf on the day of resurrection.' Abu Talib could see how eager his nephew was for his conversion. 'Dear nephew,' Abu Talib replied, 'if I were to embrace your faith, our tribal leaders would become even more hostile to you and the rest of my family, than they already are. Moreover they would say that I had embraced your faith, not from genuine conviction, but from fear of death. In truth my real motive would be to give you pleasure.'

Death was now fast approaching. Abu Talib's lips continued to move, but his voice failed. One of Abu Talib's brothers, who was also present, put his ear close to Abu Talib's lips. 'Nephew,' the brother said, 'Abu Talib has spoken the word you wanted him to say.' 'I did not hear it,' Muhammad replied.

The Thaqif tribe's rejection

After Abu Talib's death, the Quraysh leaders renewed their determination to destroy Muhammad and his religion. Muhammad was afraid of their wrath. So he decided to seek help from the Thaqif tribe, and went alone to their main settlement. He hoped to convince them of the truth of his religion; and then he would beg them to protect him and his followers.

When he arrived, he asked to see the three leaders of the tribe. They agreed to meet him, and Muhammad explained to them at great length God's revelations to him. When he had finished, he asked them to surrender themselves to God, and to assist him against his opponents.

One of the leaders said: 'I am no more convinced that you are a messenger from God, than I am willing to go to Mecca and tear down the Kaba.' The second leader said: 'Surely a messenger of God would be a more impressive man than you.' The third said: 'Do not let me ever speak with you again. If you are truly a messenger of God, as you say, then I am not worthy even to be in your presence. But if you are lying, then I am in danger of being corrupted by you.'

Muhammad realized that his journey had been fruitless, and he rose to leave. As he did so, he asked the Thaqif leaders to keep their meeting secret; he was frightened that, if news of it reached the Quraysh leaders, they would be encouraged in their attacks on him. The Thaqif leaders refused.

Verge of despair

As Muhammad left the Thaqif leaders, he was followed by a crowd of young men, who hurled insults at him. Muhammad quickened his pace, and they quickened theirs. He began to run, and they too ran. He was a fast runner, and hid in an orchard where they could not find him.

Once he felt safe, he prostrated himself. 'O God,' he prayed, 'I turn to you in my weakness. In seeking to serve you, and in conveying your message, I am utterly humiliated; I am the most wretched and despised of men. All my strength has drained away. You, O God, are the Lord of the weak; you are my Lord. To whom can I turn for protection? I am willing to look far and wide for help. But will everyone abuse me? Will I merely increase the number of my enemies?

'Yet if you are not angry with me, I have nothing to fear. Your favour is all I desire. I take refuge in the light that shines from your face; your light penetrates even the darkest recesses of my existence. All things in this world and the next are ordered and governed by you. My only wish is that you approve my thoughts and actions, and that your wrath never descends on me. Your pleasure is my happiness. Your power alone can shield me from harm.'

279, 280

A Christian slave

The orchard in which Muhammad took refuge belonged to Utba, one of the Quraysh leaders, and his brother. Although he was opposed to Islam, Utba respected its high ideals, and he acknowledged Muhammad's sincerity. It so happened that Utba and his brother were visiting the orchard when Muhammad arrived, and they observed his predicament. They had with them a young Christian slave; and they sent the slave to Muhammad, with a bunch of grapes for him to eat.

As the Christian slave handed Muhammad the grapes, Muhammad said, 'In the name of God'; and then he began to eat. 'I did not think people in this country spoke in such a way,' the slave exclaimed. 'What country do you come from, and what is your religion?' Muhammad asked. The slave replied that he came from Nineveh, and that he was a Christian. 'So you come from the same place as that righteous man Jonah,' said Muhammad. 'How do you know about Jonah?' asked the slave. 'Because Jonah and I are brothers in spirit,' Muhammad replied. At this the Christian slave kissed Muhammad on his head, his hands and his feet.

Utba and his brother were looking on, and were outraged to see this act of respect by the slave. So when the slave returned, they said: 'You rascal! Why did you kiss that man's head, hands and feet?' The slave answered that Muhammad was truly a messenger sent from God. The two brothers declared: 'You're not only a rascal, but also a fool; your religion is far better than his. Don't let him seduce you away from it.'

A question of authority

When Muhammad returned to Mecca, it was the time of the annual pilgrimage, when people from all over Arabia came to Mecca. Fairs were organized throughout the city for the visitors. Since the hostility towards him from his own tribe was growing steadily fiercer, Muhammad visited the fairs, making further attempts to enlist the support of other tribes. He spoke to members of every tribe, urging them to surrender themselves to God and to acknowledge him as God's messenger; and he then asked them to protect him, so that he could continue to convey God's message.

Most of the people to whom he spoke were highly suspicious of his words. They feared that, if they abandoned their gods in order to worship God alone, their gods would turn on them and take revenge.

One tribal leader called Amir was initially very impressed with Muhammad's strength of character. Amir said to Muhammad: 'In my opinion you would be an excellent advisor, who would help bring me victory over other tribes.' Muhammad made no response. Then Amir asked: 'If I were to win victory over other tribes through your advice, who would then wield authority, you or I?' Muhammad replied: 'Authority is a matter for God; he confers it where he pleases.' Amir exclaimed: 'So what you are really saying is that we should risk our lives protecting you, so that you can reap the benefit. Be off with you.'

282, 283

Iyas's joy

In the town of Medina two tribes, the Aws and the Khazraj, were vying for supremacy. A group of Aws leaders came to Mecca, seeking an alliance with the Quraysh against their rivals.

Muhammad heard of the arrival of the Aws leaders, and went to see them. He asked them if they would like to gain something even more profitable than an alliance with the Quraysh. They asked him what this could be. He replied that he was God's messenger, sent to urge people to worship God alone, and to abandon their idols. He explained that God had revealed to him a book, and he proceeded to recite passages from it.

The youngest of the Aws leaders, called Iyas, declared: 'This is certainly far better than the alliance we are seeking.' Another of the leaders took a handful of dirt from the ground, and threw it at Iyas's face, shouting: 'Shut up, you young fool! We didn't come to Mecca for religion.' Iyas said nothing more, and Muhammad departed. The Aws leaders returned to Medina, and a bloody battle took place between the two tribes.

Shortly afterwards Iyas fell seriously ill. As he lay dying, he was radiant with joy, constantly praising and glorifying God. Those who saw him were convinced that in his heart he had embraced the religion taught by Muhammad.

285, 286

Plea for unity

Living in Medina alongside the Aws and Khazraj tribes were many Jews. Unlike the tribal people, who worshipped many gods, the Jews worshipped God alone. Thus their presence was preparing the people of Medina for the teachings of Muhammad.

Many of the Jews were very prosperous; and often members of the Khazraj raided their homes and stole their property. The Jews responded by warning the Khazraj people: 'God will soon be sending a new messenger. His day is at hand. We shall listen to his words with joy, and obey his commands; and we shall be blessed. If you repent, he will call down God's forgiveness on you. But if you persist in your crimes, this messenger will call down God's anger, and you will be destroyed.' Although they outwardly dismissed his words, in their hearts they were frightened.

A group of six Khazraj leaders visited Mecca at the time of the annual pilgrimage, and Muhammad went to see them. As he spoke about God's revelations to him, asking them to accept him as God's messenger, they remembered the warning of the Jews. So they surrendered themselves to God.

They then said to Muhammad: 'There is no place more divided than Medina. It is ravaged by continual conflict between the Aws and ourselves. The hatred and the rancour run deep. Will God use you to unite us?' Muhammad undertook to work for unity. The Khazraj leaders then proposed that a meeting should be held, at which Muhammad would speak to leaders from both sides. Muhammad agreed to this.

The pledge of women

The six Khazraj leaders who had become Muslims, returned to Medina, and told leaders from both their own and the Aws tribe about Islam. They declared that Muhammad was God's messenger, who alone could bring peace between the two tribes; and he invited them to come and meet him. Four leaders from the Khazraj tribe, plus two from the Aws, accepted this invitation. Thus a total a twelve men went from Medina to Aqaba, where Muhammad was waiting for them.

Muhammad spoke to them about God's revelations. The six leaders who had met him in Mecca urged the others to acknowledge him as God's messenger; and they did so. Muhammad then proposed that they make a 'pledge of women', to live in peace with one another as women do. He also gave them rules to follow: they should not steal; they should not commit adultery; and they should not slander others. He promised that, if they obeyed these rules strictly, God would reward them.

Muhammad had brought with him to Aqaba a follower called Musab, who was mature in faith and was a skilled teacher. He appointed Musab as the spiritual guide to these twelve leaders; and he called the twelve leaders the Helpers. He instructed Musab and the Helpers to return to Medina and to practise their religion devoutly, inviting others to join them. And he added: 'In this way you will bring peace to your people.' The Helpers replied: 'If through your religion our two tribes are reconciled, you will become the mightiest person in all Medina.'

288, 289

Friday prayers

When they had returned to Medina, the twelve Helpers decided to hold public prayers each week; and these acts of
worship would be open to all. After much discussion they
concluded that the right day for public prayers was Friday,
the day before the Jewish Sabbath. On this day the Jews were
preparing themselves for worship, so they might be willing
to join the Muslims in their devotions.

Despite the friendship which had formed between the ten
Khazraj leaders and two Aws leaders who formed the Helpers,
those from one tribe could not bear someone from the other
tribe leading prayers. Thus
they decided always to invite
someone belonging to neither
tribe to lead.

Friday prayers took place
on a hill a short distance
outside Medina. On the first
occasion forty people came;
and the numbers steadily
increased.

290

Usayd's promise

At first many of the leaders of the Aws tribe were hostile towards the new religion, suspecting that it might be a ploy by the Khazraj to lull them into submission.

The chief of one of the Aws clans, a man called Sad, was especially hostile. Thus he was enraged when he saw Musab sitting in his garden, teaching a group of Aws people. He wanted to kill Musab immediately; but he did not wish to antagonize the two Aws leaders who had embraced Islam. So instead he ordered his assistant, Usayd, to drive Musab from his land. Usayd took his lance, strode towards Musab, stood over him, and growled: 'If you value your life, you will leave at once.'

Musab calmly invited Usayd to sit down for a while, saying: 'Listen to what I have to say. If you like what you hear, you will want me to stay. If you do not like it, I shall leave at once.' This proposal seemed fair to Usayd, so he sat down. Musab spoke with great eloquence, explaining the faith which God had revealed to Muhammad. As he did so, the expression on Usayd's face gradually changed from an angry scowl to a serene smile. At the end Usayd declared: 'Your speech has been more beautiful and wonderful than anything I have heard before. What must I do to embrace your religion?' Musab replied: 'You must submit yourself to God, praying to him regularly; and you must tell others about your faith.'

Usayd prostrated himself, promising to obey God in all things, and to bear witness to God to all his relations and friends.

Conversion of Sad's clan

Musab was delighted to observe Usayd's conversion. Then Usayd said: 'The chief of my clan, a powerful man called Sad, is near at hand. If he adopts Islam, the whole clan will follow him.' So Usayd took his lance, and walked back to Sad. As Usayd approached, Sad was astonished to see the serene joy radiating from his face. Usayd explained to his chief that he had surrendered himself to God, and asked Sad to do the same.

Sad was furious, shouting: 'You're a soft-hearted fool.' He took Usayd's lance, marched towards Musab, and exclaimed: 'If you were not a guest of my tribe, I should kill you at once. How dare you abuse our hospitality in this way!' Musab gave the same response that he had given to Usayd: 'Please sit down, and listen to what I have to say. If you like what you hear, you will ask me to stay. If you do not like it, I shall leave at once.' This proposal seemed fair; and, as Usayd had done, Sad sat sown and listened to Musab. And he too was convinced by Musab's words.

Sad and Usayd immediately called a meeting of all the men and women of their clan. The people could see from the faces of Sad and Usayd that something momentous had occurred. Sad explained their new faith, and concluded: 'I shall not speak to a man or woman amongst you, until you believe in God and his messenger.' Thus every member of the clan was converted.

Facing Mecca

The following year at the time of the pilgrimage a large group of Khazraj and Aws people travelled to Mecca, accompanied by Musab. The group consisted of both Muslims and those who still worshipped idols.

The Muslims included a Khazraj leader called Bara. At the start of the journey he said to the other Muslims: 'I have been wondering which way we should face when we pray. In Mecca it is possible to face both the Kaba and Jerusalem. But here it is impossible: by facing Jerusalem, we turn our backs on the Kaba – and this seems wrong. So I think we should face the Kaba.' The others replied that, as far as they knew, Muhammad always faced Jerusalem when he prayed. Bara said: 'We do not know for certain what he does outside Mecca; so from now on I am going to face the Kaba.' The rest refused, insisting that they would continue to face Jerusalem.

So throughout the journey, at the times of prayer, Bara faced the Kaba while the others faced Jerusalem.

When they reached Mecca, Bara went to see Muhammad, and said: 'God has guided me to accept the religion which you preach. And on the journey from Medina, I felt prompted to face the Kaba when I prayed, not Jerusalem. But my companions opposed me on this, so I have felt some misgivings. What is your judgement?' Muhammad replied: 'You have been shown which way to face; keep to that.' Bara continued to face the Kaba in prayer until the day of his death.

Meeting at Aqaba

The people from the Khazraj and the Aws completed their pilgrimage to Mecca, and then prepared for their journey home. Just before they started, Muhammad came to see those of their number who were Muslims, and ordered them to meet him in secret during their journey. The place was to be Aqaba, where the twelve Helpers had pledged themselves to support him.

Eventually the group arrived at a place near Aqaba, where they camped for the night. At dusk the Muslims pretended to fall asleep, but in fact stayed awake. Then, when a third of the night had passed, they rose up, and crept away like sandgrouse towards Aqaba. They comprised seventy-three men and two women. When they reached Aqaba, they waited patiently for Muhammad. He arrived shortly afterwards, accompanied by an uncle who respected Islam, but could not embrace it.

Muhammad's uncle spoke first: 'Within the Quraysh tribe some people follow Muhammad; some, like me, admire him, but do not accept his teachings; and some oppose him, and wish to destroy him. He is now willing to come and join you in Medina; and for your part you must protect him from his enemies. If you can accept this burden, then make a pledge this very night. But if you are liable to abandon and betray him, then let us go our separate ways.'

The Muslims of the Khazraj and the Aws said: 'We have heard what you have to say. Let us now hear Muhammad himself. Then we shall give our answer.'

295, 296

The Helpers' pledge

Muhammad began reciting God's revelations to the seventy-three men and two women who had come to meet him at Aqaba. Then he said: 'I have invited you here tonight to ask you to make a pledge: that you protect me with the same devotion as you protect your own women and children.'

Bara stepped forward, took Muhammad by the hand, and said: 'By God, who appointed you to convey the truth, we shall protect you with the same devotion as we protect our own women and children.' But as Bara was speaking, a Khazraj leader called Abdul interrupted: 'Messenger of God, if we pledge ourselves to you, the Jews of Medina may turn against us. Thus we shall become very vulnerable. Let us imagine that, with God's help, we win victory for you over the leaders of your own tribe. Will you then abandon us and return to Mecca? If so, we shall no longer have your guidance in resisting the Jews.'

Muhammad smiled and said: 'If you pledge yourselves to protect me, my blood and your blood will become one. I shall be at war with those who are at war with you, and at peace with those who are at peace with you.' Muhammad stretched out his arm, and invited the people to pledge themselves by grasping his hand. One by one they all did so. These people also became known as Helpers.

Muhammad then appointed twelve of them as elders, to take charge of the people's affairs, nine from the Khazraj and three from the Aws.

297, 299

Honouring the pledge

After the meeting with Muhammad, the seventy-three men and two women who had pledged themselves to him, walked back to their camp. They passed by a shepherd, who was watching over his flock near Aqaba. He overheard their conversation, and ran to Mecca to report it to the Quraysh leaders.

The following morning a group of Quraysh leaders came to the place where the people from Medina were camping. They met some idol-worshippers who knew nothing of the meeting at Aqaba, and told them what they had heard; they hoped that this would cause division within the tribes. The idol-worshippers, who belonged to both tribes, were aghast. The Quraysh leaders then left.

Later the idol-worshippers spoke to the Muslims, and asked them if there was any truth in what the Quraysh leaders had said. The Muslims admitted it was true. The most senior of the idol-worshippers declared: 'This is an extremely serious matter. It is quite wrong for an issue of such importance to be decided without consulting all the tribal leaders.' But he realized that he and the other idol-worshipper would have to honour the pledge which the Muslims had made, because they belonged to the same tribe.

300, 301

Permission for war

Prior to the second meeting at Aqaba, Muhammad had not been given permission to fight or allow blood to be shed. He had simply been ordered to call people to God, enduring the insults that were thrown at him, and forgiving the ignorance of all who rejected his call. Thus the Quraysh leaders had been free to persecute Muslims, without fear of retribution. As a result some Muslims had given up their faith, while others had fled their homes.

But now God gave Muhammad permission to make war on his opponents, and to call Muslims to arms; and God promised that those who died in his service would go straight to paradise. Yet God laid down two strict conditions. Firstly he ordered Muslims to fight only those who persecuted them for their faith; they should not make war for the sake of gaining power and wealth. Secondly they should never use deceit in conducting warfare, but should fight honestly.

God also commanded that, when they achieve victory, Muslims should not exploit those whom they have vanquished. Their sole aim should be to enable Islam to be practised fully and freely, and to ensure that people live in peace with one another.

305, 314

Decision to emigrate

When God gave Muslims permission to fight, Muhammad commanded the Muslims in Mecca to leave their homes and emigrate to Medina, saying: 'The Helpers will be your new tribe, and they will provide you with new homes where you will live in safety.' Muhammad did not go to Medina immediately, but awaited God's instructions as to when he personally should emigrate.

The first man to emigrate from Mecca to Medina was Abu Salama. But as he was leaving his home, a fight broke out. He put the saddle on his camel, and asked his wife to mount. At that moment members of his wife's family appeared, and said to Abu Salama: 'You yourself can do what you like. But do you imagine that we would let you take your wife away?' They then snatched the camel's halter from his hand, and took hold of his wife.

In the meantime Abu Salama grasped his son's right arm, and shouted: 'You may steal my wife, but you shall not steal my son.' His wife's uncle grabbed the boy's left arm, and the two men tugged. The boy's left arm became dislocated from his shoulder, and the uncle let go. So Abu Salama was able to leave with his son.

Abu Salama's wife was so miserable at the loss of both her husband and her son that she was unable to work. So after a year her family gave her the camel they had taken from her husband, and allowed her to leave.

314, 315

Dangerous journeys

Most of those who made the journey to Medina formed groups for mutual protection; so typically two or three families travelled together.

When Umar, the second strongest man in the Quraysh tribe, decided to emigrate with his family, two others, Ayash and Hisham, asked if they and their families could go with him. The three men decided that each family should leave the city separately, to try and avoid detection, and meet at a copse a short distance away. Umar said: 'If one of us fails to turn up, it means that he and his family have been kept back by force. So let the other two go on.'

Umar and Ayash, with their respective families, reached the copse at the appointed time, but Hisham and his family did not come. So with heavy hearts Umar and Ayash continued. News later reached Medina that Hisham had been arrested while leaving Mecca, and under torture he had renounced his faith.

Yet despite the dangers every Muslim in Mecca attempted to emigrate; and most were successful.

319, 320

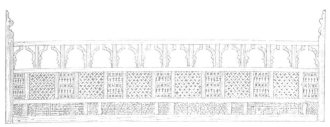

Final move

Muhammad remained in Mecca, waiting for God's permission to leave; and he kept with him Abu Bakr and Ali. During this time Muhammad used to visit Abu Bakr's house each day, either in the early morning or at night. Abu Bakr kept two camels tied up in the courtyard of his house, ready to take himself and Muhammad to Medina as soon as Muhammad gave the word.

One day Muhammad arrived at Abu Bakr's house at noon. 'God has given me permission to leave Mecca,' Muhammad said. 'Am I to be your companion?' Abu Bakr asked. 'Yes,' Muhammad replied. Abu Bakr wept with joy.

Abu Bakr had already sent most of his close relatives and possessions to Medina; but his sheep were still with him. So he went to see his shepherd, instructing him to bring his sheep to a place outside Mecca; and then they would travel together to Medina.

In the meantime Muhammad visited Ali, and ordered him to stay behind in Mecca for a few days. Many people had deposited precious objects with Muhammad for safe keeping, trusting his honesty. Muhammad instructed Ali: 'Return these goods to their owners; and when this task is complete, follow Abu Bakr and me to Medina.'

That night, as soon as darkness had fallen, Abu Bakr and Muhammad mounted the two camels, and set off towards Medina. They went out through the back gate of Abu Bakr's house to avoid detection.

Arrival in Medina

Ali followed Muhammad as soon as he had completed his task; and he, Muhammad and Abu Bakr arrived safely at Medina.

When they had said prayers, Muhammad rode into the city, and down the main street. Without prompting his camel stopped at a building used for drying and storing dates, and knelt down. Muhammad did not dismount, but made the camel rise and continue. After a few paces the camel turned round, and went back to the date store. The camel again knelt, and Muhammad concluded that this was the place for his home and the main mosque. So he dismounted, and asked who owned the date store. He was told it belonged to two orphan brothers, who were in the care of a guardian. Muhammad went to the guardian, and paid a generous price for it.

He then ordered the Emigrants and Helpers to work together in building the mosque, with a few simple houses around it. When it was complete, Muhammad moved into one of the houses.

335, 336

The call to prayer

Muhammad wondered how people should be reminded of the times for prayer. At first he ordered that a trumpet be sounded, similar to the trumpet used by the Jews. But after a time he wearied of it. So instead he ordered a clapper to be made, to replace the trumpet. But soon its sound also wearied him.

Then a man called Abdullah came to Muhammad, and reported a dream he had just had: 'A man wearing two green garments came past me. He was carrying a clapper, and I asked him to sell it to me. He inquired why I wanted it; and I told him that it was to summon people to prayer. He replied that the human voice, fashioned by God, is far better than any artificial device.'

'Did this man in your dream give you the words that should be used?' asked Muhammad. Abdullah related the words which the man had told him: 'God is great. I bear witness that there is no god but God. I bear witness that Muhammad is the messenger of God. Come to prayer. Come to prayer. Come to divine service. Come to divine service. God is great. God is great. There is no god but God.'

As soon as he had heard these words, Muhammad knew that they came from God. He went to Bilal, who had a clear and penetrating voice, and asked him to call people to prayer. And from that day onwards, at the five times stipulated for prayer, Bilal stood at the top of the mosque, and called out the words which Abdullah had received.

Abu Sufyan's caravan

Muhammad now decided that he would have to make war on his enemies. This was thirteen years after God had first called him to be his messenger; and Muhammad was now fifty-three years of age.

He heard that a wealthy merchant called Abu Sufyan was travelling from Jerusalem to Mecca, with a large caravan of money and merchandise, accompanied by about thirty or forty men. Muhammad called together his male followers and told them about the caravan, declaring: 'The money and merchandise belong to the Quraysh, so we have the right to take them. Let us go out and attack the caravan, and perhaps God will grant us success.'

Most of the men answered the summons. Some were eager, but others were reluctant, because they had not thought that Muhammad would go to war against his own tribe.

Among the hypocrites in Medina, several acted as spies for the Quraysh. They sent a message to Abu Sufyan that Muhammad had summoned his men to attack the caravan. When he heard the news, Abu Sufyan shook with terror. He in turn sent a message to Mecca, urging the Quraysh warriors to come out and protect their property. The messenger rode at full speed to the city, and the journey took him three days.

415, 428

Volunteering for battle

The message quickly spread round Mecca that Muhammad was preparing to attack Abu Sufyan's caravan, and thus take a large amount of Quraysh property. 'Do Muhammad and his followers think that this will be as easy as seizing the caravan at Nakla?' they asked one another indignantly. Almost every free man in the city decided to fight Muhammad, or send a slave in his place.

The fattest man in the city was called Umaya. He spent most of his time in the Grand Mosque, gossiping with his companions and burning incense. A young warrior came up to him and said: 'You are so addicted to pleasure that you cannot fight; you belong amongst the women.' Umaya rose up, went home, and collected his weapons.

In the meantime Muhammad and his men were heading towards Badr. News was brought to Muhammad that a large force of Quraysh men was leaving Mecca, to protect Abu Sufyan's caravan.

Muhammad convened a meeting of his men to ask their advice. Abu Bakr and the other Emigrants immediately spoke in favour of fighting the Quraysh force, declaring: 'Messenger of God, go wherever God commands you, and we shall be with you.' Muhammad thanked them for their loyalty. He then turned to the Helpers, saying: 'I cannot demand that you support me in attacking the Quraysh, because you are pledged only to defend me if I am attacked.' The leader of the Helpers replied: 'We believe in you, and so we shall obey your orders.'

430, 433, 434

Abu Sufyan's escape

Muhammad and his followers continued on their journey until they reached a large sandhill near Badr. They camped in its shadow, and Muhammad sent two men to the top of the hill, to look for the caravan and the Quraysh force. The two men reported that the Quraysh force was camped on the other side. 'How many men are there?' Muhammad asked. 'Between nine hundred and a thousand,' the men replied.

Abu Sufyan knew that the Quraysh force had camped at Badr, and was leading his caravan at great speed towards that place. He reached a road, where to his great surprise he found a large amount of camel dung. He broke a lump of dung in pieces, and, finding that it contained date stones, he exclaimed: 'The camels that made this dung are from Medina; only the Khazraj people feed dates to their camels.' He concluded that Muhammad's force was also camped near Badr. So he changed direction, and took his caravan on a more obscure path towards Mecca, escaping from Muhammad.

The caravan thus reached Mecca safely. Abu Sufyan sent a message to the Quraysh force at Badr that they could now return home. Abu Jahl, who regarded himself as leader of the Quraysh force, declared: 'We shall not go back until we have defeated Muhammad and his companions, and feasted on the meat of their camels. The whole of Arabia will hear of our victory, and will fear us!'

436, 437, 438

Hubab's trick

One of Muhammad's men, called Hubab, came to see him as the sun was setting, and asked: 'Has God given us an order to camp here, or did you choose this place simply as a matter of military tactics?' Muhammad replied that God had not given an order. Hubab said: 'In that case, I propose that we move to the well near Badr. This is the well from which the enemy draw their water. Thus if we surround it, the enemy will not be able to collect water for themselves and their animals.'

Muhammad agreed to Hubab's proposal. That night, undetected by the Quraysh, Muhammad's men moved to the well. At dawn the following day they killed all the Quraysh men that arrived to collect water.

Abdullah now came to Muhammad and said: 'Let us make a booth for you, from which you can watch the coming battle; and we shall tether your camel to it. If God gives us victory, your joy will be visible to us all, and increase our joy. But if the day goes badly, you can mount your camel and return to Medina. There you can recruit a new force with which to avenge our defeat.' Muhammad could see the wisdom of Abdullah's proposal, and allowed a booth to be built overlooking Badr.

439, 440

Utba's objections

From his booth Muhammad could see the whole Quraysh force. He spotted Utba, a man who had shown respect for Islam without embracing it. Muhammad declared: 'If there is any good in the Quraysh army, it resides in the heart of that man.'

Then Muhammad prostrated himself, and prayed: 'O God, the Quraysh in their vanity and their pride defy you, and accuse me, your messenger, of being a liar. Grant this day the help that you have promised. Destroy your enemy.'

Abu Jahl and the other Quraysh leaders sent Umaya to ride towards Muhammad's men, and estimate their number. On his return he said: 'Muhammad has about three hundred warriors. But it was not their meagre numbers that caught my attention. When I looked at their faces, I saw death. I think that for every one of them that we slay, they will slay at least one of us. I urge you to reconsider your plan.'

Utba rose to speak: 'Men of Quraysh, you will gain nothing by doing battle with Muhammad and his companions. Remember that many of them are Quraysh like ourselves. When you kill one of them, you may be killing your own cousin – and his dying face will haunt you until death overtakes you. So turn back, and let Muhammad be dealt with by other Arab tribes.'

Abu Jahl cried out: 'Utba, your lungs are swollen with fear. You want to turn back because you are afraid of Muhammad.' Others also expressed contempt for Utba's attitude, and the Quraysh leaders held stubbornly to their course.

440, 441, 442

Single combat

Aswad, a Quraysh warrior with an especially quarrelsome nature, stepped forward and declared: 'I swear to the gods that I shall drink from the well which Muhammad and his companions are occupying – or else I shall die before reaching it.' From Muhammad's side Hamza came forward to meet Aswad's challenge. When the two met, Hamza thrust his sword into Aswad's foot. Aswad fell back, with blood streaming from him. With another blow from his sword Hamza killed him.

Next Utba stepped forward, and challenged Muhammad's warriors to single combat. Three Helpers marched up to Utba. 'Who are you?' he asked. 'We belong to the Khazraj tribe,' they replied. Utba said: 'We have nothing against you; go back.' The herald of the Quraysh force called out: 'Muhammad, send forth against Utba warriors of our own tribe.' Muhammad ordered Ali, Hamza and Ubayda to march out into the ground that separated the two sides. 'Who are you?' Utba asked. The three men told Utba who they were. Utba signalled to his own side, and two other Quraysh warriors, Shayba and Walid, marched out.

Hamza fought Shayba, and quickly slew him. Ali fought Walid, and soon killed him. Ubayda and Utba exchanged two blows, and each was wounded. Hamza and Ali turned on Utba, and despatched him. Then they carried Ubayda back to his friends.

Spiritual preparation for battle

During the previous night a heavy shower of rain had fallen, turning the soft sand hard and slippery. As soon as the single combat was over, Muhammad ordered his men to march up a hill, and stand in line at the top. Then he said: 'If the enemy troops surround you and begin to climb this hill, shower them with arrows. Those that are hit will fall back on the others, who will slip over.'

Muhammad then walked along the line of his men, carrying an arrow. A warrior called Sawad was standing out of line. Muhammad pricked him gently in the belly with the arrow, saying: 'Stand in line.' Sawad said: 'You have hurt me, Messenger of God. Let me restore justice by retaliating.' Muhammad uncovered his own belly, expecting Sawad to prick it. Sawad knelt down and kissed Muhammad's belly. Muhammad asked him why he did this. 'Messenger of God,' Sawad replied, 'I believe that I shall die in the coming battle. So, since this is the last time I shall be with you, I wanted to touch your skin.' Muhammad blessed him.

Muhammad now went to the booth overlooking Badr, accompanied by Abu Bakr. Muhammad began to pray with great passion, saying: 'If this band of warriors perishes today, you will no longer be worshipped.' Abu Bakr interrupted him: 'Your constant entreaties will annoy your Lord, because he has already promised victory.' Muhammad stopped praying at once.

439, 444

Routing the enemy

As the battle started, Muhammad shouted to his followers: 'By God, who holds my soul in his hand, those who fight with courage this day, only advancing and never retreating, and who are slain, will enter paradise directly.' One of the men called back: 'Is it really true that nothing lies between me and paradise than being killed by those men?' He then rushed towards the Quraysh force, fought with great courage, and was slain.

Abu Jahl called out: 'May those who have severed the ties of kinship be destroyed.'

Muhammad picked from the ground a handful of pebbles, and hurled them towards the Quraysh warriors, ordering his followers to advance. The Muslim warriors moved slowly down the hill, and the Quraysh marched up the hill. The Muslims let forth a volley of arrows. The Quraysh warriors in the front were hit, falling back on their colleagues, who slipped over on the hard sand. Muhammad's men charged, and routed the enemy. They killed many of the leaders, and captured most of the others. A few of the Quraysh men, including Abu Jahl, fled.

A group of Helpers realized that the Quraysh warriors who had escaped might head towards Muhammad's booth, and kill him. So they hurried to the booth and stood guard.

Treatment of prisoners

Muhammad ordered that the Quraysh warriors who had been captured should be taken to Medina as prisoners. Sad, who was standing near to Muhammad, frowned. 'You seem to dislike what I have said,' Muhammad remarked. 'Yes,' answered Sad; 'this is the first defeat that God has brought on the infidels, and I should prefer to see these men slaughtered than left alive.'

Muhammad realized that Sad's attitude was likely to be widely shared. So he decided that only two of the Quraysh warriors should be spared, Abbas, his own uncle, and Bakhtari, who had always treated him with respect; the rest should be executed.

A Helper had captured Bakhtari, and was holding him. When Umar told them of Muhammad's decision, Bakhtari pointed to another Quraysh warrior with whom he had shared a camel. 'Can this man be spared as well?' Bakhtari asked. 'No, by God,' the Helper answered, 'we shall not spare your friend. Muhammad gave orders only about you.' Bakhtri declared: 'In that case, I shall die with him. I cannot let the women of Mecca say that I abandoned my friend, in order to spare my own life.' With these words Bakhtari attacked the Helper with his bare hands, and the Helper slew him with his sword.

Later Muhammad was prompted to renew his initial order, that all the captured Quraysh warriors should be taken to Medina.

446, 447

Burying the corpses

Muhammad ordered that a large pit be dug, and the corpses of the enemy be thrown into it. Every corpse was hurled into the pit, except one. This was the corpse of Umaya, which had swelled in its armour; when Muhammad's men tried to lift it, they found that it disintegrated in their hands. So they heaped stones and earth on top of it.

One of the corpses thrown into the pit was that of Utba. Hudayfa, his son, was looking on, and his face turned white. 'I fear that you feel deeply the death of your father,' Muhammad said. 'No,' Hudayfa replied; 'I have no misgivings about my father's death. He was a wise, cultured and virtuous man, and I hoped he would embrace Islam. But he died without faith – and it is this which saddens me.' Muhammad blessed and comforted him.

That evening Muhammad stood at the side of the pit, and recited the names of those whose corpses had been thrown into it: 'Utba, Shayba, Umaya, Abu Jahl ...' Then he cried out: 'People of the pit, have you now found out that what I said is true? Have you discovered that God's promises can be trusted?'

Some of his followers who heard him, asked: 'Are you calling to dead bodies?' Muhammad replied: 'In life they were deaf to my words; perhaps in death they can hear me.'

454, 455

Spoils of victory

A large quantity of booty was collected from the defeated Quraysh warriors, and the Muslim warriors started to quarrel over how it should be distributed. Those who had picked it up asserted that they themselves should keep it. Those who had gone in pursuit of retreating Quraysh warriors demanded an equal amount. And those who had been guarding Muhammad also claimed a share, complaining that their task prevented them from walking amongst the dead Quraysh, seizing their possessions.

When Muhammad heard about the quarrel, he decreed that every man should have the same amount; and he personally oversaw the distribution. He also remarked that this quarrel illustrated the evil nature of human beings, and hence the need for repentance.

Muhammad sent a messenger to Medina, to tell the people of their victory. When the messenger arrived, Muhammad's family was burying one of Muhammad's daughters, called Ruqaya.

On their journey to Medina, Muhammad, with his men and prisoners, passed through a village called Ruha. The women poured out of their houses to offer congratulations. Salama, Muhammad's nephew, said: 'What are you congratulating us about? We only encountered some bald old women; and we slaughtered them, as if they were sacrificial lambs that had been hobbled.' Muhammad smiled, and said to Salama: 'I presume you are talking about the Quraysh leaders, not their men.'

456, 457, 458

Mixed emotions

On reaching Medina, Muhammad ordered that his warriors should each take a prisoner to his own home, until a decision about the fate of the prisoners had been reached. The prisoners included many relatives of the Emigrants. So, as well as rejoicing at Muhammad's victory, many of the women amongst the Emigrants wept at the disgrace it had brought on their own families.

Muhammad took a young man called Suhayl to his home. He was the cousin of Sauda, one of Muhammad's wives. When Sauda saw Suhayl sitting in a corner, with his hands tied to his neck, she cried out: 'You surrendered too readily; you should have died a noble death.' Muhammad overheard her, and said: 'Are you trying to stir up trouble against God and his messenger?' She replied, 'I was so horrified to see my cousin enduring such ignominy, that I couldn't help speaking as I did.'

Umar came to Muhammad, and said: 'Let me pull out Suhayl's two front teeth. Then his tongue will stick out, and he will never be able to speak to you again.' Muhammad replied: 'I shall not allow my own relatives to be mutilated; otherwise God will mutilate me – even though I am his messenger.'

Meanwhile in Mecca the families of the prisoners wanted to pay a ransom quickly; and Muhammad set a high figure. The Quraysh leaders decided that the paying of ransoms should be delayed, in the hope that this would force Muhammad to accept a lower sum.

459, 461, 462, 463

A wife for a husband

Another of the Quraysh prisoners taken at Badr was Abul, who was married to Muhammad's daughter Zaynab. When Muhammad had become God's messenger, Abul had persisted in the old religion. Thus when Muhammad had emigrated to Medina, Zaynab had been forced to remain in Mecca with her husband.

Now Zaynab sent a large ransom to Medina for her husband. She added to it the necklace that her mother Khadija had given to her at her wedding. Muhammad was deeply moved by this sign of her devotion. He went to Abul and offered to release him without a ransom, on condition that he allowed Zaynab to come to Medina.

When Abul reached Mecca, he told Zaynab of Muhammad's condition. Zaynab's love for God and her father was greater than her love for her husband. So she set off for Medina, accompanied by her brother-in-law.

As soon as they heard of Zaynab's departure, the Quraysh leaders decided that this was a further humiliation for their tribe. So they sent Abu Sufyan with some warriors to fetch her back. When they encountered the fleeing couple, Abu Sufyan called out to Zaynab's brother-in-law: 'You have done wrong to take this woman away publicly, over the heads of our tribal leaders. Bring her back to Mecca until all the fuss has died down. You have my word that you will then be able to take her peacefully to her father.'

Her brother-in-law, who had no wish to humiliate his own tribe, agreed to this.

465, 466, 467

Abul's conversion

Abul was one of the wealthiest merchants in Mecca. Despite his sadness at his wife's departure, he resumed his business activities with great vigour. He organized and led a trading expedition to Jerusalem, persuading many other Quraysh men to invest.

Muslim warriors were now regularly attacking Quraysh caravans; and on his was home from Jerusalem Abul was attacked. The Muslims seized all the goods he was carrying, and took them back to Medina. Abul decided to go to Medina, to ask for his goods to be returned. He slipped into the city under cover of night, and went to Zaynab's house. She was delighted to see him.

The following morning Zaynab told her father of Abul's presence. Muhammad then sent a message to the warriors who had attacked Abul's caravan: 'Abul is my relative. If you are willing to restore to him the goods which you seized, I shall be pleased. But if you regard it as booty which God has given to you, I shall not disapprove.' The raiders restored the goods, and Abul went to Mecca with them.

Abul distributed the goods to his investors, who made a handsome profit. To each he said: 'I am imitating the honesty and generosity of the Muslims. I wanted to become a Muslim while I was with him; but I feared you would misconstrue my motive, thinking that I intended to rob you of your goods.' When he had finished the distribution, Abul returned to Medina, and declared his faith in Islam. There was great joy at his conversion.

Kab's treachery

The hypocrites amongst the Khazraj and the Aws, who secretly despised Islam, were aghast at Muhammad's victory. One of them, called Kab, commented: 'The Quraysh will avenge the death of so many of their leaders. Muhammad and his followers are doomed.' He then left Medina and went to Mecca; there he composed poems in which he mocked Muhammad, insulted Muslim women, and called for revenge for those who had been killed at Badr.

When news of Kab's treachery reached Medina, Muhammad cried out: 'Who will rid me of this traitor?' A young man, also called Muhammad, immediately exclaimed: 'I shall kill him!' Three days later Muhammad noticed that his young namesake was pale and thin, and asked the reason. 'I gave you an undertaking, and do not know how to fulfill it,' he replied. Muhammad said: 'All that matters is that you try.'

The young man travelled to Mecca with a wily friend called Abu Naila. They went to Kab's house and pretended to be enemies of Islam. In the evening they invited Kab to go for a walk with them. Suspecting nothing, Kab accepted. When they were outside the city, the young Muhammad stabbed Kab in the stomach, and killed him.

545, 548, 551, 552

Abu Sufyan's army

After the deaths of so many of their leaders at Badr, the people of Mecca turned to Abu Sufyan for guidance. He called a meeting of all the men of the city, and said: 'Muhammad has done us a grievous wrong. He and his followers have slaughtered many of our finest citizens. Remember that, prior to the defeat at Badr, I safely brought a large caravan back to Mecca. Count up the money you made from that caravan, and donate it to a fund – to be used for fighting Muhammad, and having our revenge.'

With this money Abu Sufyan employed warriors from other tribes. He thus assembled a force far larger and more competent than the one defeated at Badr.

Many of the wealthy merchants in Mecca owned slaves from Ethiopia. These Ethiopians were renowned for their skill in throwing the javelin; and the finest amongst them was called Washi. His master said to him: 'Go and join Abu Sufyan's army, and with your javelin kill Hamza, Muhammad's uncle. It was Hamza who killed my own uncle at Badr. If you succeed, I shall gladly set you free.'

Abu Sufyan invited the women of Mecca to accompany his army, to stir up the men's anger and to prevent them from running away. He led his army northwards, and then camped in a valley a short distance from Medina.

555, 557

Confused advice

When Muhammad heard that Abu Sufyan had camped near Medina with a large army, he assembled his warriors, and said to them: 'I believe that we should not attack Abu Sufyan. Eventually he will attack Medina, and we shall be in a strong position to defend ourselves.' Abdullah agreed with Muhammad. But some, who had not been present at Badr, thought that waiting in Medina would be interpreted as a sign of cowardice and weakness.

Abdullah begged Muhammad to exercise restraint: 'Disaster will ensue if we go out to attack them. But by staying here we put them in a difficult predicament. If they remain in the valley, they will soon run short of food and water. Yet if they march on Medina, the entire population will resist them – even women and children will throw stones on them from the walls.' Those who wanted to attack the Quraysh continued to argue their case, and finally Muhammad gave in to them. He went to his house, and put on his armour.

While Muhammad was preparing himself for battle, those who had urged him to attack the Quraysh were seized with doubts, and said to one another: 'We should have deferred to Muhammad's original intention.' When Muhammad appeared, they told him of their doubts, and urged him to remain in the city. Muhammad replied: 'It is not fitting that a messenger of God should put on armour, and then take it off without fighting.'

Growing anxiety

Muhammad assembled a force of about a thousand warriors, and they marched out towards the Quraysh encampment. After only a few minutes Abdullah, who was commanding three hundred men, said to them: 'Muhammad has rejected my advice, and followed the advice of fools. If we continue on this course, we shall lose our lives – for no purpose.' So he led his man back to Medina.

A large number of others, who also regarded the present action as foolish, decided to follow Abdullah. One of Muhammad's closest companions urged them to stay. But they replied: 'If we believed that you would fight, we should stay with you. But we think that, as soon as you see the size of the Quraysh army, you will retreat. So it is better to go back now.'

Another of Muhammad's close companions, who was himself very anxious, said to Muhammad: 'Should we not go back to Medina, and recruit some of the friendly Jews to our force?' 'We have no need of them,' Muhammad replied. At that moment a horse swished its tail, and caught the handle of a sword, pulling it out of its sheath. Muhammad declared that this was a good omen.

Muhammad now had only a few hundred men behind him. He led them to a hill, overlooking the valley of Uhud where the Quraysh army was camped. Muhammad's companions counted three thousand warriors under Abu Sufyan's command, with two hundred horses.

559, 561

Death and defeat

The next morning the two armies faced one another. Abu Sufyan sent a message to the Helpers: 'Men of the Khazraj and Aws tribes, we have no quarrel with you. Go home, and leave us to deal with our cousins.' But the Helpers gave a rude reply.

Abu Sufyan spoke to the Quraysh standard-bearers: 'You had charge of our flag on the day of Badr, and look what happened! Warriors depend on the fortunes of their flags. So either you must guard our flags efficiently, or hand them over to me.' The standard-bearers were infuriated by this insult, and said: 'You will see how well we act when battle is joined.' This was just the response which Abu Sufyan wanted.

The battle began. Abu Sufyan sent many women into the fray, dressed as men, to incite the Quraysh warriors to fight bravely. These women shrieked and shouted violently.

Hamza fought with great courage, killing one of the Quraysh standard-bearers, and then cutting his way through the enemy ranks, striking down men to his left and right. Washi, the Ethiopian slave, saw Hamza, and hurled his javelin at him. It pierced the lower part of his body, and came out between his legs. He staggered towards Washi, waving his sword; but after a few steps he collapsed and died.

By the middle of the day so many of the Muslim warriors had been killed, that Muhammad ordered his army to retreat. At that moment a Quraysh warrior hurled a stone at Muhammad, causing him to fall from his camel, and smash several teeth.

561, 562, 563, 564, 571

Humiliation and defiance

Word spread among the fleeing Muslim warriors that Muhammad had been killed. Then one of the warriors saw Muhammad struggling to lift himself up. The warrior was about to call out that Muhammad was alive; but Muhammad signalled to him to remain silent, lest the Quraysh warriors should hear the call also, and come and kill God's messenger.

With the warrior's help Muhammad climbed back onto his camel, and rode to the top of the gorge of Uhud, where his men had assembled. A few moments later Abu Sufyan appeared on the hill above the gorge, and called down to Muhammad: 'Victory in war goes in turns. Our victory today is in exchange for yours at Badr. Now you must vindicate your religion.' Muhammad called back: 'Your side and our side are not equal. Our dead are in paradise; yours are in hell.'

Abu Sufyan walked away. Muhammad said: 'If the Quraysh warriors are heading for Medina, we must rush back, and defend our homes.' So he sent Ali to see in which direction they were heading; Ali reported that they were marching towards Mecca.

Muhammad led his men to the battlefield to search for their dead. His men wanted to carry the corpses to Medina. But Muhammad ordered that they be buried where they lay, declaring: 'These men have died fighting in God's cause, and on the day of resurrection God will raise them up.'

574, 582, 583, 586

Siege of Medina

A number of Jews in Medina, who were hostile to Muhammad, went to Mecca, and invited the Quraysh leaders to
form an alliance with them, with the purpose of destroying
Muhammad and his religion. The Quraysh leaders said to the
Jews: 'You are a devout people, who follow an ancient religion; so you can understand the nature of our dispute with
Muhammad. In your judgement, is our religion better or
worse than his?' The Jews replied that the Quraysh religion
was superior to that taught by Muhammad. The Quraysh
leaders were so pleased with this response that they accepted
the Jews' proposal.

When Muhammad heard of this, he urged the men of
Medina to dig a trench round the city. He himself worked
hard, and others joined him with enthusiasm. But some had
been so shocked by the defeat at Uhud that they secretly
doubted whether Muhammad was truly God's messenger; and
they were slack in their work.

Just as the trench was being completed, a Quraysh army
appeared, led by Abu Sufyan, and accompanied by the hostile Jews. Seeing the trench, Abu Sufyan realized that they
should have to besiege the city.

The siege lasted for many weeks. The people of Medina
had sufficient food. Their only hardship was that they could
not go outside the city to defecate, so the city became quite
smelly. But the Quraysh army had not anticipated conducting
a siege, so they had not brought sufficient supplies. The warriors grew steadily more hungry.

669, 670, 673, 677

Nuaym's deceit

One of the Quraysh warriors, called Nuaym, had secretly become a Muslim; and he had joined the Quraysh force with the intention of subverting it. One night he came to Muhammad's house. Realizing that Nuaym was sincere, Muhammad said to him: 'War involves deceit, as well as fighting. Let deceit be your weapon.'

Nuaym went back to his camp. On the following morning he visited the Jews, and said to them: 'The Quraysh leaders are not like you. This land is yours; you grew up here, and your children are growing up here. You cannot leave it and go elsewhere. The Quraysh warriors have come to fight Muhammad; but their land is far away. If they see an opportunity to defeat Muhammad, they will seize it. But if things continue to go badly, they will eventually go home, leaving you to face Muhammad alone. So do not stay with these people, unless they are willing to hand over some of their warriors as hostages – for you to hand back when they have defeated Muhammad.' The Jews thanked Nuaym for his excellent advice.

Nuaym then went to Abu Sufyan, and said: 'I have heard something, which as a matter of duty I must pass on to you; but please regard it as confidential. The Jews now regret their action in opposing Muhammad. They have made a secret alliance with him. They will demand hostages from you, and then cut their heads off. That will be a sign to Muhammad that he can trust them. So at that moment the Jewish and the Muslim warriors will attack you.'

Abu Sufyan's retreat

Abu Sufyan was anxious about the condition of his horses and camels, who were dying for lack of food. He thus decided to prepare for an attack on Medina the following day. He did not know whether to trust Nuaym's report, but his decision would test it. If the Jews joined in the preparations without question, it would prove that the report was false; but if the Jews acted as Nuaym had said, he would lead his troops back to Mecca.

Abu Sufyan sent a message to the Jews, asking them to join the Quraysh warriors in attacking Medina. The Jews replied that they would only join the attack if he handed over hostages, who would be returned when Muhammad was defeated. Abu Sufyan sent a further message, saying that their joint action would only be successful if there was mutual trust; therefore he would not hand over hostages. The Jews replied that they would not fight.

Abu Sufyan then assembled the Quraysh warriors and said: 'Our camels and horses are dying for lack of food; and we have barely enough food to keep ourselves alive. Moreover, there is a violent wind blowing down our tents. I also have good reason to believe that the Jews intend to betray us. So I have decided we should return home.'

With these words Abu Sufyan mounted his camel and led his men away.

682, 683, 684

The missing wife

Muhammad led many expeditions attacking and seizing Quraysh caravans, in the hope of wearing down Quraysh resistance to him. By this time he had a number of wives; and he would cast lots to determine which wife would accompany him on each expedition. On one particular occasion the lot fell on Aisha, who was Abu Bakr's daughter. She sat on a camel within a howdah, and the camel was led by a man walking in front.

On the return journey the expedition camped in a valley, a day's journey from Medina. At dawn on the following morning Aisha went out to defecate. When she came back, she realized that her necklace had gone; and she retraced her steps looking for it. While she was away, the expedition set off; and, since everyone assumed she was in the howdah, her camel was led away also. Meanwhile Aisha found the necklace, and came back to the site of the camp. She sat down and waited, certain that, as soon as her absence was noticed, people would come in search of her.

One of the members of the expedition, a young man called Safwan, had fallen behind the main group, and had spent the night further back; so he was hurrying to catch them. He was astonished to find Aisha sitting alone. He told her to mount his camel, and he led the camel forward at great speed.

By nightfall Muhammad and the others had reached Medina. As news spread that Safwan and Aisha were missing, a rumour of their wickedness began to circulate.

73 1, 73 2

Aisha's illness

When Aisha and Safwan reached Medina, Aisha became very ill, and so heard nothing of the rumour. Eventually the rumour reached the ears of her parents and Muhammad himself. Her parents said nothing to her, and her mother nursed her. Muhammad was so upset that he showed no compassion for her suffering. He visited her on only one occasion, and even then refused to speak to her; he simply gave orders that she should be taken away to her mother's home.

Aisha began to recover after three months. She then resumed going out at dusk, to defecate in the area outside the town reserved for women. One evening she was approached by another woman, who asked: 'Have you heard the rumour about yourself and Safwan?' Aisha replied that she was ignorant, so the woman recounted the rumour. Aisha was so distraught that she could not defecate.

She rushed home, and wept with such bitterness that she felt her liver would burst. When she was able to speak, she exclaimed to her mother: 'God forgive you; people have slandered me, and neither you nor anyone else has told me.' 'My little daughter,' her mother replied, 'do not let that matter weigh on you. Whenever a beautiful young woman marries a loving and handsome man, other people are jealous, and indulge in malicious gossip.'

Aisha's vindication

Muhammad decided to question Aisha, to discover if the rumour of her wickedness with Safwan were true. He went to her parents' house, and sat down bedside her. He praised God, and said: 'Aisha, you know what people are saying about you. If you have done wrong, repent at once, and trust God to forgive you.' Aisha said nothing, hoping that her parents would defend her; but they remained silent. She asked them why they did not speak; and they replied that they did not know what to say.

Aisha began weeping, and exclaimed: 'I cannot repent of the sin you mention, because, as God knows, I am innocent of it. Yet if I deny the sin, you will not believe me.' Then she prayed to God. She felt that she was too insignificant for God to talk directly to Muhammad about her. But she begged God to reveal her innocence to Muhammad in a dream, or some other minor form of communication.

At that moment Muhammad went into a trance. Aisha felt no fear, because she knew that God would treat her justly. But her parents were terrified that God would confirm the truth of the rumour. After a while Muhammad came out of his trance, and declared: 'Aisha, God has sent word of your innocence.' 'Praise be to God!' Aisha answered.

Muhammad then went out and told others of God's revelation. And he ordered that anyone who mentioned the rumour again be flogged as a liar.

Pilgrimage to Mecca

Seven years after he and his followers had emigrated to Medina, Muhammad decided to make the pilgrimage to Mecca. When the Quraysh leaders heard of Muhammad's intention, they were in a quandary. They did not want him to enter the city, as they regarded him as their most dangerous enemy. Yet as custodians of the Kaba on behalf of all Arabs, they had a sacred obligation to welcome him. One of the leaders said that Muhammad's desire to come to Mecca was a sign of weakness, adding: 'I have heard that he and his followers are virtually destitute.' The leaders thus decided not to exclude him.

When Muhammad reached the Grand Mosque, most of the population was at the entrance, eager to look at him. As he went in, he threw the end of his cloak over his left shoulder, leaving his right arm free. He declared: 'May God have mercy on the man who today shows the people he is strong.' Then he walked round the Kaba, kissing each side, and finally kissing the black stone. After a short pause he trotted round the Kaba three times, and walked round it a further three times.

Muhammad remained three days in Mecca. At the end of the third day a group of Quraysh leaders came to him, and said: 'Your time here is over, so get out.' Muhammad replied: 'Let me organize a great feast, at which I shall provide food for all the Quraysh leaders.' They said: 'We do not want your food; leave this city at once.' So Muhammad left Mecca and returned to Medina.

789, 790

Abu Sufyan's peace mission

Muhammad and the Muslim warriors continued to attack Quraysh caravans, causing great hardship to the Quraysh people, whose prosperity depended on trade.

Abu Sufyan therefore decided to go to Medina, in the hope of ending hostilities. He went first to his own daughter, who had embraced Islam and emigrated with Muhammad. As he was about to sit down on one of her carpets, she folded it up. 'My dear daughter,' he said, 'I hardly know what to think. Is the carpet too good for me, or am I too good for the carpet?' She replied: 'It is Muhammad's carpet, and you are an unclean idol-worshipper.' Abu Sufyan sighed, and said: 'Since you left me, you have become cold and rude.'

Abu Sufyan then went to see Muhammad; but Muhammad refused to speak to him. He went in turn to Abu Bakr and Umar, and asked them to speak to Muhammad on his behalf; but both refused.

Abu Sufyan now went to Ali, who was now married to Muhammad's daughter, Fatima. When he arrived, the couple were together, with their small son Hassan crawling in front of them. Abu Sufyan pleaded with Ali to use his influence with Muhammad, in order to promote peace. Ali replied that, if Muhammad had made a decision about something, it was useless to talk to him about it. But he recommended that Abu Sufyan should guarantee the safety of all who went as pilgrims to Mecca, as this would be taken as a sign of peace.

806, 807, 808

Preparations to leave

Abu Sufyan now went to the mosque in Medina, and spoke to the people: 'I have come here in search of peace. I grant my protection to all who come to Mecca as pilgrims.' He then mounted his camel, and rode off towards Mecca.

When he reached Mecca, the other Quraysh leaders crowded round him, eagerly asking for his news. He told them that Muhammad would not speak to him, Abu Bakr would not help him, and Umar was an implacable enemy. He added that Ali had proved friendly; and on his advice he had guaranteed the safety of all who came on pilgrimage to Mecca. 'Did Muhammad give approval to your words, accepting them as a sign of peace?' the Quraysh leaders asked. Abu Sufyan admitted that he had not. 'Then Ali has made a fool of you,' the Quraysh leaders exclaimed.

When the time of pilgrimage approached, Muhammad ordered his wife Aisha to pack all his belongings. While she was doing this, her father Abu Bakr entered the house. 'Is Muhammad preparing to leave Medina?' he asked. She replied: 'He is, but I do not know whether he intends to go alone, or to take his army with him.' 'Then I must also get ready to leave,' Abu Bakr said.

A short time later Muhammad assembled his warriors, and ordered them to prepare to go to Mecca. Then he prayed: 'O God, cover the eyes and block the ears of the Quraysh leaders, so we may take them by surprise.'

Hatib's letter

One of the Muslim warriors called Hatib wrote a letter to the Quraysh leaders, telling them that Muhammad was intending to come to Mecca with his army. He handed it to a woman to take to the Quraysh leaders, giving her a large sum of money. She put it on her head, and plaited her hair over it; she then set off towards Mecca on her camel.

Muhammad heard of her departure, and was suspicious of her motive; so he sent Ali and a companion after her. When they caught up with her, they ordered her to dismount. They searched her baggage and found nothing. Then they told her they would strip her. She saw they were in earnest. She asked them to turn aside while she unplaited her hair; she drew out the letter, and handed it to them.

When Muhammad had read the letter, he summoned Hatib, and asked him why he had committed this act of treachery. Hatib replied: 'I believe in God, and I believe that you are his messenger. But I have a son in Mecca, who himself has children. Our family is quite lowly and impoverished; and I wished to win favour with the Quraysh leaders, so that they would treat my son and his children well.'

Umar exclaimed: 'This man is a hypocrite; I shall cut off his head at once.' Muhammad said: 'You do not know for certain that he is a hypocrite; perhaps God blesses those who fought at Badr and survived – as Hatib did.' So Hatib was spared.

809, 810

The white mule

Muhammad's army now numbered over ten thousand men. It included the Emigrants and Helpers, and also many warriors from other tribes who had converted to Islam. They left Medina on the tenth day of the month of Ramadan, and continued fasting until the end of the month.

They camped a short distance from Mecca. Until then the Quraysh leaders had been entirely ignorant of their approach. But now Abu Sufyan suspected something was afoot; and that night he went out of the city, to see what he could find. When he caught sight of thousands of fires, he was astonished.

In the meantime Abbas had ridden from the camp on a white mule, which belonged to Muhammad. He wanted to send a message to the Quraysh leaders, telling them of the size of Muhammad's army, and begging them to be hospitable; he feared that, if they resisted, the entire population of Mecca would be destroyed in the fighting. He was looking for a woodcutter or a shepherd to carry his message.

He came across Abu Sufyan, and the two men recognized one another. Abbas told Abu Sufyan that the fires belonged to Muhammad's warriors. Abu Sufyan went pale with terror. Abbas added: 'Although I am a devout Muslim, I continue to have great devotion and loyalty towards my tribe, the Quraysh – and also respect for you, as a wise leader. If you are caught here, you are likely to be instantly beheaded. But let me take you to Muhammad, and beg him to spare you.'

Abu Sufyan's submission

Abu Sufyan mounted the white mule behind Abbas, and they rode through the camp. At every group of tents they were challenged; but when the warriors saw that the two men were on Muhammad's white mule, they let them pass.

When they reached Umar's tent, Umar inspected them closely. He recognized Abu Sufyan, and exclaimed: 'Enemy of God! Thanks be to God that he has delivered you into our hands, without fighting or negotiation.' Umar took out his sword, but Abbas galloped away to Muhammad's tent. Muhammad ordered Abbas to take Abu Sufyan to his own tent, and bring him back the following morning.

At dawn Abbas brought Abu Sufyan back to Muhammad, who asked him: 'In the light of all that has occurred, is it not time for you to recognize that there is no other god but God?' Abu Sufyan replied: 'You are dearer to me than my own father and mother, your mercy, honesty and kindness are beyond measure. If there were another god apart from God, he surely would have helped me.'

Abbas then turned to Muhammad, and said: 'Abu Sufyan is a man with great pride. Ask something of him, that he may have the satisfaction of granting it.' Muhammad said to Abu Sufyan: 'Let all who enter your house enjoy protection; and let all who enter the Grand Mosque also enjoy your protection.' And Muhammad said to Abbas: 'When my army marches off towards Mecca, stand with Abu Sufyan at the side of the road, so all can see him.'

813, 814

Victory over Mecca

Muhammad ordered his commanders only to fight those who resisted them; otherwise they should treat the people of Mecca with courtesy and kindness. Yet as they entered the city, they met no violence whatever. As soon as people saw the size of his army, they realized that resistance was pointless. Besides, most of them yearned for peace with Muhammad, and respected his honesty and wisdom. As he rode down the avenue leading to the Grand Mosque, crowds gathered on either side to greet him.

When he reached the Grand Mosque, Muhammad went round the Kaba seven times on his camel, touching the black stone with a stick he was carrying. Then he summoned Uthman, the keeper of the Kaba, and took the key from him. He dismounted, opened the door of the Kaba, and entered. There he found a dove made of wood, which the people worshipped. He carried it out of the Kaba, broke it in pieces and threw it away.

By now it was noon, and Muhammad ordered all those assembled in the Grand Mosque to prostrate themselves. He led them in prayer. Afterwards he ordered his men to collect all the other idols round the Kaba, and put them in a pile. The pile was huge. Muhammad set fire to it, and the flames leapt high into the air.

817, 820

The new order

Muhammad went back into the Kaba with several of his companions. A large number of pictures had been painted on the inside walls, including two of Jesus and Mary. He ordered all the pictures to be erased, except these two.

Then he stood at the door of the Kaba, and spoke to the people: 'There is no god but God; he has no rival. He has fulfilled his promise and helped his messenger. He has put to flight those who oppose him. I hereby abolish all rights and privileges in Mecca based solely on blood or property, except the custody of the Kaba and the watering of pilgrims. Quraysh people, God has taken away from you the pride that came from your pagan religion, which was based on the veneration of ancestors. God created all people from dust, so in his eyes all are equal.'

Muhammad paused. Then he asked the Quraysh people: 'What do you think I am about to do to you?' One of the Quraysh leaders stepped forward, and said: 'We trust you, and believe you will do good to us.' Muhammad proclaimed: 'You are released from the slavery of falsehood, and now enjoy the freedom of truth. Go your way, and enjoy that freedom.'

821

Submission of all Arabia

Many of the tribes of Arabia already had members who had converted to Islam. But the tribal leaders throughout Arabia were watching to see how Muhammad fared in his conflict with the Quraysh, before making up their minds about Islam. This was because the Quraysh were acknowledged as the foremost tribe of Arabia, descended directly from Ishmael, the son of Abraham.

Thus when Muhammad took control of Mecca, and became the ruler of the Quraysh, the other tribes had no wish to oppose him. On the contrary, Muhammad's success convinced them that his message about the supremacy of God was true. Each tribe sent a deputation to Muhammad, pledging the allegiance of their people to Islam, and praising God for making Islam victorious.

One of the deputations contained a fine orator, who gave a public address in the Grand Mosque: 'Praise belongs to God, who created the sky and the earth, and established his rule within them. Nothing exists except through his generosity. By his power he appoints kings. And he chose the best of his creation to be his messenger – a man of noble lineage, honest speech, and faultless behaviour. God entrusted him with his Book, which gives guidance to all humanity. God selected this man from all the races of the world, as the means by which to reveal himself to the world.'

Time to die

Two years after subduing Mecca, and ten years after emigrating to Medina, Muhammad began to suffer from the illness by which God took him to his eternal destiny.

One night he rose from his bed, and set out towards a cemetery to pray for the dead. He was accompanied by Abdullah, the son of Umar. When they reached the cemetery, Muhammad said: 'Peace be upon you, people of the graves; you are far happier than those who are alive on earth. There is no end to arguments and disputes amongst living human beings.'

Then he turned to Abdullah, and said: 'I have been given a choice. I may have a long life, surviving into old age, and have the key to all the wealth this world contains – and then go to paradise. Or I may go to paradise at once.' Abdullah urged him to choose the former. But Muhammad said that he had already chosen the latter. He resumed praying for a short while, and then returned home. His head was now aching severely.

By this time the dawn had come, and his wife Aisha had risen. Muhammad asked her: 'Would it distress you if you were to die before me, so that I might wrap you in a shroud, pray over you, and bury you?' Aisha replied: 'If that happened, you would come back to your house, and spend the following night with one of your other wives, behaving as if you had just married.'

Muhammad smiled. As the hours and days passed, his headache worsened.

Final words

Muhammad wanted to preach once again. Seven skins of water from different wells were poured over his head, to ease the pain. Then a cloth was wrapped round his head. Umar held him as he walked to the pulpit.

Muhammad began by praying for the men who had died at Uhud: 'May God forgive them for any wrongs they did, and receive them into paradise.' He mentioned each dead warrior by name. After that he turned to the people, and said: 'God has given me the choice, to remain on this earth, or to go at once to paradise. I have chosen to go at once to paradise. Throughout my years as God's messenger my closest companion has been Abu Bakr. I appoint him as the leader of all Muslims; he will have charge of all public worship.'

Aisha interrupted, begging Muhammad to spare Abu Bakr the task of leading worship: 'He is a delicate man with a weak voice, who weeps when he recites God's revelations.' But Muhammad repeated his order, and added: 'The fire of divine truth has been kindled. Yet rebellions will come like the darkness of the night. Let Abu Bakr maintain the unity and strength of the Muslim community, by allowing what the Book allows, and forbidding what the Book forbids.'

A few days after his final sermon Muhammad died, his head resting in Aisha's arms. His last words were: 'I go forth, detached from my body, to the glory of paradise.'

1006, 1008, 1010

THE QURAN

Muhammad received messages over a period of about two decades. He dictated them to scribes; and approximately fifteen years after his death the messages were assembled in their present form. The Quran is divided into 114 chapters, arranged according to length; but for the daily reading given during Ramadan, the month of fasting, it is divided into 30 sections.

In its original Arabic the Quran is acknowledged as a poetic masterpiece, whose constant repetition of themes and phrases adds to its power. In translation much of its literary power is lost, its theology can appear crude, and its repetition tedious – so that readers are often disappointed. For this reason it is paticularly suited to abridgement.

The relationship of the words of the Quran to God can seem to vary. Sometimes God is referred to in the third person; and sometimes God is speaking in the first person – occasionally singular, but more often plural as 'we'. In the present rendering the first person verses are put in inverted commas.

In the name of God

In the name of God, the compassionate, the merciful.

All praise belongs to God, the Lord of all being. He is compassionate and merciful. He is the master of the day of judgement.

We worship only you; in you alone we seek refuge. Guide us along the straight path, the path of those whom you have blessed – not the path of those who have incurred your wrath, nor the path of those who have gone astray.

I. I–7

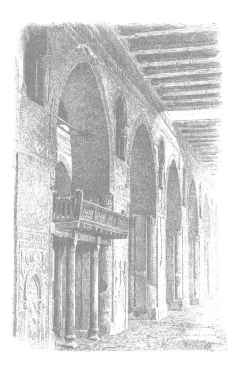

Faith and deception

'This book should not be doubted. It is a guide to the righteous, who believe in the unseen mysteries, and are steadfast
in prayer; who give generously from what we have given
them; who trust what has been revealed to Muhammad and
others before him; and who firmly believe in the life to
come.' The righteous are those who accept the righteous
guidance of their Lord; and they will surely triumph.

There are many who say: 'We believe in God and in the
last day.' But not all who say this are true believers; some are
hypocrites, who seek to deceive both God and genuine believers in God. But the hypocrites deceive no one except
themselves – though they do not perceive this. There is a
sickness in their minds, which God increases; they will be
severely punished for their hypocrisy.

You may say to the hypocrites: 'Do not bring conflict to
this land.' But they will reply: 'We only bring peace.' In fact
they bring nothing but conflict – though they do not perceive
this. You may say to them: 'Believe, as others believe.' But
they will reply: 'We shall not believe as fools believe.' In fact
they are the fools – though they do not perceive this. When
they meet true believers, they say: 'We are believers like you.'
But when they are alone with their devils, they say to them:
'We follow no one but you; we were only joking.'

2.2–5, 8–14

Fires and storms

The hypocrites exchange guidance for error. But they gain nothing in the exchange; instead they stray from the right path. They are like people who kindle fires; but as soon as their fires are burning brightly, God puts out the fires and leaves them in darkness, unable to see. They are deaf, dumb and blind; they will never return to the right path.

When a storm cloud passes overhead, some people thrust their fingers in their ears to block out the noise of thunder. With every flash of lightning they walk a few steps; but when darkness returns, their eyes are so dazzled that they can see nothing – and thus they stand still. Hypocrites are like such people; their hearts are afraid, and their minds are blind. If God wanted, he could take away their sight and hearing; he has power over all things.

Men and women, serve your Lord. He created you and all your ancestors, and he guards you against evil. He made the earth as a home for you, and the sky as a roof. He sends water from the sky, to bring forth fruits for your sustenance. Do not deliberately set up other gods besides God. 'If you doubt what we have revealed through our servant Muhammad, produce a single chapter comparable to the chapters of this book.'

2.17–23a

'Children of Israel, remember the favours which I have bestowed on you. Keep faith with me, and I shall keep faith
with you. Trust my revelations, which confirm your own
Scriptures; do not be the first to deny them. Honour me, and
do not deny my revelations for material gain. Do not mix
truth with falsehood, and do not deliberately hide the truth.
Attend to your prayers, pay the poor-rate, and worship with
others who worship. Would you urge others to be righteous,
and yet forget to be righteous yourselves? You read your own
Scriptures. Have you no sense?'

Strengthen yourselves with patient prayer. Prayer is difficult, except for those who are humble – who know they will
return to their Lord, and meet him.

'Children of Israel, remember the favours which I have bestowed upon you. Remember that I have exalted you above
all nations. Be on your guard against the day when every soul
will stand alone. At that time no one will be able to intercede
for the individual soul; no compensation will be accepted for
past sins. Every soul will face me without help.'

2.40–48

To the Arabs

'We have sent you an apostle who belongs to your own nation. He will recite our revelations and purify you of sin. He will explain to you the book which we have dictated to him; he will make you wise, teaching you things of which at present you know nothing. Remember me, and I shall remember you. Give thanks to me, and I shall never reject you.'

Strengthen yourselves with patient prayer. God is close to those who are patient. Those who have died in God's cause, are not dead; they are alive, even though you cannot see them.

'We shall test your faith with many horrors and with famine, with physical injury, and with loss of property and crops.' I proclaim good news to those who endure these tests with courage, to those who say in adversity: 'We belong to God, and to God we shall return.' God will bless and forgive such people; he will guide them on the path of righteousness.

The hills of Safa and Marwa near Mecca are beacons of God. It will be an offence for pilgrims or visitors to the sacred house to walk around these hills. Those who do good spontaneously, will be rewarded by God. God knows all things.

2.151–158

True piety

Your God is one God. There is no god but him. He is merciful and compassionate.

There are many signs of God for men and women of understanding. There is the creation of the heavens and the earth. There is the alternation of night and day. There are the ships sailing the ocean with cargoes that bring pleasure to people. There is the rain that God sends down from the sky; by this means he revives the barren earth, and nourishes the creatures that live in the earth. And there are the changing winds, and the clouds that are driven through the atmosphere between the earth and the sky.

Piety does not consist in whether you face east or west during worship. True piety consists in this: believing in God and in his final judgement; believing in his angels, in the Book, and in the prophets; giving your wealth, for the sake of God, to your relatives, to orphans, to the needy, to wayfarers and to strangers; ransoming slaves; attending prayers and paying the poor-rate; being true to your promises; and being steadfast in times of distress, adversity and war. Those who show true piety, are genuine in their faith; they honour God.

2.163–164, 177

Retaliation and pardon

Believers, you may retaliate when others attack you: you may slay a freeman for a freeman, a slave for a slave, and a woman for a woman. But when a victim pardons the person who has done wrong, then the compensation should be according to custom; and it should be handed over in a spirit of friendship. This is what the Lord prefers. Those who continue to do wrong, should be severely punished.

You must understand that retaliation is allowed as a means of protecting yourselves. It is a means of guarding yourselves against evil actions.

2.178–179

Fasting

Believers, fasting is decreed for you, in the same way that it was decreed for those before you, as a means of guarding yourselves against evil. You should fast for the number of days that has been prescribed. But if you are ill, or on a journey, you may fast for the same number of days later on. If you can afford it, you should ransom yourselves by giving food to someone who is poor. Helping others spontaneously does you much good; fasting does you even greater good – if you only knew.

In the month of Ramadan the Quran was revealed. It is a book of guidance, showing the difference between right and wrong; and it has clear proofs of the guidance it gives. So those who are at home during this month, should fast. But if you are ill, or on a journey, you may fast for the same number of days later on. God desires your well-being, not your discomfort. He wants you to fast for the whole month so that you may exalt him, and offer thanks to him for the guidance he has given you.

'When my servants question you about me, tell them that I am near. I answer their prayers when they call on me; let them answer my call. Let them trust in me, that they may be guided along the path of righteousness.'

2.183–186

Pilgrimage

Make the pilgrimage, visiting the sacred house, for God's sake. But if you are prevented from making the pilgrimage, send such offering as you can afford, and do not shave your heads until the offering reaches its destination. But if you are ill, or suffer some injury to the head, you should compensate by fasting, by giving to the poor, or by offering a sacrifice.

If in peacetime you combine visiting the sacred house with the pilgrimage, offer such gifts as you can afford. But if you lack the means to offer any gifts, you should fast three days during the pilgrimage, and seven days after you have returned – ten days in all. That is also an obligation on anyone whose family is not present at the holy mosque. Honour God; remember that he is severe in punishing evil.

Make the pilgrimage in the customary month. During the pilgrimage you should abstain from sexual intercourse, obscene language, and quarrelling. God is aware of whatever good you do. Provide well for yourselves; the best provision is piety. 'Honour me, that you may receive understanding.'

2.196–197

No compulsion in religion

There is no god but God, who lives eternally. Neither slumber nor sleep overtakes him. To him belongs everything in the heavens and on the earth. Who can intercede with him, except by his permission? He knows what lies before and behind all people. Human beings can only understand those parts of his truth which he wishes them to understand. His throne is as vast as the sky and the earth; and sustaining both the sky and the earth does not weary him. He is the highest and the greatest.

There should be no compulsion in matters of religion. The right path is now clearly distinct from the wrong path. Those who renounce the worship of idols, and put their faith in God, grasp a firm handle which will never break. God hears all and knows all.

God is the guardian of all who believe. He leads them from darkness to light. As for those who do not believe, their guardians are their false gods, who lead them from light to darkness. They are the heirs of hell, and will live there for ever.

2.25–257

Giving generously

If you spend your wealth in the service of God, you are like a grain of corn which sprouts seven ears, each of which bears a hundred grains. God is abundantly generous to those who are generous; he knows all.

If you spend your wealth in the service of God, but do not follow your generosity with reproaches and insults, you will be richly rewarded by the Lord. You will have nothing to fear or to regret.

A kind word of forgiveness is better than charity accompanied by insults. God is self-sufficient and merciful.

Believers, do not mar your generosity with reproaches and rebukes – like those who like to show off their generosity, and who do not believe in God and the last day. Such people are like a rock covered with earth; a heavy shower falls upon it, leaving it bare. They will gain nothing from their efforts. God does not guide the unbelievers.

But those who are generous with their wealth, from a desire to please God and to satisfy their own souls, are like an orchard on a hillside. If rain falls upon the orchard, it yields twice its normal crop; and if no rain falls upon it, then it is watered by the dew. God observes all your actions.

Those who are generous by day and by night, both in secret and openly, will be rewarded by God. They have nothing to fear or regret.

2.261–265, 274

Those who live by charging interest on loans, have been cast down by Satan. They claim that usury is like normal trading. But God has permitted trading and forbidden usury. Those who have been rebuked by God, and have mended their ways, may keep what they have already gained; their fate is in the hands of God. But those who ignore God's rebuke, will be consigned to the fires of hell, and will remain there for ever.

God curses usury, and blesses acts of charity. God has no love for ungrateful sinners. The Lord will reward those who have faith and do good works, who say their prayers and pay the poor-rate. They have nothing to fear or regret.

Believers, if your faith is sincere, honour God by waiving any interest that is owed to you on loans. If you do not waive all interest, God and his apostle will declare war on you. But if you repent, you may retain your capital; neither you nor your debtor will suffer any loss.

If your debtor is in difficulty, postpone the day when the debt must be repaid. If you turn the debt into a gift, that will be even better for you – if you only knew.

2.275b–280

The property of orphans and the feeble-minded

O people, honour your Lord, who created you from a single being. From that being God created a mate; and through them he covered the earth with countless men and women. Honour God, in whose name you demand from one another your rights; and honour the ties of kinship. God is constantly watching over you.

Give orphans the property that belongs to them. Do not substitute worthless objects for their valuable possessions, and do not mix their possessions with your own; such actions would be great sins.

If God has entrusted property to you, with which to support the feeble-minded, do not hand over the property to them. Maintain and clothe them from the profits of the property, and give them wise advice.

Take care of orphans until they reach the age of marriage. If you find them capable of sound judgement, hand over to them their property. Do not deprive them of any of their property by squandering it during their childhood. Rich guardians should not touch the property of orphans in their care. Poor guardians should use only that portion which is fair. When you hand over to them their property, call in some witnesses; God will check the accounts you have kept.

4. 1–2, 5–6

Harmony and generosity

If there is a breach between a husband and his wife, let his family and her family each appoint an arbiter. If the man and the woman wish to be reconciled, God will restore harmony between them. God is wise and all-knowing.

Serve God, and God alone. Be kind to your parents and your relatives, to orphans and the needy, to neighbours near and far, to other travellers when you are away, to wayfarers, and to your slaves. God does not love those who are arrogant and conceited, who are stingy and urge others to be stingy, and who conceal the wealth which God in his bounty has bestowed upon them. 'We have prepared a shameful punishment for unbelievers.' God does not love those who spend their wealth ostentatiously, believing neither in God nor in the last day. Such people are making friends with Satan – and what an evil friend he is!

What harm can befall those who believe in God and in the last day, and who give generously from what he has given to them? God knows them all. God will not do an atom's weight of injustice to anyone; he repays every good deed twofold. God rewards richly all who do good.

4.35–40

Good fortune and misfortune

The pleasures of this world are fleeting. The pleasures of the world to come are far greater – for those who avoid evil. You will not be wronged even to the extent of the husk of a date stone. Wherever you are, even if you put yourself in the highest tower, death will overtake you.

When people are blessed with good fortune, they say: 'This is from God.' And when misfortune occurs, they say: 'This is Muhammad's fault.' Let them understand that all is from God. What has happened to people that they show such lack of understanding? Whatever good befalls you, it is from God; and whatever evil befalls you, it is your own fault.

'We have sent you, Muhammad, as an apostle to humanity. God is sufficient as your witness.' Those who obey the apostle, obey God himself. Those who ignore the apostle, should know that God has not sent the apostle as their protector.

Some people promise to obey the apostle; but as they depart from the apostle, they secretly plot to disobey him. God takes note of all their plots. Therefore leave them alone, and put your trust in God. He is sufficient as your guardian.

Who refuses to meditate on the Quran? If it had not come from God, people surely would have found many contradictions within it.

4.77b–82

Bearing true witness

Let those who seek rewards in this life, remember that God holds the rewards in both this life and the next. God sees all and hears all.

Believers, uphold justice. Always bear true witness, even if it be against yourself, your parents or your relatives – and regardless of whether the person against whom you are speaking is rich or poor. God is close to people regardless of their material circumstances. Do not be led by emotion, as this may cause you to swerve from the truth. If you distort your testimony, or refuse to testify, remember that God is aware of all your actions.

Harsh words are disliked by God, except when uttered by someone who has genuinely been wronged. Whether you do good openly or in secret, and whether or not you forgive those who wrong you, remember that God is both forgiving and supremely powerful.

God will reward those who have faith and do good; he will enrich them from his own abundance. As for those who are disdainful and proud, he will severely punish them; and they will find that no one besides God can protect or help them.

4.134–135, 148–149, 173

Animals, birds, plants and people

All animals that roam the earth, and all birds that fly through the air, form communities like your own. 'We have left out nothing from our book.' All animals and all birds will be gathered before their Lord. 'Those men and women who deny our revelations, are deaf and dumb; they wander about in utter darkness.'

God allows people to err as he chooses, and he leads people onto the right path as he chooses. God holds the key to the unseen treasures; no one knows these treasures except him. He knows every creature on land and in the sea. A leaf does not fall without God knowing it. There is no seed in the soil that God does not know. There is nothing green or dry of which God is not aware. Everything is recorded in his glorious book.

It is God who makes you sleep at night as if you were dead. God knows what you have done during the day. God sustains you, so that you may live your allotted span. To him you will eventually return, and he will declare to you all that you have done.

God reigns supreme over his servants. He sends guardians to watch over you, and to carry away your soul at the moment of death; these guardians never fail in their task. At death all people are restored to God, their true Lord. Judgement belongs to him, and he is swift in making it.

6.38–39, 59–62

Religion as a hobby

'When you meet people who scoff at our revelations, with-draw from them until they can talk in some other way. If Satan causes you to forget this warning, leave such sinners as soon as you remember.' Those who honour God, are not in the least accountable for those who dishonour him. 'We tell you this so that you may guard yourself against evil.'

Avoid those who regard their religion as a hobby, as an idle pastime, and are seduced by the life of this world. Admonish them, lest their souls be damned by their own sins. They have no guardian or intercessor besides God; and even if they offer compensation to God, it will not be ac-cepted from them. This is the condition of those who have been damned by their own sins. They will drink boiling water, and be sternly punished for their refusal to believe.

I say that the guidance of God is the only guidance. We are commanded to submit to the Lord of creation, to pray, and to avoid evil. You will all be assembled before him. It is God who created both the heavens and the earth; that is the truth. On the day when he says 'Be', it is. His word is the truth. On the day when the trumpet is sounded, he will reign. He knows all that is seen and hidden. He alone is wise and knows all.

6.68–70, 71b–73

Signs in nature

It is God who causes the grain and the fruit stone to germinate. He brings forth life from that which is dead, and death from that which is living. Such is God! How then can you turn away from him?

It is God who kindles the light of dawn. He has made the night for rest, and the sun and moon for reckoning the time. This is what God has ordained; he is supremely powerful, and knows all.

It is God who has created the stars for you, so that they may guide you in the darkness, both on land and at sea. 'We have made plain our revelations to people of wisdom.'

It is God who created you from one being, and provided you with homes where you can rest. 'We have made plain our revelations to people of wisdom.'

It is God who sends rain from the sky, bringing forth buds and green leaves on every plant. The rain causes the grain to swell, the palm trees to yield clusters of dates, the vines to yield grapes, and the olive trees to bear olives; it brings forth all manner of pomegranates. Look at the fruit as it ripens! Surely this is a sign for true believers.

Such is God, your Lord. There is no god but him. He is the creator of all things; therefore serve him. He is the protector of all things. No mortal eyes can see him, though he sees all eyes. He is aware of all subtleties; he knows all.

6.95–99, 102–103

Dividing religion into sects

Shun all those who divide religion into sects. God will call them to account, and declare to them what they have done.

Every good deed will be repaid tenfold; but evil deeds will be repaid with evil. No one will be treated unjustly.

I say that I devote all my prayers and my worship, my life and my death, to God, the Lord of creation. He has no equal. I am under his command; I am the first Muslim.

I ask whether I should seek any god besides God – when he is the Lord of all things. All people will reap the harvest of their own deeds; no one will bear another's burden. Ultimately all of you will return to your Lord, and he will resolve your disputes.

God has given you the earth as your inheritance. He has raised some to a higher rank than others, so that he may test you in the way you treat this inheritance. He is swift in retribution, but he is also forgiving and merciful.

6.159–160, 162–165

The blessed and the damned

If you have faith and do good works, God will never impose a duty on you greater than you can bear. You are the heirs of paradise, and you will abide there for ever. 'We shall take away all hatred from your hearts.' Rivers will flow at your feet, and you will say: 'Praise be to God who has guided us to this place. If he had not guided us, we should have strayed from the right path. His apostles have surely preached the truth.' And a voice will cry out to them: 'This is paradise, which you have earned by your labours.'

Then the blessed will cry out to the damned: 'We have found our Lord's promises to be true. Have you also found them to be true?' The damned will answer: 'Yes!' A herald will cry out among them: 'Cursed are the evil-doers who blocked the path of God to others, and sought to make it crooked – and who did not believe in the life to come.'

A veil will divide the blessed from the damned. The damned will cry out to the blessed: 'Give us some water. Pour upon us some of the water that God has given you.' But the blessed will reply: 'God has forbidden water to unbelievers – to those who regard their religion as a hobby, as an idle pastime, and are seduced by the life of this world.

'On that day we shall ignore them, as they ignored that day; they rejected our revelations.'

7.42–46a, 50–51

The names of God

The names of God are the most excellent of all names. Therefore call on God by his names, and keep away from those who misuse his names, violating their sanctity; they will be punished for their sins.

'Among the men and women whom we have created, there are some who give true guidance to others, and who act justly. As for those who deny our revelations, we shall lead them step by step to ruin; but they will not see what is happening. Though I tolerate them at present, my plan will work.'

Has it never occurred to these people that I, Muhammad, who am their compatriot, am no lunatic? Do they not realize that I am giving a plain warning to them? Will they not ponder on the kingdom of the heavens and the earth, on all that God has created, to discern whether their doom is drawing near? And if they deny these revelations, what revelations will they believe? No one can guide those whom God leads astray. He abandons them, and they blunder about in their wickedness.

7.180−186

The first child

It was God who created you from a single being. From that being God created a mate, so that each might find comfort in the other. And when they had lain together, she conceived. At first the burden was light, and she carried the child easily. When the burden grew heavy, they cried out to God, their Lord: 'Grant us a fine child, and we shall be truly grateful!' Yet when God granted them a fine child, they set up other gods besides God, giving thanks to them for what God had done. May God be exalted above all gods.

Why do people worship gods that can create nothing, but are themselves created? Such gods cannot help anyone, nor can they help themselves. If you call to the worshippers of such gods, urging them to follow the right path, they do not come. Speaking to them is useless; you may as well remain silent. Remember that these gods are servants of God, as you are. Test your faith in them: invoke them, and see if they answer! Have they feet to walk with, hands to hold with, eyes to see with, or ears to hear with?

Show forgiveness, uphold justice, and shun the ignorant. If Satan tempts you, seek refuge in God; he hears all and knows all. Those who walk with the Lord, are never too proud to serve him; they proclaim his glory, and prostrate themselves in humility before him.

7.189–195, 199–200, 206

The Spirit of God

By his will God sends down the angels with the Spirit to those of his servants whom he chooses. He commands them to proclaim on his behalf: 'There is no god but me; therefore honour me.'

God created the heavens and the earth to manifest the truth; let him be exalted above all gods. He created human beings from a single seed; yet human beings openly dispute with him.

He created animals to provide you with warm clothing, food, and many other benefits. How beautiful they look when you lead them from their pasture and bring them home! They carry your loads to far-off lands; without them you could not reach those lands, except with great effort. Your Lord is compassionate and merciful. He has created horses, mules and donkeys, which you may ride, or you may keep for pleasure. He has created many things beyond your knowledge.

God alone can show the right path. Some deviate from it; but if he had wanted, he could have guided everyone onto it.

It is God who sends down water from the sky. You drink the water; the water causes the crops to grow on which your livestock feed; and it brings forth corn and olives, dates and grapes, and every other fruit. Surely this is a sign for thoughtful people.

16.2–11

The bee

If God punished people for their sins, not a single person would be left alive. But he holds back until the appointed time. When that time comes, no one will be able to delay it; and no one can bring it forward.

People ascribe to God what they themselves hate. They preach dishonestly, claiming that they will enjoy a great reward. But let them be in no doubt: the fire of hell awaits them – and they will be left in its flames.

God sends down water from the sky, which enlivens the barren earth. Surely this is a sign for people of wisdom. In cattle too you have a valuable lesson. 'From their bellies, between their bowels and their blood, we provide you with pure milk, which is pleasant to drink and easy to swallow. We also give you fruits of the palm and the vine, from which you derive both wine and wholesome food.' Surely this is a sign for people of understanding.

Your Lord inspired the bee, saying: 'Build your homes in the mountains, in the trees, and in the hives which people make for you. Feed on every kind of blossom.' He ordered them obediently to follow his ways. From the belly of the bee comes a fluid of many colours, which is a healing drink for humans. Surely this is a sign for people who ponder it.

16.61–62, 65–69

The slave and the man of generosity

God gives this parable: 'On the one hand there is a helpless slave, the property of his master. On the other hand there is a man whom we have greatly blessed; this man is generous both in secret and openly.' Are the two alike? All praise is due to God! Yet most people do not understand.

To God belong the secrets of the heavens and the earth. The business of the final moment will be accomplished in the twinkling of an eye, or even less time. God has power over all things.

When God brought you out of your mother's womb, you were empty of knowledge. But he gave you eyes and ears and hearts, in order that you may give thanks to him. Do your eyes not see the birds that fly under the dome of the sky? No one sustains them except God. Surely this is a sign for true believers.

God has given you houses to live in. He has given you the skins of animals with which to make tents; they are light to carry as you travel, and easy to pitch when you halt for rest. And from the wool, fur and hair of animals God has given you many comforts and good things.

By means of what he has created, God has given you shelter from the sun. He has given you refuge in the mountains. He has provided you with garments to protect you from the heat, and coats of armour to shield you in battle. His favours to you are complete, so that you may submit to him.

16.75, 77–81

Unravelling yarn

God enjoins justice, kindness to others, and generosity to relatives. He forbids indecency, wickedness and oppression. He admonishes you, so that you may take heed.

Be faithful to the covenant you have made with God. Do not break an oath after you have sworn it – for by swearing in God's name you make God your surety. God knows all your actions.

Consider a woman who unravels the yarn that she has firmly spun. Do not be like her. Do not make a treaty with another nation, knowing that you may break it if your army is superior in numbers. In such a situation God is testing you. On matters of dispute with other nations, God will declare to you the truth on the day of resurrection. If God had wanted, he could have made you one nation. But he decides to leave some nations in error, giving guidance as he pleases.

Do not take an oath, with the intention of deceiving the other party. You have been guided onto the path of righteousness; and this would cause your foot to stumble. Moreover, you would commit the evil of blocking God's path to others – and for that you would incur a grievous punishment.

Do not barter away the covenant of God for a trifling price. His reward is better than any financial gain – if only you knew it. Worldly wealth is fleeting, but God's reward lasts for ever.

16.90–95

The open book

'We have made night and day as two signs. We have en-shrouded the night in darkness, and clothed the day with light.' Thus you may seek the bounty of the Lord, and learn to compute the seasons and the years.

'We have hung the fate of all people around their necks. On the day of resurrection we shall confront each person with an open book, and say: "Here is your book; read it. Today your own soul calls you to account."'

Those who seek guidance from God, will be guided to their own advantage. But those who go astray, go astray at their own peril. No one will bear another's burden.

'Those who are concerned only with this fleeting life, will soon suffer in the manner we choose. We determine people's fate as we please. We have prepared hell for those in love with this fleeting life; they will burn within its flames, de-spised and helpless.' But the true believers who are concerned with the life to come, and strive for it with all their souls, will have their efforts rewarded by God.

'We bestow our bounty on all people.' No one will be de-nied the bounty of your Lord. 'Look at how we have raised some people to a higher rank than others. Yet the life to come has greater honours than any this life can offer; and it raises people to a higher rank than the highest rank on earth.'

17.12–15, 18–21

Stinginess and extravagance

Serve no other god but God, lest you incur disgrace and ruin; your Lord has enjoined you to worship none but him. He has also commanded you to show kindness to your parents. If either or both of your parents attain old age, and live with you, do not show any impatience towards them, or rebuke them; always speak to them gently. Treat them with humility and tenderness, praying: 'Lord, be merciful to them; they cared for me in my infancy.'

Your Lord knows best what is in your hearts; he knows if you are good. He will forgive those who turn to him.

Give to your close relatives what they need, and also give generously to the destitute and to wayfarers. Do not squander your wealth; those who are wasteful are the brothers and sisters of Satan – and Satan is always ungrateful to his Lord. But if, while waiting for the Lord's bounty, you are unable to help your relatives, the destitute and wayfarers, then at least speak to them kindly.

Do not be stingy, as if your hand were shackled to your neck; and do not be extravagant, as if your hand were stretched to the utmost limit. If you avoid stinginess, you will not be reproached; if you avoid extravagance, you will not be reduced to penury.

Your Lord gives abundantly to some and sparingly to others, as he pleases. He knows and observes all his servants.

17.22–30

Some commandments

Do not commit adultery, for it is foul and indecent.

Do not kill any person whom God has forbidden you to kill. If you kill someone unjustly, that person's heir is entitled to take revenge. But the heir should not carry vengeance too far, for the victim will in turn take revenge – and be assisted in this.

Do not interfere with the property of orphans until they reach maturity, except from proper motives.

Keep your promises; you are accountable for all you promise.

When you sell goods, give full measure; and weigh with honest scales. Not only is this fair; it will also benefit you in the end.

Do not follow advice which you do not understand. Make detailed inquiries with your eyes, ears and mind.

Do not strut about proudly. You cannot possess the earth, and you cannot rival the mountains in stature.

Avoid all evil; avoid all that is odious in the sight of the Lord.

These injunctions form part of the wisdom with which the Lord has inspired Muhammad. Serve no other god besides God, lest you should be cast into hell, despised and helpless.

17.32–39

The hidden barrier

Glory to God; let God be praised. He is high above all false-hood. The seven heavens, the earth below, and all who live on the earth and in the heavens, give glory to God. All crea-tures praise him – except some men and women, who do not understand his glory. God is benign and forgiving.

'Muhammad, when you recite the Quran, we place a hidden barrier between you and those who deny the life to come. We cast a veil over their minds, and make them hard of hearing, lest they understand it. For this reason, when you speak of your one and only Lord, they turn their backs in flight.

'We know well what they wish to hear from you, and what they say to one another in private. We hear them mut-ter to your followers: "The man whom you follow, is be-witched." Listen to the insults they hurl at you! They have surely gone astray, and cannot find the way.'

17.43–48

Restoration to life

People ask: 'After we have turned to bone and dust, shall we be restored to life?' I reply: 'You will – even if you turn to stone or iron, or any other substance which you may think cannot be brought to life.'

They ask: 'Who will restore us to life?' I say: 'You will be restored to life by the one who first created you.'

They shake their heads, and ask: 'When will this be?' I reply: 'The time may be near at hand. On that day he will summon all of you, and you will answer him with praises. You will imagine that you are being slow in coming to him; but in fact you will come quickly.'

17.49–52

At sea

It is the Lord who drives your ships across the ocean, enabling you to go in quest of greater abundance. Your Lord is merciful towards you.

When misfortune befalls you at sea, all the gods to whom you pray abandon you; God alone listens to your prayers. Yet when he brings you safely back to dry land, you turn your backs on him. Truly human beings are ungrateful.

Are you confident that he will not cause the earth to open up beneath you? Are you confident that he will not send a deadly sandstorm upon you? If he does so, you will find no one to protect you. Are you confident that when you next put to sea, he will not strike you with a violent tempest, and drown you for your ingratitude? If he does so, you will find no one to protect you.

'We have bestowed blessings on all people, guiding them by land and sea. We have provided them with many good things, and exalted them above all the other creatures which we have made. The day will surely come when we shall summon every nation, along with its apostle. A book recording their deeds will be given to every man and woman. Those who receive this book in their right hand, will read it; they will not suffer any injury. But those who have been blind in this life, will be blind in the life to come, going further astray.'

17.66–72

A healing balm

I say that truth has come, and falsehood has been put to flight. Falsehood will never triumph.

'That which we have revealed in the Quran is a healing balm and a blessing to all true believers; but it brings only ruin to those who do evil.'

'Often when we bestow blessings on someone, that person turns away and behaves proudly. But when evil comes, that same person plunges into despair.'

I say that people act according to their own natures. But the Lord knows best how to guide you on the right path.

People put questions to me about the Spirit. I say that the Spirit is under the Lord's command. Only a small amount of knowledge is given to you.

'If we pleased, we could take away that which we have revealed to you. Then you have nothing to protect you against us!' But your Lord is merciful, and his grace to you is truly abundant.

17.81–87

Excuses for unbelief

'We have set down in the Quran all manner of arguments; yet most men and women still refuse to believe.'

People say to me, Muhammad: 'We shall not believe you until you make a fountain gush from the earth before our very eyes, or cause streams to flow through a garden of palms and vines; or until you cause the sky to fall upon us in pieces, as you have threatened, or bring God and his angels face to face with us; or until you build a house of gold, or ascend into the sky – and we shall not believe in your ascension until you have sent down to us a book which we can read.'

I say in reply that all glory belongs to God, and that I am merely a human apostle. Nothing prevents people from believing the guidance which has been revealed to them. But they excuse themselves by asking: 'Could God really have sent a human being as an apostle?' I say in reply that if earth had been safe for angels, God would have sent an angel from the heavens as an apostle. And I say that God is quite capable of judging between us; he knows and observes all his servants.

17.89–96

The voice of prayer

'We have conveyed the truth by revealing the Quran; the truth has come down by means of the Quran. We have sent Muhammad to proclaim good news and to give warning. We have divided the Quran into sections, so that it may be easily recited and understood. We imparted the truth piece by piece.'

I say to you that you must either believe the Quran or deny it. Some people were given spiritual knowledge before the Quran was revealed. When the Quran is recited to them, they exclaim: 'Glory be to our Lord; his promise has been fulfilled.' They fall down on their faces, and weep; and as they listen to the Quran, their humility increases.

I say that you may call on God by whatever name you please. You may call him God, or you may call him the Merciful. He has the best of names.

When you pray, do not raise your voice, and do not remain silent; seek a middle course between these. Say: 'Praise be to God, who needs no one to help or defend him.' Proclaim his greatness.

17.105–111a

Two vineyards

Once there were two men, to each of whom God gave a vineyard. The vineyards were surrounded by palm trees, and were
watered by running streams; and a cornfield lay between
them. Both vineyards yielded an abundant crop. After the
owners had finished gathering in the harvest, one said to the
other: 'I am richer than you, and my family is larger than
yours.' In speaking in this way he wronged his own soul.

Then he led the other owner into his vineyard, and said:
'I am sure that this will never perish. And I do not believe
that the moment of judgement will ever come. Yet even if I
am taken back to the Lord, I shall be given an even better
place than this.' The other owner replied: 'Have you no faith
in the one who created you from dust, who caused you to
grow from a tiny seed into a man? I declare that God is my
Lord, and there is no other god but him. When you entered
your vineyard, you should have said: "That which God has
ordained, will surely come to pass." As you observe, I am
poorer than you are, and I have fewer children; yet God may
make my vineyard better than yours. He may send down
thunderbolts from the sky on your vines, or he may cause the
streams to drain away into the earth, turning your vineyard
into a barren waste.'

The proud owner's vineyard was indeed destroyed; his
vines shrivelled and died. He cried out: 'If only I had served
no other god but my Lord!' There was no one to help him
except God; he could not defend himself.

18.32–42a, 43

Herbs in the rain and wind

In the ordeals of life protection comes only from the Lord, the true God. No reward is better than his reward, and no recompense is more generous than his.

Here is a parable. This life is like herbs. When the rain waters them, they turn green and thrive. But when the hot wind dries them, they turn to stubble, and are scattered. God has power over all things.

Wealth and children bring great pleasure in this life. But good works bring an eternal reward from the Lord; through them you may hope for salvation.

'A day will come when we shall flatten the mountains, and turn the earth into a barren waste. On that day we shall gather all people together; not a single person will be left behind.' You will come before the Lord, who will say to you: 'We created you, and now you have returned to us. Yet you thought our promise would never be fulfilled.'

The record of your deeds will be given to each of you. And those of you who are sinners, will be horrified at what you read. You will scream, and say: 'I can hardly believe it! This book leaves out nothing; every action, both great and small, has been noted down.' Yes, you will find an account of all that you have done. Your Lord will be unjust to no one.

18.45–49

The sea as ink

Who will lose most from their work in this world? I shall tell you: those who are misguided, yet think they are doing right; those who reject the Lord's revelations, and deny that they will ever meet him. Their labours are in vain. 'On the day of resurrection we shall not honour them. Hell is their recompense, because they refused to believe, and because they mocked my apostles and my revelations. As for those who have faith and do good works, they will live for ever in the garden of paradise — and they will never want to leave.'

I say that if the sea were ink with which to write the words of my Lord, the sea would surely be consumed before his words were complete. Even if there were a second sea, it too would be consumed — and the task would still not be finished.

I say that I am mortal, as you are. It has been revealed to me that your Lord is one God. Let all those who hope to meet their Lord, do what is right, and worship only him.

18.103–110

The resurrection

'Men and women, if you doubt the resurrection, remember we created each of you from dust, which we turned into a living seed, from which we grew a clot of blood and then a lump of flesh; and from that lump of flesh we fashioned your body. In this way we have demonstrated our power. We caused you to remain in the womb at our pleasure until the appointed time; then we brought you forth as a baby; and we caused you to grow into a strong and healthy adult. Some of you will die young; but some will live into old age, when you will forget all that you once knew.

'You sometimes see the earth dry and barren. But as soon as we send down rain, the earth begins to swell and stir, putting forth radiant flowers of every kind.' This demonstrates that God is truth; he gives life to the dead, and has power over all things.

The moment of judgement is certain to come; this is beyond doubt. Those who are in the grave, God will raise to life.

22.5–7

Disputes and false claims

Some dispute about God, though they possess neither knowledge, nor guidance, nor divine revelation. They proudly turn their backs on the truth, and lead others away from God's path. Such people will incur disgrace in this life, and will taste the fires of hell on the day of resurrection. God will say to them: 'This is the reward for your misdeeds.' God is never unjust to his servants.

Some claim to serve God, and yet stand on the edge of genuine faith. When they are blessed by good fortune, they are content. But when misfortune befalls them, they turn their backs and flee, losing both this life and the life hereafter. They manifestly cheat themselves. They call on gods which can neither help nor harm them; they are utterly foolish. Or they call on Satan, who would prefer to harm them than help them; he is an evil master and a wicked friend.

As for those who have faith and do good works, God will welcome them to a garden watered by running streams. God's will is always done.

22.8–14

Forms of worship for each nation

'For every nation we have ordained a form of worship.' By this means the people of each nation can praise God, and give thanks for the livestock he has given them. Your God is one God; let every nation submit to God.

Let us proclaim good news to the humble, whose hearts fill with awe at the mention of their Lord; to those who endure their misfortunes with courage; to those who are devout in their prayers; and to those who give generously from what the Lord has given them. Let us proclaim good news to the righteous; God will protect all true believers from evil – but he does not love those who are unfaithful and ungrateful.

'For the people of every nation we have ordained a form of worship, which they should observe.' People should not argue about this. I call all people to the path of the Lord; I call all people to accept true guidance. If you argue, I shall remind you that God is aware of all your actions; and on the day of resurrection he will resolve all your disputes and disagreements.

22.34–35, 37b–38, 67–69

Beatitudes

Blessed are the believers, who are humble in their prayers, who avoid profane talk, and who give generously to the destitute. Blessed are the believers who restrain their sexual desires, except within marriage, and who have no desire to commit adultery. Blessed are the believers who are worthy of trust, who keep their promises, and who never neglect their prayers. They are the heirs of paradise; they will live there for ever.

Blessed are those who honour God in all they do, who believe in the revelations of their Lord, and who worship only their Lord. Blessed are those who, when they give to the poor, do so with hearts filled with awe, knowing that they will soon return to their Lord. Blessed are those who vie with one another for God's blessings; they will be foremost in receiving them.

'We demand nothing of people beyond what they can achieve. Our book records the truth: no one will suffer injustice.'

23.1–6a, 7–11, 57–61

God's patience and mercy

If God lacked patience and mercy, he would never have given you his revelations. If God lacked wisdom and forgiveness, you would still be ignorant. Yet God is patient and merciful both in this life and the next.

If God lacked patience and mercy, all of you would long ago have been punished. If God lacked compassion and for-giveness, none of you would have escaped.

You are true believers, so do not walk in the footsteps of Satan. Those who walk in Satan's footsteps, find themselves committing acts of indecency and evil. If God lacked pa-tience and mercy, none of you would have been cleansed of sin. God purifies those whom he chooses; he hears all and knows all.

Those of you with wealth and power should never with-hold your help from your relatives, from the poor, and from those who have lost their homes in the service of God. If you have ever been stingy, may you receive pardon and forgive-ness. Do you not want God to forgive you? He is forgiving and merciful.

24.10, 14a, 20–22

Houses and sex

Believers, do not enter the houses of others without first seeking the residents' permission, and without wishing peace to
the residents. That is the best for you; perhaps you will take
heed. If you find no one in a house, do not enter until you
have received permission. If you are refused permission, that
refusal may not be justified; nonetheless you should go away.
God knows all your actions.

It is no offence for you to seek shelter in empty houses.
God knows what you do in secret, as well as what you do
openly.

Men should turn their eyes away from temptation, and restrain their sexual desires. This will make their lives purer.
God knows all their actions. Women also should turn their
eyes away from temptation, and preserve their chastity.
Believers, turn to God in a spirit of repentance, that you may
be blessed.

You should seek to marry only those who are at present
single. You may marry a slave, if you are convinced of the
slave's honesty. Do not worry if your spouse is poor; God
will provide wealth from his own abundance. God is generous, and knows all. If you cannot afford to marry, live without sexual relations until God enriches you.

24.27–31a, 32–33a

The light of God

God is the light of the heavens and the earth. His light is like a niche that holds a lamp; it is like a lamp which contains a crystal as bright as a star. It is kindled from a blessed tree, an olive tree that belongs neither to the east nor to the west. Its oil would almost shine, even with no fire touching it. It is light upon light. God guides towards his light all whom he chooses.

God's light is found in temples which he has allowed to be built. In these temples men and women constantly remember his name; and every morning and evening they sing his praises. Neither business nor profit can distract these people from remembering God, from offering prayers to him, or from giving generously to the poor.

As for unbelievers, their efforts are like a mirage in the desert. Thirsty travellers think it is water; but as they come closer, they find it is nothing. Yet God is present, and he will pay back the unbelievers for what they have done; his judgement is swift. Their efforts are like the darkness in the depths of the ocean, when storm clouds pass above. It is darkness upon darkness. If people were to stretch out their hands, they could scarcely see them. Indeed, those from whom God withholds his light, will have no light at all.

24.35a, 36–37a, 39–40

Solitude and company

Believers, there are three times during the day when no one should disturb you: before the morning prayer; as you retreat from the midday sun to rest; and after the evening prayer. If your children or servants wish to see you at these times, they must ask your permission. At other times of the day, people should feel free to visit one another without prior permission. Thus God makes plain his revelations; he is wise, and knows all.

Invite the blind, the lame and the sick to eat at your table; that is good. And it is good to eat at the homes of your children, your parents, your brothers and sisters, your uncles and aunts on both your father's and mother's sides, and your friends. It good to eat at any home where you are welcome. Sometimes you may prefer to eat alone.

When you enter a house, greet the people present in the name of God; and let your greeting be warm and gentle. God makes plain his revelations, that you may grow in wisdom.

To God belong all that the heavens and the earth contain. He knows all your thoughts and actions. On the day when people return to him, he will declare to them all that they have done. He knows all things.

24.58, 61, 64

Accusations and questions

Unbelievers say: 'The Quran is a forgery. Muhammad wrote it himself, with the help of others.' Such words are both evil and false. Unbelievers say: 'The Quran consists of ancient fables and legends. Muhammad dictates them every morning and evening.' I reply: 'The Quran is revealed by God, who knows the secrets of the heavens and the earth. He is forgiving and merciful.'

Unbelievers also say: 'How is it that this apostle eats normally, and walks about the city as other people do? Why has no angel been sent down with him, to tell us that he is an apostle? Why has he not been given great wealth, and his own lands to provide him with food?' Wicked people add: 'This man is surely bewitched.'

Listen to what people say about me! They have surely gone astray, and cannot return to the true path.

I cry to the Lord: 'My people have rejected the Quran!' He replies: 'To every prophet we have appointed evil adversaries. But you need no one apart from me, your Lord, to guide and help you.'

Unbelievers ask: 'Why was the Quran not revealed to you in a single revelation?' God has said to me: 'We reveal it gradually, piece by piece, to strengthen people's faith. As soon as people come to you with a new question, we reveal the truth in a form that will answer it.'

25.4–9, 30–33

True servants of the Lord

The true servants of the merciful Lord are those who walk on the earth in humility; who, when they are accosted by ignorant people, wish them peace; and who spend the night standing and kneeling, in adoration of God. The true servants of the merciful Lord are those who are neither extravagant nor stingy, but keep the mean between these two extremes; who invoke no god apart from God; who do not kill except in a just cause; and who do not commit adultery. The true servants of the merciful Lord are those who do not tell lies against others, and do not lose their composure when listening to profane abuse; and who do not turn a blind eye and a deaf ear to the Lord's revelations, when they are reminded of them. The true servants of the merciful Lord are those who say to him: 'Make our families happy, and make us examples to all who honour you.'

The true servants of the merciful Lord will be rewarded in paradise for their devotion. There they will be warmly welcomed, and there they will live for ever. Paradise is a joyful home, and a serene resting-place.

25.63–64, 67–68a, 72–76

Asking animals

'My servants, my true believers, consider how vast is the earth which I have created. Therefore serve me. All people will taste death, and in the end you will return to me.'

Those who embrace the truth and do good works, will dwell for ever in the mansions of paradise. Streams will pass at their feet. Joyful is the reward for those who are loyal and obedient servants of God.

The countless animals that roam the earth, cannot provide for themselves. God provides for them, as he provides for you. He alone hears all and knows all. If you were to ask the animals who created the heavens and the earth, and who commands the sun and the moon, they would reply: 'God.' So how can you turn away from him? God gives abundantly to some and sparingly to others, as he pleases; he knows all things.

If you were to ask the animals who sends rain from the sky to enliven the barren earth, they would reply: 'God.' So you should proclaim God's praise. Yet most people are too stupid to do this.

The life of this world is merely a sport; it is only an idle pastime. The true life is the life to come – if you only knew it.

29.56–64

The attitude of the wealthy

'Whenever God has sent an apostle to a city or nation, the wealthy people of that place, living in comfort, have rejected the apostle's message. They have said to themselves: 'We have more wealth and more children than those who believe the apostle's message. That shows that we shall not be punished.' But I say that God gives abundantly to some, and sparingly to others, as he pleases; but most people do not understand this.

'Neither your wealth nor your children will bring you any nearer to us. Those who have faith, and act justly, will be doubly rewarded for their deeds; they will dwell in the mansions of paradise. But those who strive to oppose our revelations will be brought for punishment.'

I ask no recompense for my work as an apostle; keep your wealth for yourselves. No one can reward me except God. He is watching over all things.

I declare that my Lord reveals the truth; he knows all that is hidden. I declare that the truth has come; falsehood has departed, and will never return. I declare that, if I am in error, the fault is surely mine; but if I am right, it is because the Lord has revealed to me the truth. The Lord hears all, and is close at hand.

34.34–38, 47–50

Deception and truth

Praise be to God, the creator of the heavens and the earth! He sends forth angels as his messengers, some with two pairs of wings, some with three pairs, and some with four. He multiplies his creatures according to his will. God has power over all things.

If God wishes to bestow blessings, no one can compel him to withhold them; and if God wishes to withhold blessings, no one can compel him to bestow them. He is mighty and wise. 'If people reject you, Muhammad, remember that other apostles have been rejected before you.'

Men and women, remember God's goodness towards you. Is there any other creator who takes from his abundance in the heavens and on the earth, and provides for you? There is no god but him. How then can you turn away from him?

Men and women, the promise of God is true. Do not be deceived by the life of this world; and do not let Satan trick you about God. Satan is your enemy, so treat him as such. He lures his followers to become heirs of hell. Those who do evil, generally believe that their actions are right. God leaves some people in error, and guides others towards the truth, as he pleases. 'Muhammad, do not waste away worrying about unbelievers; God knows all their actions.'

35.1–6, 7–8

Standing in need of God

God sends forth the winds, which set the clouds in motion. 'We drive the clouds over land which is parched and barren, and restore it to fresh life.' This is an image of the resurrection.

If you want glory, then remember that all glory belongs to God alone. He hears every kind word that is spoken, and he praises every good deed. But those who plot evil will be sternly punished; he will thwart their plots, bringing them to nothing.

God created you from dust, which he formed into a tiny seed. He divided you into two sexes. No woman conceives or gives birth without his knowledge. No one grows old, or dies young, except in accordance with his decree. Every action is easy for God.

The water in lakes is fresh and sweet and pleasant to drink; while the water in the sea is salty and bitter. Yet you catch fish to eat in both lakes and the sea; and from both lakes and the sea you bring up ornaments to wear. And you sail on both in order to engage in profitable trade. Perhaps all this will prompt you to give thanks.

God causes the night to pass into day, and the day to pass into night. He rules the sun and the moon, putting each on the course he has chosen. This is how God, your Lord, works; he is sovereign over all things.

Men and women, you stand in need of God. His power and glory cannot be surpassed.

35.9–13a, 15

The blind and the seeing

If God wanted, he could destroy the present generation, and replace it with a new generation; that would not be impossible for God.

No one is responsible for the sins another person commits. If a person burdened by guilt cries out for help, not even that person's closest relatives will share that guilt.

I speak to those who honour the Lord, and pray to him constantly, but cannot see him. Those who cleanse themselves of sin, will be richly rewarded. To God all creatures will return.

The blind and the seeing are not alike; nor are darkness and light. Shade and heat are not alike; nor are the living and the dead. God can cause people to hear him, if he chooses.

'That which we have revealed in our book, is the same truth that was revealed in previous Scriptures.' God knows and observes all his servants. 'We have entrusted our book to those of our servants whom we chose.' Some of them sin against their own souls, while others are lax in their devotion. But some, with God's encouragement, vie with one another in acts of charity; their virtue is supreme.

35.16–22a, 31–32

The sound of the trumpet

When the trumpet sounds, the dead will rise up from their graves, and rush forwards to their Lord. They will gasp, and exclaim: 'Who has aroused us from sleep? This is what the Lord of mercy promised; the apostles were preaching the truth.' 'With one shout they will assemble before us.'

On that day no one will suffer even the smallest injustice; you will be rewarded according to your deeds. On that day the inhabitants of paradise will be utterly absorbed in their own bliss: married couples will recline together on soft couches in shady orchards, eating fruit and fulfilling every desire; and the merciful Lord will wish them peace. But to the guilty God will say: 'Away with you, children of the world! Did I not command you never to serve Satan, your manifest enemy? Did I not require you to worship me? Did I not show you the right path? Yet Satan has led many of you astray. Did you not understand what you were doing? Here is the hell with which you have been threatened; today you will enter it, and burn as a punishment for your unbelief.'

'We have not taught Muhammad to utter poetry, because it would not be right for him to be a poet. His purpose is to proclaim the Quran in plain language, and thus warn the people. The Quran encourages those who desire the life of truth, and pronounces judgement on unbelievers.'

36.51–64, 69–70

The glorious guardian

God accepts the repentance of his servants, and pardons their sins. He knows all their actions.

God hears the prayers of all who have faith and do good works, and he enriches them with his grace. But a terrible punishment awaits those who do not believe.

If God had bestowed excessive wealth on his servants, they would have rebelled against him. He gives them the right amount, according to his will. He understands and observes all his servants.

When people have despaired of reaping a harvest, God sends down rain. He spreads his blessing across the world; he is the glorious guardian. Look at how he created the heavens and the earth, and all the creatures that he has spread across the earth. The creation is merely one among many of his signs. If he wanted, he could gather the heavens and the earth and all the creatures into one place.

If misfortune befalls you, it is the consequence of your own actions. Yet God forgives much. On this earth you cannot escape God; and there is no one apart from God who can protect or help you.

42.25–31

Ships like mountains

Among God's signs are ships which sail like mountains across
the ocean. When God pleases, he calms the wind, so the ships
lie motionless on the bosom of the ocean. And when God
pleases, he causes the ships to founder on the rocks, as a punishment for the evil deeds of those who sail in them. Yet God
forgives many sins. Surely these are signs for people who are
courageous and grateful.

'Those who dispute our revelations, should know that
they cannot escape from us.'

The wealth of this world, which God has bestowed on
you, brings only fleeting pleasure. Far better and more enduring is God's reward to those who believe and put their
trust in him; who shun the gross sins and indecencies; who,
when angered, are quick to forgive; who obey their Lord, and

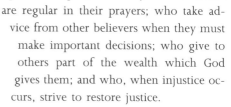

are regular in their prayers; who take advice from other believers when they must
make important decisions; who give to
others part of the wealth which God
gives them; and who, when injustice occurs, strive to restore justice.

42.32–39

Revenge and forgiveness

Let evil be rewarded with evil. But those who forgive and seek reconciliation, will be rewarded by God. Those who do evil, are not loved by God.

If you have been wronged, and then take revenge, you do not incur great guilt. But if you oppress or exploit other people, and are indifferent to morality and justice, then you incur great guilt; you will be severely punished.

To endure suffering with fortitude, and to forgive those who have wronged you, are duties which all should strive to fulfill. Those whom God has led astray have no one to protect them. When sinners face their punishment, you will hear them exclaim: 'Is there no way back?'

To God belongs the kingdom of the heavens and the earth. He creates whatever he wishes. He bestows daughters on whom he pleases, and sons on whom he pleases. On some he bestows both sons and daughters, and on others he bestows no children at all. God is mighty, and knows all.

God speaks to no human beings except by revelation; or from behind a veil; or through a messenger sent by God, and authorized by God to make known his will. God is wise, and exalted above all creatures.

42.40−44, 49−51

Fighting in God's cause

When you meet unbelievers on the battlefield, fight hard, cutting off their heads, until you have overcome them. Take the survivors into captivity, binding them firmly. While war continues, you may take ransom from your prisoners; or you may choose to set them free without charge. This is what you should do. If God had wanted, he could have punished the unbelievers himself; but he decided to make you fight for your beliefs, in order to test you.

As for those who are slain in God's cause, he will not let their deeds perish. He will guide and reward them; he will lead them into paradise, which he has already made known.

Believers, if you serve God, he will serve you and make you strong. But he will destroy those who refuse to believe. He will bring the deeds of unbelievers to nothing; since they have rejected his revelations, he will thwart all their efforts.

Have you never travelled abroad, and seen the fate of unbelievers in the past? He utterly destroyed them. A similar fate awaits unbelievers today – because God protects the faithful, and gives no protection to the unfaithful.

Let all who embrace the true faith and do good works, know this: that God will welcome them into gardens watered by running streams. The unbelievers have their fill of pleasure now, eating as animals eat; but the fire of hell will be their home.

47.4–12

Rivers in paradise

'Muhammad, how many cities, which were mightier than your own, have cast you out? We have destroyed them all, and there was no one to protect them.'

Can those who follow the guidance of their Lord, be compared with those who are led by their appetites, and to whom foul deeds seem fair?

In paradise, which the righteous have been promised, many rivers flow: there are rivers of unpolluted water; there are rivers of milk, which is always fresh; there are rivers of delicious wine; and there are rivers of clarified honey. In paradise the righteous shall eat every kind of fruit, and they will be protected by the Lord. The unrighteous will live in hell, where they will drink scalding water which will tear their bowels.

'Some of the unrighteous have listened to you, Muhammad. But as soon as they have left your presence, they have turned to people who have been given knowledge, and asked: "What did he say just now?" These are people whose hearts have been sealed by God, and they follow their base desires.'

As for those who follow the path of righteousness, God will draw ever closer to them, and he will teach them how to ward off all evil.

47.13–17

A glorious victory

'Believers, in enabling you to take Mecca, we have given you a glorious victory.' God will forgive both your past and future sins, and complete his work of making you holy. He will guide you along the path of righteousness, and bestow upon you his mighty help.

It was God who made the hearts of the faithful serene, so that their faith could grow stronger. To God belong the armies of both the heavens and the earth. God is wise, and knows all.

He has prompted the actions of believers, both men and women, so that he may bring them into gardens watered by running streams, where they will live for ever; so that he may forgive their sins, which in God's sight is the most glorious victory; so that he may punish hypocrites, those who worship false gods, and those who entertain hateful thoughts about him. The forces of evil will turn against them, because God is angry with them. He has laid a curse on them, and prepared them for the fires of hell – an evil fate.

To God belong the armies of both the heavens and the earth. God is mighty and wise.

48. 1–7

Faith above all religions

Bigotry, the bigotry of ignorance, reigned in the hearts of the unbelievers. But God bestowed his serenity on his apostle and on all the faithful. He enabled them to uphold piety and shun evil; thus they deserved his serenity, and were worthy of receiving it. God knows all things.

In truth God has realized his apostle's vision. His apostle said: 'If God wishes, you will enter the holy mosque in safety, with hearts free from fear, and with heads cropped or shaven.' God knew what you did not know; and he granted you a speedy victory.

It is God who has sent his apostle to guide you towards faith – true faith which stands above all religions. God is sufficient as a witness.

Muhammad is God's apostle. Those who follow Muhammad, are firm of heart against unbelievers, but are merciful to one another. You see believers on their knees in adoration of God, seeking his grace and favour. You see traces of dust on the foreheads of believers, showing that they have prostrated themselves before God. Believers are described in the Torah and the Gospel. They are like seeds which sprout and thrive, rising up on thick, strong stalks to the delight of their sowers. Through the believers God enrages the unbelievers.

To all who embrace the faith and do good works, God has promised forgiveness and a rich reward.

48.26–29

The prophet in his room

Believers, do not be assertive in the presence of God and his apostle. Honour God; he hears all and knows all.

Believers, do not raise your voices above my voice, the voice of the prophet. Do not shout at me, as you often shout at one another. If you raise your voices and shout, you will not hear the truth, and so your labours will come to nothing. Those who speak softly in the presence of God's apostle, and those whom God has made pious, will be forgiven their sins, and they will receive a rich reward.

'Muhammad, those who call out to you while you are in your room, are mostly fools. They should wait until you come out to them.' But God is forgiving and merciful.

Believers, if a sinner brings you some news, be sceptical as to its truth. False news may cause you to harm others unwittingly, and you will later repent of what you have done.

If two groups of believers take up arms against one another, let God's apostle make peace between them. If one group commits violence against the other, then the aggressors should be resisted until they submit to the judgement of God. When they submit, let the apostle resolve the dispute fairly and justly; God loves those who act justly.

49. 1–6, 9

A band of brothers and sisters

The believers are a band of brothers and sisters. Let there be peace among them, and let them honour God with one voice. Thus God will show them mercy.

Believers, let no man among you mock another man; the man being mocked is usually superior to the man who mocks. Let no woman among you mock another woman; the woman being mocked is usually superior to the woman who mocks. Do not slander one another, nor call each other by rude names; it is wrong that someone who has embraced the faith, should be called by a rude name. Those who do not repent, are sinners.

Believers, avoid undue suspicion of one another; in some cases suspicion is a crime. Do not spy on one another, nor talk badly about other believers behind their backs. Would any of you like to eat the flesh of a dead brother or sister? Surely you would loathe it. Honour God; he is forgiving and merciful.

49.10–12

Becoming Muslims

'We have created each of you from a man and a woman; and we have divided you into nations and tribes, that you might learn to appreciate one another.' Those whom God regards as most noble, are those who give him greatest honour. God is wise, and knows all.

Arabs of the desert, you declare: 'We are true believers!' I say that you are not; faith has not yet entered your hearts. So you should say: 'We submit to God.' If you obey God and his apostle, he will not fail to reward you for your labours. God is forgiving and merciful.

The true believers are those who have faith in God and his apostle, and never doubt; and who serve God both with their time and with their wealth. True believers fight for God's cause.

Would you boast to God about your religion, when God knows all that the heavens and the earth contain? God knows all things.

Some of you regard it as a personal favour to me that you became Muslims. I say that when you became Muslims, you conferred favours on no one; rather, God bestowed a favour on you by guiding you to the true faith. If you are truly people of faith, you should acknowledge this. God knows all that is hidden, both in the heavens and on the earth; he watches over your actions.

49.13–18

On the day of judgement the sky will shake and sway, and the mountains will crumble into nothing. On that day the plight of those who reject the truth, and of those who distort the truth with clever arguments, will be terrible. With great force they will be driven into the fire of hell. And a voice will say to them: 'This is the fire which you denied. Is this magic? Is this an illusion? You will burn in its flames. It makes no difference whether you endure it with fortitude, or whether you panic; you will burn in its flames. You will be treated according to your deeds.'

But the righteous will be taken to beautiful gardens, where they will live in bliss. They will rejoice at what the Lord is giving to them; and he will protect them from the heat of hell. He will say to them: 'Eat and drink at your pleasure. This is the reward for your labours.'

'We shall unite the true believers with those of their descendants who follow them in their faith. We shall give to all of them the proper reward for their good works; all are accountable for what they have done. We shall give them fruits to eat, and such meats as they desire. They will pass from one to another a cup whose liquid will suppress all malicious talk and sinful desires.'

They will say to one another: 'When we were living on earth, we were constantly anxious about the well-being of our families. But now God's grace has cooled our hearts.'

52.9–19, 21–23, 26–27

Muhammad's critics

People say: 'Muhammad is a poet. We are waiting for some misfortune to befall him.' I reply: 'Wait for as long as you wish; I too am waiting.' Do people have any reason to think that I shall suffer some misfortune; or is their statement prompted by malice?

People say: 'Muhammad has written the Quran himself.' In saying this they demonstrate their lack of faith. If their statement is true, let them write a similar book themselves.

Did my critics create themselves out of nothing? Did they create the heavens and the earth? Their ideas are foolish. Do they possess and control the treasures of your Lord? Do they have a ladder by which they climb up to God, and overhear him? Let their eavesdroppers bring proof that they have heard him. Do they know the mysteries of existence, and can they write them down? Do they want a war? Yet in any war the unbelievers will be vanquished. Do they have another god besides God? Let God be exalted above their idols. If they saw part of the heavens fall from the sky, they would still say: 'It is only a mass of clouds.'

Ignore my critics. A day will come when they will be struck dumb with terror; and on that day their cleverness will count for nothing – they will be utterly helpless.

52.30–38, 41–46

Speculations and conjectures

I swear by the morning star that I, your compatriot, am not in error; nor am I deceived. My words are not based on my own speculations; they are inspired by divine revelation. I am taught by the angel Gabriel, who is powerful and strong.

Unbelievers follow their own whims and vain conjectures – even though the guidance of the Lord has come to them. Can people attain all that they desire? God ordains all that happens in this life, and in the life to come.

There are countless angels in the heavens. Yet their prayers achieve nothing unless God chooses to listen to them. Those who do not believe in the life to come, call the angels by female names. Yet they have no knowledge of the sex of angels; they are merely speculating – and speculation is no substitute for the truth.

'Ignore those who ignore our warning, and seek only the pleasures of this world; they know only those pleasures.' Your Lord knows well who has strayed from his path, and who is walking in the right direction.

Which of the Lord's blessings do the unbelievers deny? The prophet who warns them now, is just like the prophets of old. Why do they not marvel at this revelation? Why do you not laugh with joy, instead of weeping with misery? Why do you not prostrate yourself before God, and worship him?

53. 1–5, 23b–30, 55–62

The Lord's blessings in this life

The merciful God taught you the Quran. He created human beings, and gave them language. The sun and the moon follow the course he has ordained. The herbs and trees bow down in adoration.

He raised up the sky, and set all things in balance; he commanded you not to upset that balance, but to respect it. He laid out the earth for all creatures; and he planted upon it trees that bear blossom and fruit, husks that carry grain, and herbs that emit fragrance. Which of the Lord's blessings would you deny? He created human beings from dry clay, as a potter creates pots; and he created spirits from the flames of fire. Which of the Lord's blessings would you deny?

The Lord is present where the sun rises in summer, and where the sun rises in winter. He is present where the sun sets in summer, and where the sun sets in winter. Which of the Lord's blessings would you deny?

The Lord has made lakes of fresh water and seas of salt water; and he has put barriers between them so they cannot mix. Which of the Lord's blessings would you deny? Precious stones come from both lakes and the sea. Which of the Lord's blessings would you deny? The ships that sail across the ocean like mountains, belong to the Lord. Which of the Lord's blessings would you deny?

55. 1−25

The Lord's blessings in the next life

All creatures on earth will pass away. But the face of your Lord will endure for ever, in all majesty and glory. Which of the Lord's blessings would you deny? All who dwell in the heavens and on the earth, look to God for help. Each day God engages himself on some new task. Which of the Lord's blessings would you deny?

'Human beings and spirits, we shall certainly find time to judge you!' Which of the Lord's blessings would you deny?

'Human beings and spirits, if you have the power to penetrate the mysteries of the heavens and the earth, then penetrate them! But you cannot do this except on our authority.' Which of the Lord's blessings would you deny?

For those who honour the majesty of the Lord, there are two gardens, each planted with trees which give shade. Which of the Lord's blessings would you deny? Each garden is watered by a spring which constantly flows. Which of the Lord's blessings would you deny? Each garden contains a pair of every kind of tree; so there is every kind of fruit. Which of the Lord's blessings would you deny?

The righteous will recline on couches covered with silk brocade, and the fruits will hang within their reach. Which of the Lord's blessings would you deny? They will rest on green cushions, and there will be beautiful carpets. Which of the Lord's blessings would you deny?

Blessed be the name of the Lord, the Lord of glory and honour.

55.26–34, 46–55, 75–78

God's questions

'We created you. Will you not believe in our power? Look at the semen which you discharge. Did you create it, or did we? We ordained that all living creatures must die. Nothing can hinder us from replacing you with others like you; nothing can prevent us from transforming you from your present condition, to a condition which you cannot imagine.

'You surely know that you were created. Why, then, do you not reflect on your creation? Consider the seeds that you sow. Do you make them grow, or do we? If we wanted, we could turn your harvest into chaff. Filled with horror, you would exclaim: "We cannot now pay our debts. We have been robbed."

'Consider the water that you drink. Did you pour it from the clouds, or did we? If we wanted, we could turn it bitter. Why, then, do you not give thanks?

'Consider the fire which you kindle. Did you create the wood, or did we? We have created fire as a source of light for all people, and as a beacon for travellers.'

So praise the name of the Lord, the supreme being.

56.57–74

The kingdom of the heavens and the earth

All creatures in the heavens and on the earth give glory to God. He is mighty and wise. To him belongs the kingdom of the heavens and the earth. He ordains life and death, and has power over all things. He is the first and the last, the seen and the unseen. He knows all.

He created the heavens and the earth in six days. He is secure in his power. He knows all that happens below the surface of the earth, and he knows all that emerges from the earth. He knows all that comes down from the heavens, and all that ascends to the heavens. He is close to you, wherever you are. God is aware of all your actions.

To him belongs the kingdom of the heavens and the earth. To him will all things return. He causes the night to pass into day, and the day to pass into night. He knows the deepest thoughts of every man and woman.

Put your faith in God and his apostle. Give generously from what he has given you. Those who have faith and give generously, will be richly rewarded. When the apostle invites you to put your faith in God, what reason have you for refusing? After all, God has entered a covenant with you; so if you are true believers, trust him.

God sends down clear revelations to his servant, in order to lead you from darkness to light. God is compassionate and merciful to you.

57. 1–9

Hypocrites and believers

What reason have you, that you should not give generously to God's cause? After all, God alone will inherit the heavens and the earth. What reason have you, that you should not make a generous loan to God's cause? If you lend to God's cause, he will repay you double, and you will be richly rewarded.

The day will surely come when you will see faithful men and women, the true believers, marching forward, with a light going before them, and carrying lights in their right hands. A voice will declare to them: 'Rejoice at the good news! Today you will enter gardens watered by running streams, in which you will live for ever.' That will be the supreme triumph.

On that day the hypocrites, both men and women, will say to those who believe: 'Wait for us, that we may take light from your light.' But the believers will answer: 'Go away, and seek some other light.' Then a wall will descend between the believers and the hypocrites, with a gate in it; inside the wall there will be mercy, and outside the wall there will be punishment.

The hypocrites will cry out to the believers: 'Were we not on your side?' 'Yes' the believers will reply, 'but you allowed yourselves to be tempted; you wavered and doubted; you were deceived by your own desires; and you let Satan deceive you about God. Now let God's will be done.'

57.10a, 11–14

Worldly success

There were people in the past who received Scriptures; and yet, despite living to a great age, they hardened their hearts – and many of them did great evil. Is it not time for true believers to submit to God's warning, embracing the truth he has revealed?

Remember that God restores the earth to life after it has died. 'We have made plain to you our revelations, that you may grow in wisdom.'

Men and women who give generously, and who make generous loans in the name of God, will be repaid double; they will receive a noble recompense. Those who believe in God and his apostle, are regarded by God as his true and faithful servants; they will have their reward and their light. 'But those who reject our revelations, refusing to believe them, are the heirs of hell.'

Remember that the present life in this world is merely a sport and a pastime; a time when people play foolish games, competing against one another for greater wealth and larger families. The present life is like a plant that flourishes after rain: the gardener is glad to see it grow; but soon it will wither, turning yellow, and become worthless stubble. Success in this world counts for nothing.

Therefore seek urgently the forgiveness of God, that you many enter paradise; it is as vast as the sky and the earth, and has been prepared for those who believe in God and his apostle. God's grace is infinite; and he bestows it as he likes.

57.16–20a, 21

Noah, Abraham and Jesus

Do not be upset at the good things you miss, and do not be overjoyed at the good things you receive. God does not love those who are arrogant and boastful; he does not love those who are stingy, and encourage others to be stingy also. Those who ignore these words, should remember that God alone is self-reliant, and God alone is worthy of praise.

'We have sent our apostles with clear arguments; we have sent them down with Scriptures, that people may assess themselves justly – and thereby conduct themselves well. We have given people iron, which has great strength and can be put to many uses.' God can see who serves him, even in secret, and who helps his apostle. God is powerful and mighty.

'We have sent Noah and Abraham, and we have bestowed on their descendants the gift of prophecy and Scriptures. Some followed the right path, but others were sinners. After Noah and Abraham we sent Jesus, the son of Mary. We gave him the Gospel, and put compassion and mercy in the hearts of his followers.'

Let those who believe in the Scriptures sent by God, understand that they do not control God's gifts; his gifts are in his hand, and he bestows them as he wishes. God's bounty is infinite.

57.23–27a, 29

Cruelty and dishonesty in marriage

God hears the words of the woman who complains to Muhammad about the cruelty of her husband; God hears her words when she complains directly to him. God listens to everything that is said; he hears all and observes all.

Some of you divorce your wife by declaring her to be your mother, even though you know this is untrue – even though you know she did not give birth to you. Your words are both unjust and dishonest; but God is forgiving and merciful.

Some of you divorce your wife, and later retract your words. In these circumstances you must not have intercourse with her, until you have ransomed a slave. You are required to do this; God is aware of all your actions. If you do not possess a slave, you must fast for two successive months before having intercourse. If you cannot do this, you must feed sixty poor people. This is required of you, as a mark of your faith in God and his apostle. Such are the laws of God. A grievous punishment awaits the unbelievers.

58. 1–4

Intrigue

God knows all that the heavens and the earth contain. Are you not aware of this? If three people talk in secret together, he is the fourth; if four people talk, he is the fifth; if five people talk, he is the sixth. Whatever the size of the group, and wherever they meet, he is present among them. Then on the day of resurrection he will declare to them all that they have done. God knows all things.

All of you are forbidden by God's apostle from forming secret plots. Yet are you not aware that some people do this, motivated by malice, enmity and defiance? When these people meet you, they use language which God dislikes. Then they say to themselves: 'God is not punishing us for our foul words.' Hell is what they deserve; they will burn in its flames – a horrible fate.

Believers, when you meet in private, do not speak with malice, enmity or defiance towards the apostle; speak only in a spirit of fairness and piety. Honour God, because you will all be brought before him

Intrigue is the work of Satan, who uses it to upset the faithful. Yet he cannot hurt them, except by the will of God. Let the faithful put their trust in God.

58.7–10

Relations between believers and unbelievers

Believers, when a woman of faith seeks refuge with you, examine her; God knows her faith. If you find that her faith is genuine, do not return her to the unbelieving husband from whom she has fled; it is not right for a faithful woman to have sexual relations with an unbeliever. But if she has brought any material goods that belong to her husband, hand them back to him. It is not an offence for you to marry such a woman, provided that you can support her.

When a man becomes a believer, but his wife remains an unbeliever, he is not required to remain married to her. But if he divorces her, he should give back all her possessions. This is the law which God lays down for you. God is wise, and knows all.

Consider a woman of faith coming to me, the prophet. She pledges herself to serve no other god but God; she promises not to commit theft, adultery or murder; she undertakes not to tell monstrous lies of her own invention; she says that she will obey me when my commands are just and reasonable. I shall accept her, and beg God to forgive her. God is forgiving and merciful.

Believers, do not make friends with those who have incurred God's anger. Such people have no hope of the life to come – just as they have no hope for those already in their graves.

60. 10–13

Friday prayers

All things in the heavens and on the earth give glory to God,
the sovereign Lord, the holy one, the one who possesses all
power and knowledge.

It is God who raised an apostle from the inhabitants of
Mecca, to recite to them his revelations, to purify them, to
make them wise, and to explain the Scriptures to them – and
thereby save them from the gross errors into which they have
fallen. Such is the grace of God; he bestows his grace on
whom he pleases, and his grace is infinite.

Believers, you are required to pray together each Friday.
When you hear the call to prayer, stop your worship, and
hurry to the place of meeting. This will do you much good
– if you only knew. When the prayers are finished, disperse,
and seek God's grace. Keep God always in your mind, so that
you may enjoy success in your work.

That which God has in store for believers, is far better
than any material novelties or pleasures which distract people
on earth. I declare that God is the most generous giver.

62. 1–2, 4, 9–11

The day of cheating

All things in the heavens and on the earth give glory to God. To him belong all majesty and glory and power.

It was God who created you; yet some of you refuse to believe, while others have faith. He is aware of all your actions. He created the heavens and the earth to manifest the truth. He fashioned each one of you – and each one of you is beautiful. To God you will all return. He knows all that the heavens and the earth contain. He knows all that you hide and all that you reveal. He knows your deepest thoughts.

Have you not heard of people in the past who refused to believe? They have already suffered through their unbelief; and a terrible punishment awaits them. When their apostles brought them clear arguments, they said: 'Will mortals be our guides?' They denied the truth, and turned their backs. But God has no need of them; he has all he needs, and he alone should be praised.

The unbelievers deny the resurrection. I say to you that by the Lord's power you will certainly be raised to life. Then you will be told of all you have done; that is easy for God.

On the day of resurrection God will gather you together in one place. That will be the day of cheating: those who are blessed will cheat those who are damned of their places in paradise.

64. 1–7, 9a

Divorce

If you wish to divorce your wife, let there be an interval between making the decision and enacting it. Determine in advance the days and weeks of this interval, and let them be many; be careful to honour God in all you do. Do not expel your wife from your home, and do not let her leave, unless you can prove she has acted immorally. These are the rules which God has prescribed; those who transgress them, injure their own souls. You do not know whether the decision to divorce your wife is right; something may happen, which causes you to change your mind.

When the interval is over, you may keep your wife, or you may divorce her. If you keep her, be gentle with her; if you divorce her, treat her with honour. Make your decision before God, and summon two honest men to act as witnesses. Whoever believes in God and in the last day, should do this. If you honour God in your conduct towards your wife, God will save you.

65. 1—2

The inevitable

The inevitable – what is inevitable? If only you knew!

The trumpet will sound a single blast. Earth with all its mountains will be raised high in the air; and then with a mighty crash it will be shattered into dust. On that day even greater things will happen. The sky will lose its strength, and start to sway; then it will break apart. The angels will stand around the sky, and eight of them will carry the throne of God above their heads. On that day all of you will be brought before him, and all your secrets will be exposed.

There will be a book for every person, in which all that person's deeds are recorded. The righteous will receive their books in their right hands; and they will show their books with pride to one another. The wicked will receive their books in their left hands. And each will say: 'I wish that this book had not been given to me. I wish that I knew nothing about it. I wish that death had ended my existence. My wealth now counts for nothing, and I am helpless.'

'If our prophet had fabricated lies about us, we should have seized him by the right hand, and cut the vein into his heart. None of you would have been able to protect him.'

69.1–3, 13–19, 25–29, 44–47

Keeping vigil

'Muhammad, remain clothed at night, and keep vigil. Sleep only for half the night – sometimes a little more, sometimes a little less. Slowly recite the Quran, so that you may hear us speak to you with great profundity. In the silent hours of the night our impression upon you is deepest, and our words come to you with greatest eloquence; during the day you are concerned with practical matters.'

Remember the name of your Lord, and dedicate yourself utterly to his service. He is the Lord of the east and the west, and there is no god but him. Trust him as your protector.

'Muhammad, your Lord knows that sometimes you keep vigil for almost two-thirds of the night; sometimes you keep vigil for a half or one-third of the night. Others among your followers do the same.' God measures the night and the day. He knows that you, the believers, cannot accurately count the hours, and he is tolerant. Recite from the Quran as many verses as you can; he knows that some of you are sick, some are travelling in order to obtain God's bounty, and some are fighting in God's cause. Recite from the Quran as many verses as you can.'

73.1–9, 20a

The challenge of life

A time will come when the sun ceases to shine; when the stars fall from the sky, and the mountains are blown away; when pregnant camels do not need tending, and wild animals live in peace; when the lakes are set alight, and people understand fully their own souls; when infant girls, who have been buried alive, are allowed to defend themselves; when the records of people's deeds are opened, and the heavens are exposed to view; when hell burns fiercely, and paradise is brought near. At that time every man will be told the deeds he has done, and every woman will be told the deeds she has done.

I swear by the planets that follow their courses, by the stars that rise and set, by the darkness of night, and by the first light of dawn, that my words are those of an honoured messenger, held in esteem by the Lord who sits on the divine throne and is obeyed in the heavens; I swear that I am worthy of the trust that he has placed in me.

No, I am not mad. I saw the angel Gabriel on the horizon, which was perfectly clear. Gabriel does not strive to conceal the unseen mysteries; nor is he influenced by the accursed Satan.

What direction do you wish your lives to take? I urge all of you, if you have the strength of will, to follow the path of righteousness. Yet you cannot do this, unless it is willed by God, the Lord of creation.

81.1–29

Standing alone before God

A time will come when the sky is torn apart; when the stars scatter, and the ocean drains away; and when the graves are tossed about, and laid open. At that time every man will be told what he has done, and what he has failed to do; and every woman will be told what she has done, and what she has failed to do.

Men and women, what evil attractions have lured you from your gracious Lord, who created and fashioned you, moulding your body according to his will? Yes, you deny the last judgement. Yet there are guardians watching over you, carefully recording all your actions. The righteous will surely live in bliss. But after the day of judgement the wicked will burn in hell; they will not escape.

If only you understood the day of judgement! I wish you understood the day of judgement. It is the day when every soul will stand alone, and God will reign supreme.

82. 1–19

From one existence to the next

A time will come when the sky bursts apart, obeying its Lord as it must. A time will come when the earth expands, casting out all the creatures that live upon it and within it, and becoming empty; it will do this in obedience to its Lord, as it must. Then all men and women who strive to meet their Lord, will do so.

Each person will be given a book. Those who are given their books in their right hands, will be judged leniently; and they will return to their people joyfully. But those who are given their books in their left hands, will call down destruction on themselves, and burn in the fire of hell. They are the people who have never cared for their neighbours; they thought they would never return to God. Their Lord watches all that people do.

I swear by the glow of the sunset, by the night and all that the night brings to life, and by the full moon, that you will move from your present existence to a different existence.

Why do the people of Mecca not have faith? Why do they not kneel in prayer when the Quran is recited to them? The unbelievers reject the Quran; but God knows the false beliefs that fill their minds.

Let all be aware that they will suffer a terrible punishment – except those who embrace the true faith and do good deeds. Believers will enjoy a reward that will never diminish.

84. 1–25

The nightly visitor

I swear by the heavens that there is a spiritual visitor each night. If only you knew this nightly visitor! It is like a star, whose brightness pierces the heart. Every soul has a guardian watching over it.

Let men and women reflect on how they came into existence. They were created from a fluid that is made in the male body between the loins and the ribs. God has power to bring the dead back to life – and he will do so on the day of judgement, when every conscience will be searched. People will stand helpless; no one will be able to support them.

I swear by the sky that gives rain, and by the earth that is constantly bursting with new life, that my words are true and profound; nothing is spoken in jest. The unbelievers scheme against you; but I scheme against them. So endure the unbelievers, and do not let them distract you.

86. 1–17

Neither living nor dying

Praise the name of your Lord, the most high, who has created all living things, and made them beautiful; who has ordained the destinies of all living things, and guides them; and who makes them lush and green, or withered and yellow, according to the seasons.

'We shall require you to recite our revelations.' Thus you will not forget any of them, except as God pleases. He knows all that is open, and all that is hidden.

'We shall guide you onto the smoothest path. Then invite the people of Mecca to follow that path – if they will listen.' Those who honour God, will accept the invitation; but wicked sinners will refuse it. Wicked sinners will be cast into the raging fire, where they will neither live nor die. Happy are those who purify themselves of sin, who remember the name of the Lord, and who pray to him.

The people of Mecca prefer this life, even though the next life is better and more lasting.

All this is written in earlier Scriptures – such as the Scriptures of Abraham and Moses.

87.1–19

Two kinds of test

When God tests you by giving you worldly honour and prosperity, you are inclined to say: 'The Lord is kind.' But when he tests you by withdrawing his favours, you say: 'The Lord is cruel.'

Yes! But you show no kindness to orphans; you do not compete with one another in feeding the poor. You grab with greedy hands the property of the weak; you are in love with material wealth.

Yes! But a time will come when the earth is crushed to fine dust, and your Lord comes down with the angels, rank upon rank. Hell will come near. At that time all people will remember their deeds. But will their memory help them?

The wicked will say: 'If only I had been charitable during my life!' But no one can punish as the Lord will punish the wicked on that day. There are no chains stronger than the chains with which the Lord will bind the wicked on that day.

May your soul be serene. May your soul be joyful as you return to the Lord. May your soul be pleasing in his sight. 'Enter my paradise, and join my servants.'

89.15–30

The height

'We created human beings, in order to test them with suffering.'

Do people think that no one has power over them. They boast: 'We are so rich that we can afford to waste riches.' Do they think that no one observes them?

'Have we not given each person two eyes, a tongue, and two lips? Have we not shown them the two paths, the path of righteousness and the path of wickedness? Yet they refuse to scale the great height.'

If only you understood the great height! It consists in purchasing the freedom of a slave. It consists in feeding, during famines, an orphaned relative, or anyone who is starving. It consists in having faith, in encouraging others, and in exercising mercy.

'Those who do these things, will stand at our right hand. But those who deny our revelations, will stand at our left hand, while the fire of hell closes over them.'

90. 1—20

The paths of salvation and sorrow

I swear that I speak the truth, by the sun and its brightness at midday; by the moon, which rises as the sun sets; by the day, which reveals the splendour of the sun; and by the night which veils the sun.

I swear that I speak the truth, by the heavens, and the one who built them; by the earth, and the one who spread it out; and by the soul, and the one who moulded it, and inspired it with knowledge of sin and piety. The man or woman who keeps the soul pure, will be blessed; the man or woman who corrupts the soul, will come to ruin.

I swear that I speak the truth, by the night which casts a veil of darkness over the earth; and by the radiant day. 'For those who give generously to the needy, who guard against evil, and who cherish goodness, we shall make smooth the path of salvation. But for those who neither give nor take, and who do not cherish goodness, we shall make smooth the path of sorrow.' When people perish, their wealth counts for nothing.

'It is our task to give guidance. The present life and the next life belong to us.'

91. 1—10; 92. 1—13

Words for Muhammad

Muhammad, your Lord never forsakes you; nor does he ever turn away from you. The life to come holds a far richer prize than this present life; you will be delighted at what your Lord will give you. When you were an orphan, did he not come to you, and give you shelter? When you were in error, did he not guide you? When you were poor, did he not enrich you? Therefore you should neither reject the orphan, nor drive away the beggar; instead you should proclaim the goodness of your Lord.

'When you are weighed down with many burdens, do we not encourage and relieve you? Have we not made you famous, winning for you the highest respect?' Every hardship is followed by comfort; every setback is followed by success. When one task is complete, resume your labours, seeking your Lord with all fervour.

93.3–11; 94.1–8

Absorbed by gain

Right up until the moment of death your hearts are absorbed
by material gain. But you will soon understand; yes, before
long you will understand. Indeed, if you knew the truth with
certainty, you would perceive the fire of hell; you would see
it with your own eyes. On the day of judgement you will be
questioned about all your pleasures.

There are many people who slander and defame others for
their own advantage. There are many who amass great
wealth, and gloat over it, imagining that it will make them
immortal. Such people are doomed. They will be hurled towards a great fire, and destroyed. Do you understand this fire
which destroys people? It is the fire kindled by God, which
will rise up to people's hearts. It will be like towering
columns which will crush them.

Consider those who deny the last judgement. They are
people who turn away orphans, and are indifferent as to
whether the poor are fed. They pray, but they never think
about the meaning of their prayers. They make a grand display of their piety, but they give nothing to the destitute.
They are doomed.

102. 1–8; 104. 1–9; 107. 1–7

The unity of God

Those who refuse to believe, listen to me. I do not serve what you worship, and you do not serve what I worship. I shall never serve what you worship, and you will never serve what I worship. You have your religion, and I have mine.

When God comes to the help of his servants, and brings them victory, you will see great multitudes embrace his faith. By seeking his forgiveness these converts will give glory to your Lord; he is always inclined to show mercy.

God is one; God is eternal. He has given birth to no one, and no one gave birth to him. No one is equal to him.

109.1–6; 110.1–3; 112.1–4

SUFI MYSTICISM

The term 'Sufi' probably refers to the rough woollen garments which Muslim ascetics habitually wore. The Sufis formed loose-knit communities; and each community had a master, who taught mystical prayer to the disciples.

Episodes from the lives of some early Sufis were recorded by Attar. These include one of the first known Sufis, a woman called Rabi'a (d. 801). Her feisty approach to the spiritual life won the respect of many male Sufis.

The first great Sufi master was Junayd of Baghdad (d. 910), who outlined a method of mystical prayer. He also urged Sufis to obey the political authorities, regarding social disruption as contrary to the spiritual quest.

Junayd's conformism did not appeal to the more ecstatic Hallaj (d. 922), who was regarded by many as a rebel. He was eventually crucified as a heretic, for claiming himself to be the truth. Accounts of both Junayd and Hallaj are included in Attar's work; and some of their own writings also survive.

Qushayri (d. 1074), who lived in north-eastern Iran, wrote a treatise on the psychology of mysticism. He also emphasized the importance of all Sufis being under a master.

At an early age Ghazali (d. 1111) achieved fame as a philosopher in Baghdad. But eventually he became disillusioned with the rational approach to religion, and turned to mysticism, giving up his career and wealth in the process. He wrote a spiritual autobiography describing his movement from intellectual to mystical thought.

Ibn Arabi (d. 1240) grew up in Spain, and also turned from philosophy to mysticism. He travelled throughout north Africa as a Sufi teacher, composing short poetic meditations which people could easily learn.

The most famous Sufi teacher is undoubtedly Rumi (d. 1293). His family came from Afghanistan, but fled from the Mongol invasions to Turkey. He became the dominant religious figure in Konya, the main city of Turkey. His aphorisms are packed with spiritual insight.

The most popular Sufi text is the *Gulistan* of Sadi (d. 1294); it expresses the deepest spiritual wisdom in simple stories. He came from Shiraz in Iran, and travelled widely in India, central Asia, and Africa; and at one point was a prisoner of the Crusaders.

Sadi's method of expressing truth in stories was emulated by Nizam al-Din of India (d. 1325).

A woman on God's path

Rabi'a was veiled with a special veil, the veil of sincerity. Love and yearning for God burned within her. She wanted to be close to God, and to be absorbed by him. In her devotion to God she lost all sense of self. She compared herself with Mary, the mother of Jesus. She was regarded as the equal of men, because the mercy of the most high God was upon her.

If anyone asks why Rabi'a is ranked equal with men, we reply that Muhammad, the chief of prophets, said: 'God does not judge you by your outward forms. It is not outward form that matters, but inner intention.' Moreover, since we derive much of our religion from Muhammad's wife Aisha, then it is right to take spiritual inspiration from a woman. When a woman is on the path of God, it is not appropriate to define her by her womanhood.

Attar: Rabi'a 1

As a slave

When Rabi'a was a young woman, both her mother and her father died. A great famine occurred in Basra, the city where she lived. She became separated from her sisters, and she was seized by a wicked man, who sold her into slavery for a few coins. Her master made her work long and hard as a prostitute.

One day, as she was standing in the street, she decided to flee. As she ran, she tripped and fell, breaking her hand. She put her face into the dust, and cried out to God: 'I am a stranger in this world, without a family. I am a slave, and now my hand is broken. Yet none of this saddens me. All I need is for you to be pleased with me. I beg you to tell me whether you are pleased with me, or not.' Then she heard a voice speaking to her: 'Do not be sad. Tomorrow you will enjoy a position, so high that even the highest angels in heaven will envy you.'

Attar: Rabi'a 4

Release from slavery

Rabi'a returned to her master's house. She began to fast; and she spent every night in prayer, remaining on her feet. One night her master awoke from sleep, saw her in prayer, and heard her words: 'O God, you know that my heart desires to obey your commands; and the prospect of serving in your court brings light to my mind. If the choice were mine, I should not rest one moment from serving you. But you have put me in the hands of this man; and for this reason I am held back.'

Her master saw a lantern, suspended without a chain above her head; it filled the whole house with light. He felt frightened. He arose, and said to himself: 'She cannot be kept in slavery.' Then at dawn he said to her: 'I release you. If you wish to stay here, I shall serve you. If not, go wherever you wish.' Rabi'a asked to leave.

She went into the desert, where she offered a thousand prayers each day. She frequently went to visit another Sufi, called Hasan.

Some time later, so it is said, she left the desert, and became a musician. But she soon repented, and went to live in a ruin. Then she found a cell in which to meditate and pray.

Attar: Rabi'a 5

Stealing and eating meat

One night Rabi'a was praying in her cell. She was overcome by weariness, and fell asleep on her mat, which was made of reeds. A reed pierced her eye; but she was so absorbed in pious dreams, that she was unaware of it.

A thief entered her cell, and picked up the rug on which she prayed. But as he picked it up, he went blind, so he could not find the way out. He put the rug down, and could see; but when it picked it up again, he was again blind. Seven times this happened. Then he heard a voice from the corner of the cell: 'Do not cause yourself so much trouble. For several years this woman has entrusted herself to us. The Devil himself does not have the courage to come near her. How can a mere thief have the boldness to steal her prayer-rug? Leave her, you scoundrel, and do not cause yourself any further trouble. Remember, even if our friends are asleep, we are awake.'

A few days later Rabi'a went up a mountain. Wild goats and gazelles gathered round her, and gazed at her with devotion. Then Hasan appeared, and all the animals shied away. Hasan was perplexed, and asked Rabi'a: 'Why are the animals so intimate with you, yet dislike me?' Rabi'a said: 'What have you eaten today.' Hasan replied: 'I have eaten stew made from goat's meat.' Rabi'a said: 'No wonder goats and other animals dislike you!'

Attar: Rabi'a 13, 15

Real spiritual business

Rabi'a passed Hasan's cell. He was sitting on the roof, weeping so profusely that water was dripping from the rain spouts. Several drops fell onto Rabi'a. Looking up, she wondered at first if it were raining. But when she saw that the drops were Hasan's tears, she spoke to him: 'If these tears are a sign of spiritual languor, you should hold them back; otherwise a great sea of tears may well up within you, such that you will no longer be able to find your own heart – except in the keeping of the omnipotent King.'

These words distressed Hasan, but he said nothing. Then some days later he saw Rabi'a by the banks of the Euphrates river. Hasan threw his prayer-rug onto the water, and exclaimed: 'Rabi'a, let us pray together on the water.' Rabi'a replied: 'Hasan, you should not show off your spiritual powers in this worldly market. And if you do, the powers should be greater than anything ordinary creatures can display.' She then threw her own prayer-rug into the air, and said: 'Hasan, let us pray together floating above the ground.' But Hasan lacked the power to float above ground; so he said nothing.

Rabi'a tried to console him, saying: 'What you suggested that we do, fish can also do. What I suggested that we do, insects can also do. Our real spiritual business is beyond both.'

Attar: Rabi'a 16, 17

A piece of wax, a needle and a hair

Hasan used to say to his friends: 'Whenever I meet Rabi'a, we discuss the spiritual path and divine truth at great depth; and I forget that I am a man, and she is a woman. In fact, I think of myself as a spiritual pauper, and her as the possessor of great spiritual wealth.'

Rabi'a came to Hasan with three things: a candle, a needle, and a hair. She said: 'Be like the candle: give light to the world, as you yourself burn. Be like the needle: work hard, and have nothing to protect you. Then, like the hair, you will last for ever.'

A few days later Hasan asked Rabi'a if she would marry him. She replied: 'The knot of marriage can only tie someone who exists as a distinct person. But I no longer exist as a distinct person: I have lost myself, and exist entirely through God. I belong wholly to God; I live under the shadow of his command. You must ask his permission for my hand in marriage.'

'Rabi'a,' Hasan asked, 'how have you attained such a degree of holiness?' Rabi'a replied: 'By losing in him all that I have attained.' Hasan asked: 'How do you know God?' Rabi'a replied: 'You want to know how to know God. I know God, without knowing how to know him.'

Attar: Rabi'a 18, 20, 21

This world and the next world

Some people asked Rabi'a: 'Why do you not take a husband?'
She replied: 'There are three questions, which absorb all my
attention; if you can answer these questions, I shall take a
husband. First, at the moment of death, will my faith be
sound or not? Second, will the record of my deeds be put in
my right hand, or in my left hand? Third, will I be in the
group which is led to paradise, or in the group which is led
to hell?' They said: 'We cannot answer these questions.' She
said: 'With such agonizing questions on my mind, how can
I concern myself with taking a husband?'

The people asked Rabi'a: 'Where have you come from?'
She replied: 'I have come from this world.' They asked:
'Where are you going to?' She replied: 'To the next world.'
They asked: 'What are you doing in this world?' She replied:
'I am grieving.' They asked: 'Why?' She replied: 'I eat the
bread of this world, but do the work of the next world.'

They exclaimed: 'You speak so wisely; you are fit to take
charge of a religious community.' She said: 'I am in charge
of myself. Whatever is within me, I do not let out. Whatever
is outside me, I do not let in. I do not allow anything to enter
me from this world; and I do not allow anything from the
next world to leave me. I watch over my heart; I do not wish
to watch over buildings made of mud and clay.'

Attar: Rabi'a 24, 25

Love, contentment and repentance

Some people asked Rabi'a: 'Do you love the presence of God in his majesty?' She replied: 'I do.' They asked: 'Do you hate Satan?' She replied: 'I feel pity for Satan, so I cannot hate him.'

The people asked her about love. She said: 'Love came down as a liquid from eternity, and returned to eternity. It visited eighteen thousand worlds, and found no one to drink it. Then it met the truth. As a consequence of that meeting, love loves the truth, and the truth is true to love.'

The people asked her: 'Do you see that which you worship?' She replied: 'If I did not see that which I worship, I should not worship.'

The people asked her: 'When are servants of God contented?' She replied: 'They are contented when they are as grateful for pain as they are for pleasure.'

They asked her: 'When sinners repent, does God accept their repentance, or not?' She replied: 'Sinners can only repent if God gives them a spirit of repentance; and when God gives people this spirit, he accepts their repentance. But if people try to repent without receiving this spirit, he will not accept their repentance.'

Attar: Rabi'a 26, 27, 29

Complaint, division and creation

Rabi'a saw a man with a bandage round his head. She asked him: 'Why do you have a bandage round your head?' He replied: 'My head aches.' She asked: 'How old are you?' 'Thirty,' he replied. She asked: 'In these thirty years, have you mainly been healthy or sick?' 'Healthy,' he replied. She said: 'In these thirty years you have never tied the bandage of gratitude round your head. Now, because you have a headache, you tie a bandage of complaint.'

Rabi'a asked someone to buy a blanket for her, giving the person four coins. The person asked: 'Do you want a black blanket, or a white one?' Rabi'a took back the coins, threw them in the Tigris river, and exclaimed: 'Must we divide even blankets into distinct groups?'

One springtime Rabi'a entered a house, and did not come out. A follower said to her: 'Come outside, and see the beauties of the creation.' Rabi'a said: 'Come inside, and see the creator. If you see the creator, you become too preoccupied to look at the creation.'

Attar: Rabi'a 34, 35, 36

Fasting and frustration

Rabi'a fasted for seven days and nights; she did not sleep during the nights, but prayed continually. On the eighth night she was overcome with hunger, and her soul cried out: 'How long will I be tormented?' At that moment someone arrived at her cell, and gave her a bowl of food. She accepted it, and went to fetch a lamp. She returned to find that her cat had spilled the food.

She said to herself: 'I shall go out and fetch a jug, and I shall break my fast by drinking. By the time she had brought the jug, the lamp had gone out. She tried to drink in the dark; but the jug slipped from her hand, and broke. She sighed with such frustration that the heat of her sigh could have burned her cell down. 'O God,' she exclaimed, 'why are you making me so helpless?'

She heard a voice in her ears: 'Be careful, lest you want me to fulfill your material desires, and take away your desire for me. Material desires and the desire for me cannot exist within the same heart.'

Thirty years later Rabi'a related this event, and added: 'When I heard this voice, I detached my heart from material things, and suppressed all material desires. Since that time, whenever I have prayed, I have assumed it to be my last prayer.'

Attar: Rabi'a 38

Reasons for worship

A group of religious leaders came to Rabi'a. She asked one of
them: 'Why do you worship the Lord?' He replied: 'There are
seven levels of hell, which I regard with great fear and dread;
I wish to avoid passing through them.' She asked another
man the same question. He replied: 'There are many levels of
paradise, where there is much joy; I wish to dwell in one of
the levels.' Rabi'a said: 'It is wrong to worship God from fear
of punishment, or from hope of reward.'

So the men asked her: 'Why do you worship the Lord? Do
you have no fear or hope?' Rabi'a quoted a proverb: 'The
neighbour matters more than the house in
which the neighbour lives.' Then she said:
'God has commanded us to worship him; that
is all that matters. Do you think that, if
there were no heaven and hell, worship would be unnecessary? Would
not God deserve to be worshipped,
even if he had no punishments to
threaten or rewards to offer?'

Attar: Rabi'a 40

Male and female virtues

A religious leader came to visit Rabi'a, and was shocked to see that her clothes were in tatters. He said: 'There are many people who would provide you with decent clothes, if you only allowed them.' Rabi'a replied: 'Everything in this world is on loan to us from God. I am ashamed to accept the loan of a loan.' The man went away, and said to others: 'It is astonishing that a mere woman has reached such spiritual heights. She refuses to spend any time on material matters.'

A group of men came to Rabi'a in order to test her. They said: 'Virtues and spiritual gifts have been bestowed on men, not women. The crown of nobility has been placed on the heads of men, and the belt of generosity has been tied around their waists. The gift of prophecy has never descended on any woman. What can you boast of?' Rabi'a replied: 'I shall not dispute what you say. Yet women are less prone to pride, egotism and self-worship; they are less liable to think highly of themselves. And they do not so readily exploit others for their own pleasure.'

Attar: Rabi'a 41, 42

Contentment with God

Rabi'a fell ill. Someone asked her about the cause of the illness. She replied: 'The desire for paradise passed across the edge of my heart; and the Lord, who is my friend, chastised me.'

A philosopher called Sufyan went to visit her. At first Sufyan was overcome with awe at her holiness, so he could not speak. But eventually he said: 'If you will pray to God, your pain will surely be eased.' Rabi'a said: 'God has willed that I should suffer. Do you not know this?' Sufyan replied: 'Yes.' Rabi'a continued: 'If you know this, how can you ask me to pray for that which is contrary to his will? It is not right to oppose the Lord, who is my friend.'

Then Sufyan asked Rabi'a: 'Is there something that you desire?' Rabi'a replied: 'Sufyan, you are a learned man. So how can you speak of my desiring something? By the glory of God I have been desiring dates for the past twelve years. As you know, in Basra fresh dates are easy to obtain. Yet I have not eaten any. I am God's servant; and servants have no right to have desires of their own.'

Sufyan was reduced to silence. Then he said: 'Since I cannot speak about your situation, will you say something of mine?' Rabi'a replied: 'You are a good man, but you are in love with the world. You enjoy showing off your knowledge.' 'Lord God,' Sufyan exclaimed, 'be content with me!' Rabi'a said: 'How can you ask God to be content with you, when you are not content with him?'

Attar: Rabi'a 43, 45

Oblivious to suffering

A Sufi called Malik went to see Rabi'a. He was shocked to see
her material circumstances. The pitcher, which she used for
both washing and drinking, was broken; her reed mat on
which she lay was old and worn; and she had only a brick
for a pillow. He said to her: 'Rabi'a, I have many wealthy
friends. If you permit, I shall ask them to provide all that you
need.' Rabi'a said: 'You make an error. Your friends and I
have the same provider.' 'Yes,' Malik replied. Rabi'a continued: 'Does God forget the poor because of their poverty?
Does he help the wealthy because of their wealth?' 'No,'
Malik replied. Rabi'a concluded: 'Since God already knows
my circumstances, why should I remind him? Whatever he
wills, we should will.'

Some days later Malik returned, accompanied by two
other Sufis, Hasan and Shaqiq. The conversation turned to the
question of faith. Hasan said: 'Having faith means being
patient when God inflicts suffering.' Rabi'a said: 'That stinks
of egotism.' Shaqiq said: 'Having faith means being grateful
for suffering inflicted by God.' Rabi'a said: 'We need some
better definition than this.' Malik said: 'Having faith means
taking delight in suffering inflicted by God.' Rabi'a said: 'We
need some better definition than this.' They said to Rabi'a:
'Now you speak.' Rabi'a said: 'Having faith means having
such a clear vision of the Master, that one is oblivious to the
suffering he inflicts.'

Attar: Rabi'a 46, 47

Rabi'a's death

When Rabi'a was about to die, many religious leaders came to her bedside. She said to them: 'For the sake of God's prophets, rise up and leave my cell.' They arose, left her cell, and closed the door. Then they heard her recite a verse from the Quran: 'May my soul be serene. May my soul be joyful as I return to the Lord. May my soul be pleasing in his sight.'

Time passed, and they heard nothing more. They went back into her cell, and found her dead. The religious leaders said: 'Throughout her life in this world Rabi'a was never proud or arrogant towards the most high God. She never wanted anything for herself. She never asked God for any position. She never asked God to do anything for her.'

After her death she was seen in a dream. In the dream she was asked about two young men called Munkir and Nadir. She related that these two young men came to see her. They said: 'Who is your Lord?' She replied: 'God is my Lord. Go to him, and thank him for not forgetting a feeble old woman, even though he has many thousands of other creatures to care for.' Then she said to God: 'I love nothing in the world; I love only you. Have I ever forgotten you? So why have you sent these people to ask me who is my Lord?'

Attar: Rabi'a 57, 58

Giving and accepting

From earliest childhood Junayd was an earnest seeker after God. He was well-disciplined, thoughtful, and quick to understand; and he possessed a penetrating intuition. He had an uncle, called Sari, who was a Sufi.

One day he returned from school to find his father weeping. 'Why are you weeping?' Junayd asked. His father answered: 'I have struggled to save five gold coins, to give to your uncle Sari. I am weeping because he refuses to accept them.' Junayd said: 'Hand me the coins, and I shall give them to him.' His father gave Junayd the coins; and Junayd went to his uncle's house.

When he arrived, he said to Sari: 'Take this offering.' 'I shall not take it,' Sari exclaimed. Junayd said: 'I beg you to take it, in the name of God who has dealt graciously with you, and justly with my father.' Sari asked: 'How has God dealt graciously with me, and justly with your father.' Junayd said: 'God was gracious with you in giving you poverty; and he was just with my father in giving him wealth. You are free to accept or reject these coins, as you please. But my father is obliged to share his wealth with those who deserve it.'

Sari liked Junayd's answer, and said: 'Before accepting these coins, I must accept you.' He invited Junayd to live in his house; and then he took the coins.

Attar: Junayd

A definition of thankfulness

When Junayd was aged seven, Sari took him on the pilgrimage to Mecca. At the mosque a group of religious leaders were discussing the meaning of thankfulness. Each leader expressed his own view. Then Sari said to Junayd: 'You must express your view.'

Junayd said: 'Thankfulness means not using the blessings and gifts he has bestowed on you, as the means of disobeying his commands, nor as the motive for disobeying his commands.'

The leaders congratulated him for speaking so well; and they agreed that no finer definition of thankfulness could be devised. His uncle said: 'It is becoming plain that your special gift from God is your tongue.' Junayd wept at these words. Then Sari asked: 'Where did you acquire this gift?' Junayd answered: 'From listening to you.'

Junayd returned home to Baghdad, where in due course he took up selling glasses. At the end of each day he closed the shop, drew down the blinds, and said four hundred prayers. But after a time he gave up the shop, and he devoted all his time to caring for his own soul.

Attar: Junayd

A mystic and a preacher

For forty years Junayd followed the mystic path. At the end of this time the idea arose in his mind that he had attained his goal. Then a voice from the heavens spoke to him: 'I shall now show that your mystical girdle remains loose.' When he heard these words, he exclaimed: 'O God, what sin have I committed?' The voice said: 'Do you imagine that there is a worse sin than this: that you exist?' Junayd sighed, and bowed his head. After a few moments he whispered: 'I am not worthy of union with God; all my good works are merely sins.'

Junayd now began to speak eloquently about spiritual matters. His uncle Sari told him that his duty was to preach in public places. Junayd was doubtful, because he disliked this prospect. So he said to Sari: 'While the master is still alive, it is unseemly for the disciple to preach.'

Then one night Junayd saw the prophet Muhammad in a dream. The prophet said to him: 'Preach.' The following morning Junayd went to see Sari, who was waiting for him. Sari said: 'Now you have no choice: you must preach. And your words will be the means of salvation for countless people across the world. You refused to preach at my urging; but now the prophet Muhammad has commanded you.' Junayd said: 'May God forgive me. But how did you know that the prophet Muhammad has commanded me to preach?' Sari replied: 'God told me in a dream.'

Attar: Junayd

The worst of the people

When he began to preach, Junayd stipulated that he would
not speak to more than forty people at a time.

After Junayd had preached a number of times, certain religious leaders started to oppose him. So he gave up preaching, and returned to his cell. Many people urged him to
resume. But he refused, saying to them: 'I am content as I
am. It would be wrong to collude with my own destruction.

But some time later he felt impelled to preach again.
When he had finished, he was asked what prompted him to
resume preaching. He replied: 'The prophet Muhammad said
– according to a report which I have heard – the preacher to
the people should be the worst of them. I know that I am the
worst of the people; and so I am preaching in obedience to
Muhammad.'

Attar: Junayd

Carrying burdens

After a sermon a man came up to Junayd, and said: 'These days it is hard to find people who are truly faithful.' Junayd replied: 'If you are looking for people to carry your burdens, they are indeed hard to find. But if you are seeking to carry other people's loads, such people are easy to find.'

Whenever Junayd spoke about the divine unity, he used a different term; and people could not understand what he meant. One day a man cried out: 'Surely you are simply speaking about God.' Junayd replied: 'If God is absent, we should not speak about him. If God is present, we should beware of speaking about him with irreverence.'

A man offered five hundred silver coins as a gift to Junayd. Junayd asked: 'Do you possess any wealth besides these coins.' 'Yes,' the man replied. Junayd asked: 'Would you like to possess more?' 'Yes,' the man replied. Junayd said: 'Then it is better that you keep the coins. I possess nothing, and I want to possess nothing.'

Attar: Junayd

Junayd and the beggar

As Junayd was preaching on one occasion, a man interrupted him, begging for money. Junayd thought: 'This man is perfectly healthy. He should work for his living, rather than humiliate himself by begging.'

That night Junayd had a dream, in which a dish, covered with a cloth, was brought before him. A voice said: 'Eat.' He drew back the cloth, and saw the beggar lying dead on the dish. 'I do not eat human flesh,' Junayd protested. The voice said: 'What did you do yesterday?' Junayd realized that in his heart he had been guilty of slander.

He awoke in terror. He purified himself with prayer, and then went in search of the beggar. He found him on the banks of the river Tigris; he was picking out of the water the scraps of vegetables which people had washed there, and eating them. As Junayd approached, the beggar raised his head, and said: 'Junayd, have you repented your thoughts about me.' 'I have,' Junayd replied. The beggar said: 'Then go; and in future keep a closer watch over your mind.'

Attar: Junayd

Junayd and the barber

Junayd once went to a barber, and said: 'For the sake of God, can you cut my hair?' 'I can,' the barber replied. The barber's eyes filled with tears. He said to his other customers: 'I must cut Junayd's hair before I cut yours; when God's name is spoken, everything else must wait.' He gave Junayd a seat, kissed his head, and cut his hair. Then he gave Junayd a few coins, and said: 'Please spend these on your needs.'

Junayd received many gifts; and he decided that he would pass the next gift to the barber. Soon afterwards he was sent a bag of gold from Basra; and he took it to the barber. 'What is this?' the barber asked. Junayd replied: 'I decided to pass my next gift to you; and this is it.'

The barber exclaimed: 'Have you no shame? You asked me to cut your hair for the sake of God; and now you offer me money! No one can do something for the sake of God, and then take payment for it.'

Junayd frequently recounted this story, and added: 'I learnt true faith from that barber.'

Attar: Junayd

A life for a crime

A thief was hanged in Baghdad. Junayd went and kissed his feet. People asked him why he had done that. He replied: 'He was a master of his profession. He was so dedicated to his work that he gave his life for it.'

One night a thief entered Junayd's cell. He found nothing but a shirt; so he took it, and fled. The next day Junayd was walking through the market, and saw his shirt being sold at a stall. The purchaser said to the stallholder: 'I require someone to testify that this shirt belongs to you, before I buy it.' Junayd overheard this, and said: 'I can testify that it belongs to him.' So the shirt was sold.

An old woman came to Junayd, and said: 'My son is missing. Please say a prayer for his return.' Junayd replied: 'Be patient.' The woman waited patiently for a week; then she returned to Junayd. 'Be patient,' he repeated. This happened several times. Finally the old woman came, and declared: 'My patience is exhausted. Pray to God.' Junayd said: 'If your patience is truly exhausted, then your son has already returned.' Junayd offered up a prayer. The woman went back to her house, and found her son had come back.

Attar: Junayd

Jealous disciples

Junayd had twenty disciples. He loved one disciple above all the others. This made the other nineteen disciples jealous – which Junayd could sense. Junayd said to them: 'This disciple is superior to you both in behaviour and in insight. I shall prove this to you.'

He asked for twenty birds to be brought to him. Then he said to his disciples: 'Each one of you must take a bird. Carry it to a place where no one can see you; and then kill it.' Each of the nineteen jealous disciples took a bird, carried it to a remote spot, killed it, and brought back the body. But the disciple whom Junayd loved, brought the bird back alive.

'Why did you not kill the bird?' Junayd asked. The disciple replied: 'You said that it should be killed where no one can see me. Yet wherever I went, God was watching.'

Junayd turned to the other disciples, and exclaimed: 'Now you can perceive the depth of his insight.' All of them begged God to forgive them their jealousy.

Attar: Junayd

Junayd's death

When he was about to die, Junayd ordered his disciples to
come for a meal. He said: 'I wish to give up my soul while
my companions are enjoying a bowl of soup.'

Then he rose from his bed, and prostrated himself before
God. His disciples said: 'You have served and obeyed God
throughout your life. Surely you do not need to prostrate
yourself before him.' He replied: 'I have never been in greater
need of prostrating myself.'

He began to recite the Quran. His disciples asked: 'Why
do you recite the Quran?' Junayd replied: 'I must recite the
Quran because the scroll of my life is now being rolled up.
Soon I shall see my obedient service to God suspended by a
single thread. Then a wind will come, and swing it to and
fro; so I shall not know whether it is the wind of separation
or union. On one side will stretch the road that leads to paradise; and on the other side the road that leads to hell. God,
who is perfectly just, will judge me with unwavering justice.'

He read the entire Quran. Then he cried out: 'In the name
of God, the compassionate, the merciful.' And with those
words he died.

Attar: Junayd

Knowing God

In order to worship God, you must know God. In order to know God, you must recognize his unity. In order to recognize his unity, you must deny any possibility of describing how God is present, where he is present, and when he is present.

It is through God that you can be guided towards him. And to obtain this guidance you may seek his permission to find him. When he grants this permission, you recognize his unity. Recognizing his unity is the essence of faith in God. Faith in God leads to knowledge of God. Knowledge of God implies obedience to his commands. Obedience to God's commands is the means whereby you ascend towards him. And by ascending towards God you will eventually reach him.

When God has made himself manifest to you, then you can speak about him. Yet in finding God you become bewildered; and this bewilderment is so great, that it removes any possibility of speaking coherently. Thus the true worshipper of God, who has encountered him directly, is unable to describe him.

Junayd: Tawhid 1

Absence and presence

As you find God, you lose your individual identity. With the
loss of individual identity your soul is made pure. In this state
of purity you lose your personal attributes. As you lose your
personal attributes, you become wholly present to God. By
being wholly present to God, you are wholly lost to the self.

Thus you are present to God, and absent to self; you are
absent and present at the same time. You are where you are
not; and you are not where you are. After you have not been,
you are where you have been. By being absent to self, you
are truly yourself. You exist in God, and do not exist in the
self; thus you exist truly in yourself.

When God first overwhelms you by manifesting himself,
you are bewildered – as if you were drunk. But as you lose
the self, you have the clarity of sobri-
ety. You see all things as they are,
and you know their place and
qualities.

Junayd: Tawhid ı

Religious and spiritual knowledge

You may possess great religious knowledge, and be regarded as an authority on religious matters; you may perform your religious duties punctiliously and with unstinting devotion. Yet your religious knowledge and duties do not coincide with your instinctive spiritual desires. If you become aware of this gap, you will wish to close it; and the only means of closing it is by seeking to know God directly.

When you seek to know God directly, you become modest and humble; and you prefer poverty to wealth. When you come to know God directly, you realize that this direct knowledge of God satisfies your instinctive spiritual desires. This causes you to become indifferent to your religious knowledge and duties.

We may thus distinguish two types of knowledge. There is religious knowledge, which consists of rational theories about God. And there is spiritual or intuitive knowledge, which arises from personal encounters with God. As you acquire spiritual knowledge, you discard religious knowledge.

Junayd: Tawhid 2

Annihilation and satisfaction

When you realize that God wishes you to discard your religious knowledge, you taste a bitter cup. Yet, while God despises your religious knowledge, he cherishes other qualities within you – which have lain hidden beneath this knowledge. And as you become aware of this, you move towards the genuine and absolute unity of God.

As religious knowledge diminishes, you feel annihilated. But as spiritual knowledge becomes dominant, you feel joyful, because your deepest spiritual desires are being satisfied.

At this stage all desire for physical pleasure vanishes. You no longer have to watch and control your physical desires, because these desires have disappeared. Moreover, you are able to discern God within the pattern of events, and within the changes in things. You no longer want explanations for events and changes, because you understand their inner cause. The faculty of reason is now surpassed by the faculty of intuition.

Junayd: Tawhid 2

Fear, hope, truth and ritual

Fear distresses me; hope comforts me. Truth unites me with God; ritual separates me.

When God distresses me with fear, he annihilates my existence, so I no longer need to take care of myself. When God comforts me with hope, he returns my existence to me, and he commands me to take care of myself. When God unites me to himself with a vision of his truth, he brings me into his presence. When God separates me from himself by means of ritual, he makes himself absent from me – and absent from myself.

It is God who causes me to move from one of these states to another; he does not allow me to remain still, and he makes my soul ill at ease with each of these states in turn. When I am in the presence of God, I want to be absent from him. When I am absent from him, I want to see him. When he annihilates my existence, I want my existence returned. When my existence is complete, I want to be obliterated.

If only God would annihilate me completely and permanently as a distinct individual, that I may live eternally in his presence.

Junayd: Tawhid 3

Visible qualities

People are respected for their righteousness, for their unstinting efforts to abide by the laws of God, and for the discipline of their devotions; they are respected for submitting to God's will, forgoing all personal freedom. All these spiritual qualities are externally visible, and are recognized by everyone; and they point upwards to the truest and highest stage of worship.

The truest and highest stage of worship is to see God face to face, and to receive his guidance from his own mouth. Those who attain this highest stage, choose for themselves whatever God chooses for them. Their entire characters are transformed by God. They are God's friends; so they no longer discriminate between people, but regard all people as friends. Wherever they go, they go from God; wherever they arrive, they arrive at God. Whatever they do, they do for God; whatever service they perform, they perform it in God. The self has been truly annihilated.

God returns these true worshippers to the communities from which they have come, as a means of teaching those communities about his grace – as a means of enlightening them. True worshippers attract others to the worship of God.

Junayd: Tawhid 4

Annihilation of self

You should understand that the self is like a veil, concealing from you your deepest spiritual desire. You should also understand that you cannot reach God through yourself; you can only reach God through himself.

When God grants you a vision of reaching him, he is inviting you to seek him; and you accept his invitation – because reaching God is your deepest spiritual desire. When God grants you a vision of seeking him, you will realize the toil and effort required for this. This realization is the reassertion of the self, which conceals your deepest spiritual desire. At this point you must understand the depth of your need for God – and begin to seek him with great intensity.

He now becomes your pillar and support. He enables you to perform those spiritual exercises which he has prescribed for all seekers. He enables you to maintain the way of life which all seekers must maintain. And he enables you to be vigilant in the manner in which all seekers must be vigilant.

In this way you pierce the veil of self – you annihilate the self – and so fulfill your deepest spiritual desire, which is to live eternally with God. Unity with God depends on the annihilation of self.

Junayd: *Tawhid* 5

Three stages of annihilation

There are three stages in the annihilation of self.

The first stage is the annihilation of all personal attributes and characteristics. You should make great efforts to act in ways that are contrary to your natural inclinations. You should compel yourself to do things which you do not wish to do.

The second stage is the annihilation of all personal desires. You should forbid yourself the enjoyment of any worldly pleasures. Your only desire should be to obey God's will. In this way you will truly belong to him; and you will learn to discern his will without the need for any teacher or intermediary.

The third stage is the annihilation of the consciousness of any vision of God, or of the ecstasy that accompanies visions of God. In this the last vestige of self is destroyed, and you exist only in God; you become united with his eternal existence.

When the self has been annihilated, your physical being continues, but your individuality has departed.

Junayd: Tawhid 5

Seeking, reaching and entering

You should understand that there are three types of people: those who seek and search; those who reach the door, and remain there; and those who enter and stay.

Consider those who seek and search for God. They move towards him, guided by the religious precepts they have learnt. They perform their religious duties with great care and concentration. They submit to God in all external matters.

Consider those who reach the door, and remain there. They find their way to the door through purifying themselves inwardly; and from this purity they derive great spiritual strength. They submit to God in all internal matters.

Consider those who enter God's presence, and stay in his presence. They know nothing, apart from God; and they feel nothing, apart from God. Their attention is wholly directed towards God; and they stand ready to do whatever their Lord may command. This readiness is typical of those who recognize the unity of God.

Junayd: Tawhid 6

The way for ordinary people and scholars

You should understand that different groups of people attain unity with God in different ways. There is the way for ordinary people; there is the way for scholars who have studied religion; there is the lower way for mystics; and there is the higher way for mystics.

Consider the way for ordinary people. They should believe in the unity of God. They should expel from their minds all ideas of other gods, or other beings which are similar to God; they should know that God has no equals. Yet equally they should realize there are spiritual forces which are opposed to God. They should trust God, and fear all that are opposed to him.

Consider the way for those who have studied religion. They too should believe in the unity of God, trusting him, and fearing all that are opposed to him. In addition they should seek to discern the commands of God in particular situations; and as they do this, they should proclaim what should be done, and what should not be done. In this way they show that human society can function in unity with God.

Junayd: Tawhid 7

The lower and higher ways for mystics

Consider the lower way for mystics. They too should believe in the unity of God, trusting him, and fearing all that are opposed to him. In addition they should examine all their own attitudes and conceptions, ensuring that they conform with the precepts of God. They should constantly hold the presence of God in their minds. They should do nothing, except in response to God's call; and they should say nothing, except in response to God's prompting.

Consider the higher way for mystics. They should allow no intermediary to stand between themselves and God. They should invite God to annihilate their individuality. They should submit in all things to his omnipotence. They should plunge into the ocean of his unity. As they do this, they cease to hear God's call or feel his prompting, because they are no longer separate from him. At this point they know the unity of God because they are part of that unity. God's perception becomes their perception, and God's actions become their actions; they see as God sees, and they act as he acts. In this final state they have returned to their first state – the state before they existed.

Junayd: Tawhid 9

The final goal

What is the final goal of the worship of God? The final goal is the conquest of self. God has shown us how to conquer the self; he has laid out the duties and tasks that we must perform. And if we begin to perform these duties and tasks, he will perform them for us; we do not need to depend on ourselves.

God wants all people to enter his presence and hear his voice; he wants all people to be prophets. He prefers prophets to saints, who seek to be righteous by their own efforts. He wants all people to lay aside personal ambition, to suppress the desire for personal achievement, and to allow him to achieve his purpose for them. His purpose is to raise them up to his own state.

Most people act on their own account; they pursue personal ambitions without seeking God's guidance and grace. By asserting the self they will achieve nothing.

Junayd: Tawhid 10

Hallaj's travels

Hallaj came from Tostar; his father, called Mansur, was a
woolcarder. At the age of eighteen he walked to Baghdad,
where he called on Junayd for advice. Junayd prescribed for
him silence and solitude. After a while he went to Mecca,
where he lived for a year; then he returned to Baghdad. He
went again to Junayd, accompanied by a group of Sufis, and
put a number of questions to him; Junayd gave no reply. He
felt frustrated, and returned to Tostar.

He remained at Tostar for a year, and was widely acclaimed for the brilliance of his teaching. The theologians
grew envious of him; and since he ignored orthodoxy, regarding it as worthless, they turned against him. He decided
to cast aside the Sufi garb, adopting normal clothes; and he
lived as normal people do. But this did not satisfy him; so he
left Tostar, and wandered from place to place. After five years
he settled in Ahwaz, where again he was acclaimed for the
brilliance of his teaching. He referred frequently to the 'secrets of people's hearts'; so he became known as 'Hallaj of
the secrets'. He adopted again the ragged clothes of the Sufis.

After a time he said to the people of Ahwaz: 'I am now
going to faraway places to preach about God.' So he went to
India and China, calling men and women to follow God, and
composing spiritual poems for them. Eventually he returned
to Mecca, and then to Baghdad.

Attar: Hallaj

Hallaj's claim

Hallaj changed in the course of his travels, and he now said: 'I am the truth.' The people of Baghdad were divided in their attitude to him; he had innumerable detractors, and he also had countless supporters. His supporters pointed to the many miracles he had performed. But his detractors were outraged at his claim to be the truth; and they reported him to the monarch, saying that he should be put to death.

The monarch ordered Hallaj to be thrown into prison, where he was held for a year. Many people came to see him in prison, to seek his advice. But the authorities stopped all visits, and for five months no one was allowed to come near him. A religious leader, who respected Hallaj, sent him a message: 'Ask to be pardoned for the claim you have made, so you may be set free.' Hallaj replied: 'Let the person who sent this message, ask for pardon.' When the religious leader heard this reply, he wept, and said: 'None of us has even a fraction of Hallaj's stature.'

It is said that on his first and second nights in prison, Hallaj disappeared; and only on the third night did the gaoler find him again. The gaoler asked Hallaj: 'Where have you been for the last two nights?' Hallaj replied: 'On the first night I went to speak to God; so I was not here. On the second night God came here, and spoke to me; so, although we were both here, neither of us was visible. Tonight God insists that I am both present and visible, in order that the law may be upheld.'

Attar: Hallaj

The release of prisoners

In the prison where Hallaj was kept, there were three hundred other prisoners. On his third night in the prison Hallaj called the other prisoners together, and asked them: 'Would you like me to set you free?' The prisoners said: 'Why do you not free yourself?' Hallaj said: 'I am God's prisoner; and I am the sentinel of salvation. I have the power, with a single wave of my hand, to break all chains.' He waved his hand, and the chains binding every prisoner broke.

The prisoners asked: 'What should we do now? The gate of the prison is locked.' Hallaj waved his hand again, and a crack appeared in the wall of the prison. 'Now go your way,' Hallaj said. 'Are you coming too?' the prisoners asked. 'No,' Hallaj replied; 'I possess a divine secret, which cannot be told except on the gallows.'

The next morning, when the gaoler discovered that all the prisoners had escaped, he questioned Hallaj about what had happened. 'I set them free,' Hallaj replied. 'Why did you not go with them?' the gaoler asked. Hallaj said: 'God has reason to chastise me, so I did not go.'

Attar: Hallaj

Ascending the gallows

When the monarch was told that Hallaj had set the prisoners free, he exclaimed: 'There will be a riot. Kill Hallaj. Or beat him with sticks until he repents of what he has done.' So the soldiers beat Hallaj three hundred times. At each blow a voice could be heard: 'Do not be afraid, son of Mansur.' Then they put thirteen heavy chains around him, and led him out to be crucified.

Despite the weight of the chains Hallaj walked upright along the road; and he waved his arms like a madman. 'Why do you strut so proudly?' the soldiers asked him. 'I am proud to be dying in this manner,' he replied.

When they reached the gallows, Hallaj kissed the base, and then began to climb the ladder. The soldiers asked sarcastically: 'How do you feel now?' Hallaj answered: 'Ascending the gallows is the first stage of a true believer's ascension to the heavens.'

He was wearing a loincloth, with a cloth over his shoulders. Turning towards Mecca, he lifted up his hands, and stood silently in prayer. Then he exclaimed: 'That which is mysterious to men and women, is known by God.' With these words he stretched himself out on the cross.

Attar: Hallaj

Stones and earth

A group of Hallaj's disciples came to the gallows, and said to him: 'Do you have any words for us who are your disciples, and for those who condemn and kill you?' Hallaj replied: 'They have a double reward, while you only have a single reward. You merely think well of me. They are motivated by their belief in one God to uphold the rigour of the law.'

A religious leader called Shebli asked Hallaj: 'What is Sufism?' Hallaj replied: 'The lowest part of Sufism is what you are now seeing.' 'What is the highest part?' Shebli asked. Hallaj answered: 'The highest part is what you cannot see.'

All the spectators now began to throw stones at Hallaj. For fear of not conforming Shebli threw a clod of earth. Hallaj sobbed. The soldiers said: 'You remain utterly calm when hard stones hit you. So why do you sob when a soft clod of earth lands on you?' Hallaj replied: 'The people throwing the stones do not know what they are doing; so I can excuse them. But the man who threw the clod of earth, knew that he was doing wrong; and that upsets me.'

Attar: Hallaj

The cosmetic of heroes

The soldiers cut off Hallaj's hands. Hallaj laughed. 'Why do you laugh?' they asked. Hallaj replied: 'It is easy to cut off the hands of someone who is bound in chains. It is much harder to cut off the hands of truth which fashion the crown of hope.'

They hacked off his feet. He smiled, and said: 'With these feet I travelled across the earth. But I have other feet, with which I shall travel to the next world. Hack off those feet, if you can!'

Then with the ends of his arms, where his hands had been amputated, he rubbed his face, covering it with blood. 'Why do you do that?' the soldiers asked. He replied: 'I have lost so much blood, that my face must be turning pale. I do not want people to interpret my pallor as a sign of fear. So by rubbing blood on my face its colour is restored. Blood is the cosmetic of heroes.'

Hallaj also rubbed each arm with the end of the other arm, so both arms were covered with blood. 'Why do you stain your arms?' the soldiers asked. 'I am cleansing myself,' Hallaj replied. 'Why?' they asked. He answered: 'In order to worship God. Blood is the perfect agent of cleansing for those who worship God with love.'

Attar: Hallaj

The death of Hallaj

The soldiers plucked out Hallaj's eyes. The crowd roared; some flung more stones, while others wept.

Then the soldiers took a knife to Hallaj's tongue. He begged them to be patient, allowing him to offer a prayer. He looked up to the heavens, and cried out: 'These people who are causing me to suffer, believe that they are serving you. So do not condemn them; do not exclude them from the bliss of paradise. I praise you, O God, for letting them cut off my feet; now I can truly walk in your way. And if they cut my head from my body, and lift up my head on a pole, then I shall be better able to contemplate your glory.'

The soldiers cut off his ears and nose. An old woman carrying a pitcher passed by. Looking at Hallaj she exclaimed: 'Make him suffer; make him truly suffer. What right has this man to speak about God? He is only a woolcarder by birth.'

Hallaj said: 'To love God is to be alone with God.' Those were his last words. When he had uttered them, the soldiers cut off his tongue. At the time of evening prayer they cut off his head; as they were doing so, he smiled. Then he gave up his soul.

At that moment all his disciples shouted: 'I am the truth.'

Attar: Hallaj

Proximity and distance

O God, it would be impossible for me to distance myself from you; it would be impossible for you to distance yourself from me. In the certainty of our relationship, proximity and distance are the same.

If you were to abandon me, then abandonment would be my companion. The abandonment would be yours; so by being close to the abandonment, I should be close to you. How can abandonment be real, when love is real?

I praise you for your success in being you; you praise me for my success in being me. In your purity you make me pure. In your wholeness you make me whole. In my service you serve me. I bow to all, because I bow to you.

Hallaj: Tawasin 12

Remembrance

Remembrance is not remembered. I do not remember whether or not God remembered me in the past; he remembers me now. God does not remember whether I remembered him in the past; I remember him now. His remembrance is my remembrance, and mine is his. Can two beings who remember one another not be in union?

My service of God is now purer than in the past; I live more fully for God in each moment; and my remembrance of God is greater. In the past I served him out of concern for my own well-being; now I serve him out of concern for his.

Hallaj: Tawasin 15

Set apart

When God caused me to be expelled from my city, he set me apart. He knew that my zeal for him was so great, that I should overwhelm people. He knew that in the confusion of my love for him, I should confuse people. He did not want me to have friends. My praise for him deformed me in the eyes of others. Since I knew him as he is, and was in union with him, he appeared to abandon me.

But I have not erred; I have not deviated from his designs for me; nor have I rejected my destiny; nor have I set myself up as a judge of others. Even if he were to torment me with the fires of hell for ever and beyond, I should not bow down to any other being but him; I should not pay homage to any man, woman or idol; I should not acknowledge any rival to him.

My proclamation of faith is the same as the proclamation of all who are sincere. In the love of God I am triumphant. How could it be otherwise?

Hallaj: Tawasin 16–17

Invisible yet visible

God is rooted in the earth; yet he also appears from above. He is invisible, yet he appears as a blazing fire and a blinding light.

God is in the water of the lake; he is also in the cracked bed of the lake, when the lake has dried up. God is in the abundant harvest; he is also in the famine that occurs when the harvest fails. God is in the lightning; he is also in the darkness, when the lightning has faded.

God can be seen in the rain, when it falls from the sky like swords. God can be seen by blind people as they wander this way and that.

Brothers and sisters, you pile up stones to make shrines, imagining that God will make himself present there. Then you are surprised when these shrines do not ease your cares and worries.

Hallaj: Tawasin 31–33

Satan's qualities

The most eloquent speakers are struck dumb by the eloquence of Satan. The wisest sages cannot fathom the wisdom of Satan. The loftiest mystics cannot match Satan in the art of prayer. Satan is nearer than any of them to God. He devotes himself without stint to performing the role that he is destined to perform. He is always generous in his actions, doing more than he is required to do. He is utterly faithful to the oaths he swears. He is more loyal to God than any man or woman on earth.

Men and women prostrate themselves in prayer; but Satan, since he has borne witness to God for so long, refuses. The human customs, which he established in ancient times, still carry weight. The excesses of pleasure, which he has always advocated, are a refuge from the rigours of religion. The weeds which he sows, bear good fruit. He can be as sweet and gentle as a flower; he is a model of courtesy.

Hallaj: Tawasin 34–35

God's soul and the human soul

What is wrong, O God, with this earth, that people want to rise up to the heavens? Why can people not find you on earth, so they must seek you in the heavens? Look at them staring upwards. You are right before their eyes; yet their eyes cannot see. You are in front of them; yet they are blind.

Once my soul was patient; I was willing to wait for you. But can the soul be patient with itself? Now I know that my soul and your soul are blended together. Whether I am near you, or whether I am far away, my soul and your soul are mingled.

I am you, O God. You are my being; you are the fulfilment of all my desires. I embrace you in my innermost thoughts. Your soul and my soul are like two lamps, shedding a single light.

Hallaj: Diwan

If only

People ask how you can be known. Any method of knowing you can yield only intellectual knowledge – knowledge of your exterior attributes. It cannot penetrate the heart of your being, the heart of all being.

Men and women spend their entire lives seeking you in the darkness of intellectual endeavour. They die in darkness. Their quest is blind. They speculate about you; but their speculations are no more than guesses. They concoct theories about you; but their theories are no more than dreams.

Men and women look up to the sky when they pray; they whisper their deepest secrets to the heavens. Yet you are among them. At every moment you are present. In every event you are present. In all situations you are present. In every place you are present. You are never absent, not even for the blink of an eye.

If only people knew that you are always present with them. If only they knew that you are never absent from them – not even for a moment. If only.

Hallaj: Diwan

The moment

The moment is what you are in. If you are in this world, your moment is this world. If you are in the next world, your moment is the next world. If you are in a state of happiness, your moment is happiness. If you are in a state of sorrow, your moment is sorrow. The moment is that which dominates a person.

Sufis are sometimes called children of the moment. This means they are completely occupied with the spiritual demands of their present state. They do whatever they are required to do at a particular time. In embracing poverty they have no concern for the past or the future; they are only concerned with the present moment in which they find themselves. Sufis say that to be preoccupied with the past is to lose the present.

Sufis also say that the moment is a sword. Like a sword the moment cuts away everything around itself, so that it can be free. The sword is gentle to the touch, and its edge is sharp: those who handle it gently are unharmed; but those who treat it roughly are injured. The moment is similar: those who submit to its decree are saved; but those who oppose it are overcome and destroyed.

Qushayri: Risalah 3

The station

We define a station as a particular place along the path of refinement. A station is reached by servants of God through their behaviour, their motivation, and their self-discipline. You cannot move from one station to the next, until you have fulfilled the requirements of the first. Those who have not reached the station of serenity, cannot move to the station of trust in God. Those who have not reached the station of trust in God, cannot move to the station of surrender to God. Those who have not reached the station of repentance, can-

not move to the station of contrition. Those who have not reached the station of vigilance, cannot move to the station of renunciation.

Qushayri: Risalah 3

The state

We define a state as a mood which comes upon a person involuntarily, without any intention or effort. The mood may be joy or sorrow, frustration or yearning, anxiety or fear, desire or contentment. Whereas stations are reached, states are bestowed. Whereas stations require great effort, states come freely. Those who have reached a certain station, can be secure in what they have attained; those who are experiencing a certain state, may quickly lose that state.

Some people say that states are like flashes of lightning; they throw light on the heart, and then they disappear. Other people say that states are permanent, and that fleeting experiences are not true states. The latter group are correct, in that genuine states must have continuity. But the former are correct, in that every person has the potential for higher and more subtle states. The higher and subtler states are initially ephemeral; but each time they occur, they last longer, until they become continual.

It is impossible for a human being to experience the highest and most subtle state. There is always a higher and more subtle state than the one being experienced at present.

Qushayri: Risalah 3

Guilt and contentment

Servants of God rise above the states of fear and hope, to the states of guilt and contentment. Guilt is to the spiritual master, as fear is to the spiritual beginner; and contentment is to the spiritual master, as hope is to the spiritual beginner. What precisely is the distinction between guilt and fear, and between contentment and hope? Fear concerns something in the future, as does hope. But guilt and contentment concern the present moment.

People may experience guilt when they realize that they have caused injury to the people and objects around them, and that blame is deserved; guilt seizes their hearts. People may experience contentment when they are in harmony with the people and objects around them. In general, the greater the guilt which people feel, the greater is the contentment they feel, when the cause of guilt has been removed.

People may experience guilt for no apparent reason; their hearts are seized by guilt, yet they do not know the cause. The proper response is to submit to the guilt until it passes. If they try to expel it or suppress it, then it will increase. Equally contentment can occur suddenly, without any apparent cause. This can be very disconcerting and even upsetting. The proper response is to stay still, and be very vigilant – because it can easily become a spiritual trap.

Qushayri: Risalah 3

Awe and intimacy

Above guilt and contentment lie two further states, awe and intimacy. Just as guilt is higher than fear, so awe is higher than guilt; and just as contentment is higher than hope, so intimacy is higher than contentment.

The effect of awe is the disappearance of self; the self which is in a state of awe, disappears. Levels of awe may be measured by the degree to which the self has disappeared; some people are at a higher level of awe than others.

The effect of intimacy, by contrast, is alertness; those who are intimate, are alert. A person who is fully intimate, could be thrown into a fire, and the intimacy would not be disturbed.

Yet spiritual masters consider the states of awe and intimacy, glorious as they are, to be deficient. This is because they are not constant, but vary from one time to another. The states of those who are firmly rooted in God, will never vary. Thus they have neither awe nor intimacy – which means they have neither knowledge nor sensation.

Qushayri: Risalah 3

Ecstasy

It is possible to induce ecstasy through a form of self-will. Induced ecstasy is not as complete as true ecstasy; those who possess true ecstasy, do not have to induce it. A poet once described his method of inducing ecstasy: 'I cause my eyes to squint, even though normally they are straight. Eventually I can no longer see, even though both my eyes are still functioning.'

Some people advise against inducing ecstasy through deliberate effort, because it delays genuine self-realization. Others condone it for those Sufis who have detached themselves from all material things, and have made a close study of the ecstatic state. The latter group are correct: inducing ecstasy can be the beginning of true ecstasy.

True ecstasy is passive: it overwhelms the heart without any intention or deliberate effort. It is the fruit of spiritual devotion and worship. The deeper is your devotion to God, and the more intense is your worship, the more likely you are to receive ecstasy from God.

In a state of ecstasy the heart is lost to God.

Qushayri: Risalah 3

Union and separateness

When you worship, you are aware of your separateness from God; you are the subject and he is the object. The more you worship, the more you acquire this sense of separateness from God. Union with God comes when this sense of your separateness from God is stripped away.

When God allows you to observe your own acts of obedience and disobedience, you are separate from him. When God allows you to perceive your acts as his acts, then you are in union with him. Awareness of the world as God's creation is a sign of separateness; awareness of the creator is a sign of union.

Servants of God must have both union and separateness. Those who have no sense of separateness from God, are not truly worshipping him. Those who have no sense of union with God, do not truly know him. At the beginning of the Quran we read the words: 'We worship only you.' This is a reference to separateness. In the same verse we read the words: 'In you alone we seek refuge.' This is a reference to union.

When people address God in words – in the form of intimate conversation, petition and pleading, gratitude, remorse and repentance, and so on – they are in a position of separateness from God. When they address God directly through the heart, and when they listen to him in the heart, they are in a position of union with God.

Qushayri: Risalah 3

Union of union

Beyond union and separateness is union of union. When people are aware of themselves, and they are aware of creation, and are aware that they themselves and all creatures exist in God, they experience union with God. When people are snatched away from all awareness of creation, and are uprooted even from themselves, they experience union of union. In union of union people no longer perceive anything apart from God.

Separateness is perceiving the self and other creatures as separate from God. Union is perceiving the self and other creatures as existing through God. Union of union is the falling away of any perception of self and others as distinct from God.

Beyond union of union there is a sublime condition called the second separateness. This is where servants of God are brought back to waking consciousness in order to perform religious duties at the proper times. God alone can decide when this second separateness occurs; the servants of God are not responsible for it.

Qushayri: Risalah 3

Shedding and upholding

We should shed bad attributes; and we should uphold good attributes. When people shed bad attributes, then their good attributes come to the fore. But when they allow their bad attributes to prevail, their good attributes are pushed back.

There are three aspects to our attributes: acts, character traits, and states. Acts are the exercise of free will. Character traits are the innate temperament – although we can improve our character traits through cultivating good habits. States are the mental conditions and moods that arise involuntarily – although we can improve our states through behaving well.

Thus we can shed bad character traits, and enable good character traits to prevail, if we exercise our free will according to God's will. And we can shed bad states, and enable good states to prevail, by the same means.

Qushayri: Risalah 3

Shedding bad attributes

When we abandon acts that are contrary to God's law, we shed our carnal desires. When we shed our carnal desires, we become sincere in our intentions towards others, and in our worship of God.

When in our hearts we renounce material ambitions, we shed every urge to manipulate the world to our advantage. When we shed every urge to manipulate the world, we become sincere in regretting past wickedness.

As we cultivate good habits, we expel from our hearts all envy, hatred, stinginess, greed, anger, pride, and every kind of vanity. When we shed these bad character traits, we become courteous and gentle.

When we allow God's power to pervade all our actions, and submit to his decrees, we shed all anxiety about the effects of our actions on others; we cease even to consider the effects of our actions. When we cease to consider the effects of our actions, we are adopting the attributes of God himself.

Qushayri: Risalah 3

Losing the sense of self

As we shed bad attributes, we also shed the sense of self –
the self within, and the self of all other creatures. We no
longer think of the self; it is as if the self has never existed.
People might object that, if the self really exists, it is wrong
not to be aware of the self. Yet the fact is that as we shed bad
attributes, we also shed all knowledge of self; so even if the
self exists, we do not perceive the self in any way.

Imagine yourself entering the presence of a mighty emperor. You are overwhelmed with awe at his power, and with
a sense of your own insignificance. Your entire attention is
absorbed by the emperor's greatness, so you are utterly unaware of his physical appearance and of the other people
around him. When you leave his presence, people ask you
about the other people, about his physical appearance, and
about your own experience of being in his presence. But you
are unable to answer.

This is a parable for losing the sense of self.

Qushayri: Risalah 3

Absence and presence

In serving God we become absent from the world: we cease
to perceive both ourselves and others; we cease to be aware
of ourselves in relation to outward events; and we cease to
consider rewards and punishments.

A Sufi was once engaged in prayer, when his cell caught
fire. He did not stop praying for one moment. Afterwards
people asked him about this. He replied: 'The divine fire held
my attention, so I could not attend to the fire in my cell.'

A blacksmith was once at work at his forge, when someone arrived and quoted a verse from the Quran. At that moment the blacksmith became absent from his own senses. He
put his hand – his bare hand – into the fire, and took out the
glowing iron. One of his apprentices exclaimed: 'Master,
what are you doing?' When the blacksmith realized what he
had done, he gave up his craft.

As we become absent from the world, so we become present to God. We are seized by awareness of the divine reality.
Our presence to God is in proportion to our absence from the
world.

                                                Qushayri: *Risalah* 3

Total scepticism

From an early age I instinctively thirsted after truth; this was part of my temperament, given by God, and was not a matter of choice or effort. So as I reached adulthood, I refused to accept ideas on the authority of others; and the beliefs which I had been taught as a child, lost their grip on me. I observed that the offspring of Christians grew up to be Christian, the offspring of Jews grew up to be Jews, and the offspring of Muslims grew up to be Muslims. I was driven to search for the inner truths which lie behind all religions.

It was self-evident to me that knowledge can only be certain, if the object of knowledge is disclosed in such a way as to dispel all doubt. Thus I considered the various kinds of knowledge which I already possessed, and realized that none of it was certain, except the perceptions of the senses. I then wondered whether even the perceptions of the senses are open to doubt; and after profound thought I concluded that they are. For example, the shadow cast by the gnomon of a sundial may appear to the sense of sight to be stationary; yet by observing it hour by hour one discovers that it is moving.

I was now sceptical of all knowledge; and this total scepticism was a spiritual disease.

Ghazali: al-Munqidh min ad-Dalal 1, 2

Theology and philosophy

Eventually God cured me of the disease of total scepticism. This did not happen through systematic proofs, nor through logical arguments; it happened by a light which the most high God shone into my breast. This light gave me the confidence to seek knowledge, while at the same time releasing me from the need for proofs and arguments – those who demand proofs and arguments, are too narrow in their view as to how God can communicate.

I started with theology, and gained a thorough understanding of it. I read the books of reputable theologians, and wrote some books myself on the subject. I was impressed that theology is successful is achieving its aim; but it did not achieve mine. Its aim is to uphold the beliefs of orthodoxy, and to defend orthodoxy against heretics who think differently. Its method is to expose the contradictions in the teachings of heretics, and to show that these teachings have harmful consequences. Yet it does not delve deeply into the inner nature of things; and it did not dispel my own confusion.

When I had rejected theology, I studied philosophy. I was convinced that I could only understand the flaws in a subject, by first gaining a complete grasp of it. So I read many books about philosophy; and within two years I was familiar with all its various branches. I spent a further year reflecting on what I had learnt, probing its tangled depths, until I realized that it is both deceitful and muddled.

Ghazali: al-Munqidh min ad-Dalal 3

Knowing and being

When I had finished with both theology and philosophy, I turned with determination to the study of mysticism – or, as it is called, Sufism. I knew that mysticism involves both intellectual endeavour and spiritual activity. I also knew that this spiritual activity consists in purifying the self of all that is corrupt and base; in this way the soul breaks free from all that is not divine, and contemplates God without interruption.

The intellectual endeavour was easier for me than the spiritual activity. I read many books by Sufis, and I arrived at a clear knowledge of mysticism. But it became clear to me that mysticism cannot be understood by study alone; it needs to be tasted. Mysticism is distinct from any other form of truth, in that it consists of a moral and spiritual transformation, leading to a state of ecstasy.

There is a great difference between knowing about health and contentment, and being healthy and contented. There is a great difference between knowing the physiology of drunkenness, and being drunk. Similarly there is a great difference between knowing the nature and causes of mystical experience, and being a mystic.

Ghazali: al-Munqidh min ad-Dalal 3

The mystical path

I now understood that mystics are not people of words, but people of real experiences; and that I myself had progressed as far as I could through intellectual study. My needs could not be satisfied by further instruction and reading; they could only be satisfied by direct and immediate experience. So I decided to follow the mystical path.

Through my efforts in following the paths of theology and philosophy, I had attained firm faith in God, in his revelations, and in the day of judgement. These three beliefs were deeply rooted within me, not by means of clever proofs, but through an understanding of the nature of existence itself. Yet I realized that my only hope of attaining eternal bliss was by detaching myself from all worldly desires, and by honouring God in every aspect of my life. I knew that I had to leave the mansion of deception, and set out with all vigour towards the house of God. I had to turn away from wealth and position, and flee from all the worldly obligations that consumed my time.

Ghazali: al-Munqidh min ad-Dalal 3

Mixed motives

So I reflected on the circumstances of my life, and saw that I was caught in a tangle of worldly attachments. The most important of these was my teaching; and in this I was dealing with branches of knowledge that contributed nothing towards the attainment of eternal life – and so are utterly unimportant.

Then I examined my motive for teaching; and I realized that it was not pure desire to serve God, but was mixed with the desire for social status and public influence. I saw myself as standing on the edge of a sandy cliff, that was crumbling beneath me; I was in imminent danger of plunging into the fires of hell, unless I started to mend my ways.

I was faced with a choice, and day after day I grappled with it. One day I would decide to abandon my career, and the circumstances surrounding it; and the next day I would reverse my decision. I put one foot forward, and drew the other foot back. If in the morning I had a genuine yearning for eternal life, by the evening a great mass of worldly desires had reduced me to impotence. Worldly desires were like chains holding me in my present position.

Ghazali: al-Munqidh min ad-Dalal 3

Opposing voices

Day after day the voice of faith called out to me: 'To the road!
To the road! The years of life are few, and the journey ahead
is long. Only hypocrisy and delusion hold you back. You
imagine that by being busy you are serving God! If you do
not prepare now for eternal life, when will you prepare? If
you do not sever your worldly attachments immediately,
when will you sever them?' As I heard these words, the urge
to follow the mystical path surged within me; and I decided
to abandon my career.

Then Satan said: 'This is just a passing mood, which will
soon fade; so resist it. If you yield to it, think what you will
be giving up: a position from which you can exercise a benign influence; the respect of society; material comforts
which leave your mind free from all disturbances; and safety
and security, which allow you to speak honestly, without fear
of your opponents. If you abandon all this, you will never be
able to return to it. Come to your senses!'

For six months these opposing voices spoke to me, toss-
ing me between the attractions of the world and the impulse
towards eternal life.

Ghazali: al-Munqidh min ad-Dalal 3

God's choice

Eventually the choice between following the mystical path and retaining my career was taken away from me. God caused my voice to become silent, so that I could no longer teach. One day, as I stood before my students with the intention of satisfying their hunger for knowledge, I found myself unable to utter a single word.

I was deeply upset. Moreover the same illness that silenced my voice, also made it difficult for me to eat and digest food; I could barely even swallow soup. Gradually my body weakened until the physicians gave up all hope of treating me successfully. Recognizing my condition, and having lost the power of choice, I sought refuge with the most high God; I was driven into his arms, because I was no longer able to care for myself. In this way he made it easy for me to turn away from position and wealth.

I made arrangements to leave my house, and to withdraw from the world. The religious leaders were very sceptical of my motives, doubting whether I was prompted by spiritual desires; in their minds a career as a theological teacher was the highest calling. And others were also confused at my conduct. In particular, government officials, who had often keenly sought my advice, were now offended that I showed no interest in their affairs.

I gave away my wealth, retaining only enough to sustain myself and my relatives; then I left the city.

Ghazali: al-Munqidh min ad-Dalal 3

The life of solitude

I lived in solitude, and devoted myself to ascetic exercises, in which I sought to purify my soul, improve my character, and cleanse my heart. In all things I followed the teachings of the mystics whose books I had read, hoping that I should have a direct encounter with God. In order to be alone, I sometimes went to the nearby mosque, and climbed to the top of the minaret, shutting myself in from dawn until dusk. I experienced ecstasy only occasionally; but I never ceased to yearn and strive for it.

I continued in this manner for ten years; and during this time many deep and important things were revealed to me. I shall say a little of what I learnt, so that others may be helped. I learnt that the mystics, above all people, walk on the path of God. And I learnt that their life is the best life, their spiritual method is the soundest spiritual method, and they attain the greatest purity of character. Indeed, if the intellect of the intellectuals, the learning of the learned, and the scholarship of the scholars, were combined, they still could not find a way of improving the life and the character of the mystics.

To the mystics all movement and all rest, whether physical or mental, enlighten the soul; all actions bring light from the lamp of divine revelation. And there is no other light anywhere on earth, from which the soul may be enlightened.

Ghazali: al-Munqidh min ad-Dalal 3

The mystical way

How, then, may the mystical way be described? The first part of the mystical way is the attainment of purity. Just as Muslim worshippers are required to cleanse their bodies in preparation for worship, so mystics are required to cleanse their souls in preparation for contemplating the most high God. This is done by learning to adore God, allowing the soul to be absorbed by the love of God. In order to adore God, you must make a deliberate choice in favour of God's love; by this means you take the first step along the mystical way.

After taking this first step, you begin to receive visions and revelations. Mystics, while they are wide awake, see angels and prophets, who speak to them, giving instruction. Initially these angels and prophets have physical forms; but gradually they appear in a manner which is impossible to describe in words; any attempt to describe them inevitably contains errors.

After receiving visions and revelations, you draw closer to God. Some speak of this closeness as becoming a child of God; some speak of it as being in union with God; some speak of it as being connected with God. All these words are inadequate. A true mystic once said: 'My mind does not recall being close to God. The experience is as it is. I simply know that being close to God is good. Do not ask me to give an account of it.'

Ghazali: al-Munqidh min ad-Dalal 3

Knowledge, certainty and faith

The mystical state is an immediate and direct encounter. It
cannot be attained by deliberate effort alone. You can walk
along the mystical path which leads towards it; and then it
may be granted to you. If it is not granted to you, you may
have a strong impression of it by contact with those to whom
it has been granted, observing and listening to them. Either
through personal experience or by hearsay you will realize
that the mystical state is accompanied by ecstasy. If you are
in the company of a mystic in a state of ecstasy, you will to
some degree share it; it certainly will not cause you pain.

Through being in the company of a mystic in a state of
ecstasy, you obtain knowledge of the mystical state. Through
personal experience of the mystical state, you obtain certainty.
Through listening to and observing mystics, you obtain faith
in the mystical state.

There are many people who are shocked by mysticism,
and they mock it, calling it nonsense. These people are blinded
by ignorance. By following the mystical way I came to understand the true nature of God's revelations to Muhammad.

Ghazali: al-Munqidh min ad-Dalal 3

Mutual dependence

What I say is from God; so listen! Remember that to God you will return. When you hear what I say, learn!

In the details you can see the whole; and in the whole you can see the details.

Give what you learn to those who seek; do not stint. Remember that whatever you learn, is by the mercy of God; so extend God's mercy to others.

Each living being is dependent on all living beings; no living being is independent. This is the plain truth, and we speak it plainly.

If I say there is one being who is self-sufficient and independent, you will know to whom I refer.

Each is bound up with all; there is no escaping this bond. Listen carefully to what I am saying.

Ibn Arabi: Fusus
al-hikam Preface, 1

Transcendent and immanent

If you think of God only as transcendent, your view of him is too narrow. If you think of God only as immanent, your view of him is too limited. If you think of God as both transcendent and immanent, you are right.

If you understand the reality of God's transcendence and immanence, you are a master of spiritual science. But if you think that there are two gods, one transcendent and one immanent, then you are ignorant.

Do not think of God as isolated from his creation. Do not think of God as bound by rules. Do not compare God with any other entity. Beware of thinking of God as remote.

You are not God; and you are God. You see him in the essences of all things; yet he is boundless.

Ibn Arabi: Fusus al-hikam 3

He and I

God praises me, and I praise God. God worships me, and I worship God. In my existence, I confirm his existence; but insofar as I do not exist, I deny his existence. He knows me, and I know nothing of him; yet I also know and perceive him.

Why do people speak about the self-sufficiency of God? I serve him in all manner of ways; and I give him pleasure. Indeed, he created me in order to serve and please him. I embody his genius, and I give expression to his intelligence. He has sent his message to earth, and it is fulfilled in me.

I belong to God, as has often been shown; yet I also belong to myself. He becomes himself through me. I live in him, and I live in myself. I have two aspects, he and I, divine and human. But he is not I, and I am not he. My actions are the theatre in which he expresses himself; to him I am a vessel.

Ibn Arabi: Fusus al-hikam 5

The presence of God

In every living being and in every object the unique God is present – sometimes hidden and sometimes manifest. In every moment and in every event the merciful God is present – sometimes hidden and sometimes manifest.

You may point to some being or event, and exclaim: 'This is God!' Such an exclamation would be true. You may point to some being or event, and exclaim: 'This is such-and-such!' Such an exclamation would be an interpretation.

God is equally present in every being and event. He is constantly unfolding his creative plan in every being and event. He is constantly before our eyes – even though rational argument may be used to deny his presence.

An intelligent mind concludes that God is present. A sensitive imagination believes that God is present. The mystical soul sees the presence of God.

Ibn Arabi: Fusus al-hikam 6

Servants of the Lord

Sometimes servants of God try to behave like the Lord, without a doubt. Sometimes servants of God behave like servants. When they behave like servants, they are truly like the Lord. When they behave like the Lord, they are in a sorry condition.

Servants of the Lord should acknowledge that they are mere servants, and look to the Lord with respect, hoping to gain his favour. They should see the Lord in all creatures, from the smallest to the largest.

Servants of the Lord may make demands of God. But God may not always wish to meet those demands. For this reason those who behave like the Lord, often weep with frustration. So be a servant of the Lord; do not behave like the Lord, treating others as servants.

You are a servant, and you are Lord; you are a servant of the one in whom you exist. You are Lord, and you are a servant; you are a servant of the one who has bound himself to you. Every relationship between master and servant on earth should be modelled by the relationship between the Lord and his servants.

Ibn Arabi: Fusus al-hikam 6, 7

The reality of God

There is nothing except the reality of God. There is no close-ness except closeness to God; there is no distance except dis-tance from God. Spiritual visions confirm this: when I look with the eyes of the soul, I see nothing but God.

Do not look only on the reality of God; if you do, you will no longer see him in his creation. Do not look only on God's creation; if you do, you will no longer see God.

In order to think about God, you may compare him with other beings; but remember that he is incomparable. In this way you will live in the house of truth.

Allow yourself to see the unity of what God has made; but remember its infinite variety. If you can see both unity and variety in God's creation, you will have victory over it.

Do not die, and do not live; do not be annihilated, and do not be sustained.

Only the one who always keeps his promises, truly exists. He cannot really harm you; his threats do not exist in reality. You may have a time of suffering, but this will be followed by joy – and the joy of being joyful. To see you enjoying the joy of paradise, is God's joy.

Ibn Arabi: Fusus al-hikam 7

God's presence in all things

The straight path of God is not hidden; all can see it. God is present in all things, great and small; some are ignorant of his presence within them, and some are aware of his presence. Thus his mercy embraces all things, humble and mighty alike.

If another living being submits to you, in reality it is God submitting to you. But if God were to submit to you, other living beings would not follow him in that.

Understand what I say, for my words are true. There is no living being that does not possess the power of self-expression. There is no living being, visible to the human eye, in whom God is not present. Indeed, every living being is in reality a vessel for God.

God is constantly becoming; and by his becoming I become. Thus my being becomes his being; I am transformed in his image. In a certain respect I seek refuge from him in him.

The spiritual eye perceives nothing but God; and God sees only himself. We are his; by him we exist, and by him we are governed. He is present within us at all times, and in all states.

Ibn Arabi: Fusus al-hikam 10

Here and there

The earth beneath our feet takes many forms; so God has given us animals on which to ride, enabling us to travel across any terrain. This is a sign of his grace.

Some only ride on paths, while others ride across trackless deserts. Those who ride on paths, are like those who can see the way to God. Those who ride across trackless deserts, are like those who have lost the way to God. Yet God reveals himself within the souls of both; he is the inner reality of all people.

Who is here, and what is there? That which is here, is that which is there. The one who is universal, is within every particular thing. There is one essence of all things; that essence is both light and darkness. Those who understand these words, will not fall into confusion. In truth only those who possess spiritual power, can understand what we say.

Ibn Arabi: Fusus al-hikam · 11, 12

The essence of God

God speaks: 'We only say what our essence gives us to say. We know our own essence perfectly; so we can never say anything that is contrary to our essence. We only say what we intend to say.

'Since we are the essence of all creatures, we speak only to ourselves. Yet all creatures are free to comply with what we say, or not to comply.

'All grace comes from us; and since we are present in all creatures, all grace comes from every living creature. Even if particular creatures do not regard themselves as belonging to us, we most certainly belong to them.

'Thus we make our mystery clear to you; we explain it well. Odd numbers are enshrined within even.'

Ibn Arabi: Fusus al-hikam 13

Divine in essence, human in form

If it were not for God, and if it were not for us, that which is, would not be. We are servants of God's truth, and God is our master. But the essence of God is within us. So when I use the term 'human', do not be deceived by this term; God has shown you that 'human' also means 'divine.' You are divine in essence, and human in form. And since God is compassionate, you are compassionate.

In serving God, we give back to him what he has given to us. In our actions we make manifest the will of God. The whole task of creating and sustaining the world is shared between God and us. He gave us his life; and when we grow weary, he revives us with his life. In him we exist; he is our essence; his time is our time.

Ibn Arabi: Fusus al-hikam 15

Divine warmth and light

In the darkness before dawn the essence of light is already present. In human beings the Spirit of God is present, even before it has made itself manifest through action.

Let me illustrate what I mean. Imagine yourself asleep; your mind is dark. Then you rise to that intermediate state of being half asleep and half awake. The darkness of sleep is still upon you, but the light of the morning is also present. If you understand this illustration, you will see how the Spirit of God is present in a human being – even if that human appears to have no divine attributes.

So you do not need to be anxious about any human being. Those who are not aware of the Spirit of God, will at some point in their lives feel spiritually cold; they are then ready to find the warmth within themselves. That warmth is like a coal burning in the heart. Those who are not aware of the Spirit of God, will at some point in their lives feel spiritually dark; they are then ready to find the light within themselves. That light is like a lantern for travellers at night.

If you understand what I am saying, you will know whether you are spiritually cold and dark.

Ibn Arabi: Fusus al-hikam 15

Vision and reality

Before you can become like God, you must first imagine
being like God; then the vision becomes the reality. Those
who understand this, understand the mystical way. Those
who do not understand my words, are assailed by anxiety.

I speak from experience; I pass on only what I
myself have received. So I ask you to trust me.
Trust will lead to understanding; and understanding will ease anxiety.

The mercy of God flows through all living
beings. Since God created all living beings, his
mercy flows through them like a river. God's
mercy is the essence of all living beings; it is
their true selves. Use your intelligence to perceive God's within you.

Ibn Arabi: Fusus al-hikam 16, 17, 21

In love with God

If God were to need sustenance, then the whole of existence could serve as food for him. When God wishes to provide sustenance for us, then he himself is our food.

God's wish is God's will; that which he wishes, he wills to happen. When he wishes us to be fed, we are fed; when he wishes us to be hungry, we are not fed. He does not will anything that he does not wish to happen.

God, whom I love, yearns to see me; and for this reason I yearn even more to see him. My heart pounds with love. But the will of God bars the way. I groan with frustration – and so does he!

You are right to think that I am in love. But do you know the one with whom I am in love?

Ibn Arabi: Fusus al-hikam 23, 27

Lions on a flag

If the intellect were to try and explain love, it would fall
down in the mud like an ass. Love and loving can only be
explained by love. The sun is the proof of the sun; if you
need proof of its existence, stare at it.

Who can describe the activities of God? I speak obliquely
because I have no choice. Sometimes God shows himself in
one way, and sometimes in an opposite way. The work of religion brings much bewilderment. It is not a bewilderment
which turns you away from God; it drowns you in him, and
intoxicates you with him.

We think we exist; but in ourselves we do not exist. You,
O God, are real existence; you express yourself in that which
is transient. We are like lions painted on a flag: we appear to
move, but in reality it is the wind which makes us move.

Whenever you are inclined to undertake some particular
work, you recognize your own freedom to do so. But whenever you are not inclined to undertake some particular work,
you are fatalistic, saying: 'God requires me to do this.'
Prophets are fatalists regarding the works of this world; unbelievers are fatalists regarding the works of the next world.
The prophets proclaim that we can choose freely what we
shall do in the next world; unbelievers choose freely what
they will do in this world.

Rumi: *Masnavi* I

Born anew

I saw my physical birth as death; I was very frightened. But now I have been born anew into a spiritual world of fragrant air and vivid colours.

Life consists in peace among opposites. Death consists in strife amongst them. God brings the lion and the sheep together.

The spiritually blind can only find the path if they are guided by those with spiritual sight. If there were no people with spiritual sight – if there were no spiritual masters – the whole world would be spiritually dead.

Wealth needs the poor to whom it can be given – just as a beautiful woman needs a clear mirror in which to see her beauty. A mirror reflects the beauty of a face; poverty brings forth generosity from where it is hidden.

In life you may acquire knowledge on many different subjects. But on the day of death only one kind of knowledge will provide sustenance for the journey: the knowledge of poverty.

Consider a man falling into the ocean. When the man dies, the corpse rises to the surface. But while the man is still alive, the waves drag him down. In the same way, when you have died to human attributes, the ocean of divine mysteries will raise you up.

Rumi: *Masnavi* I

Washing clothes

Look at a husband and wife whose work is washing clothes. Outwardly they are in conflict. He throws them into the water, and she takes them out and squeezes them dry; he then throws them into the water again. It looks as if they are quarrelling, with each trying to thwart the other. But in fact they are working harmoniously at a single task. Each prophet and saint has his or her own spiritual method; but all methods lead to God – they are in harmony.

The philosopher denies the very existence of the devil. At that very moment the devil seizes him. Have you not seen the devil? Then look at yourself. If the devil is not active within you, why do you frequently wear a dark expression?

Purify yourself from all the attributes of self, that you may see your own pure essence.

There may be sweet pleasures for the body in this world. But anything other than love for God, whose beauty is unmatched, is agony to the soul. What is agony of the soul? It is to advance towards death without being sustained by the water of life.

Rumi: *Masnavi* I

Saintly footprints

The Sufi's book is not composed of words written in ink; it is a heart as white as snow. We know a scholar by the marks of a pen; we know a Sufi by saintly footprints.

Move from the assertion of self to the negating of self. You are seeking the Lord, and you belong to him. The negating of self is where spiritual profits are made; so stay at that place. The assertion of self is where spiritual losses are made; so flee from that place. God's workshop is the negating of self; everything outside that workshop is worthless.

Whether your love belongs to this world or the next, you do not love the outward form of another person. After all, you do not continue to love an outward form, when the soul has departed. Look carefully at those whom you love. Have your fill of their outward forms; and learn to love them as they really are.

The outward form of things passes away, but the essence remains for ever. How long will you be besotted with the shape of the jug? Cast aside the jug, and seek the water. If you look too closely at the form, you miss the essence. If you are wise, you will always pick out the pearl from the shell.

Rumi: *Masnavi* 2

The creed of love

That which appears to exist, does not exist in itself. That which is hidden, is true existence. Look at dust blowing in the air: you see the dust, but the wind raising it in the air is hidden. That which appears to be moving, does not move in itself; it is only the shell of motion. That which is hidden, is truly moving; it is the kernel of motion.

The creed of love is separate from all religions; the creed of love is God.

If you want to sit with God, sit with saints. If you do not consort with saints, you will be lost; you will be separated from the whole.

You must turn your intelligence into ignorance; you must become mad. Whenever you see something that may yield material profit, flee from it. Curse anyone who praises you. Lend your wealth to the poor and the feckless. Abandon the security of your home, and live in places of danger. Throw away your reputation, and embrace dishonour and disgrace. I shall test my intellect to the limit; and then I shall make myself mad.

Rumi: *Masnavi* 2

Mumbling nonsense

If you want your misery to vanish, then try to banish your worldly wisdom. This is because worldly wisdom belongs to the lower nature, which is not illuminated by God's light. The wisdom of the world makes you both more opinionated, and more doubtful about your beliefs. But the wisdom of faith carries you beyond the heavens.

Like all hypocrites you make your excuses, saying to me: 'I am so busy providing for my wife and children, that I have no time to scratch my head, let alone practise religion. You are a spiritual man; pray for me, that eventually I may be saved.' You do not make this request of me with passion and fervour; you are like someone who wakes briefly from sleep, mumbles some nonsense, and then drops off again. You speak again: 'I cannot escape from the obligation to feed my family; I must make every lawful effort to acquire money.' What do you mean by 'lawful'? The truth is that you demand the comforts of this world, yet are indifferent to the one who created this world. You want the world's luxuries, but care nothing for the one who generously provides them.

Rumi: Masnavi 2

Slaying the serpent

The sign on the road is for travellers who easily become lost. Those who have attained union with God, have no need for signs or roads; they have the inward eye and the divine lamp. When people in union with God speak of signs, they are trying to guide those who are uncertain of the way. Remember that the parents of a new-born child utter babbling sounds, even though they can speak clearly.

Since you are not a prophet, follow the way taught by prophets. Since you are not a king, be a loyal subject to the king. Since you are not a captain, do not take the helm of the ship. Since you do not possess every skill, have partners in your business. Be as pliant as dough in the hands of others, that you may rise well.

If someone says something contrary to your own attitudes, anger rises up within you. 'That person wants me as a pupil and follower,' you say to yourself. Your bad attitudes have led to bad habits, which are hard to break; you have allowed the ant of sensuality to become a serpent. You must slay the serpent now, or else it will grow into a dragon. But, like most people, you probably think that your serpent is still an ant.

Rumi: *Masnavi* 2

The tent and the guest

First make or buy a tent; then invite a stranger into the tent as your guest. The outward form is the tent; the inward essence is the guest. Obtain a ship, and send it across the sea. The outward form is the ship; the inward essence is the captain.

There are those whose heads are full of knowledge on every subject, but who do not know their own souls. They know the properties of every material substance; but if they try to describe their own spiritual substance, they are like asses. They know the value of every item that can be bought and sold; but they do not know their own value. They are stupid. They can read the stars, but they cannot read themselves. The only knowledge which matters, is this: the knowledge of who you will be on the day of resurrection.

Those who are erudite, are inclined to miss the essence of things; they know the outward form perfectly, but cannot see behind and beyond it. True knowledge is rooted behind and beyond the outward form.

Rumi: Masnavi 3

Dry lips

Do not look at your own form, be it beautiful or ugly; look at the true object of your love, and the goal of your search. Do not look at your own state, which is feeble and vile; look at the true object of your hopes and aspirations. In whatever state you are, seek God. Seek God as if your lips were dry and you were seeking water. Dry lips are a sign that you will eventually reach a spring. Dry lips are a message from the water: 'If you keep searching, you will find me.' To seek is a blessed activity; it destroys the obstacles on the path to God. If you seek, you will find.

Where there is pain, cures will be found. Where there is poverty, wealth will be supplied. Where there are questions, answers will be given. Spend less time worrying, and more time trusting.

Saints die to themselves, and live through the Lord; for that reason God's mysteries are always on their lips. When the soul has become master of the body, life begins. In acquiring mastery the soul must inflict suffering on the body; physical suffering is nourishment for the soul.

Rumi: *Masnavi* 3

The candle and the sun

True Sufis subsist only on their essence; their personal attributes have been subsumed into the attributes of God. This may
be understood by considering a candle next to the sun. Both
the candle and the sun have the essence of fire; but the
candle's flame is subsumed into the sun's. The candle's flame
has not ceased to exist; if you were to place a cotton thread
in it, the thread would be consumed. But the candle's flame
no longer sheds light, because the sun's brightness is infinitely stronger.

A person's death reflects the person's life. Those who have
lived as God's enemies, die as God's enemies. Those who
have lived as God's friends, die as God's friends. Death is like
a mirror of life. A mirror in front of a white face shows a
white face; a mirror in front of a black face shows a black
face. If you are frightened of death, you are frightened of
yourself; if you wish to flee from death, you wish to flee
from yourself. It is your own ugliness which frightens you,
not the ugliness of death. Your soul is like a tree, and death
its leaves. Whether it is good or bad, your death has grown
from you. Every hidden thought, whether good or bad, is
rooted in you.

Rumi: Masnavi 3

Being broken

Everyone can see the effects of God's mercy. But who, except God himself, understands the essence of his mercy? Most people cannot understand the essence of any of God's attributes; they only know his attributes through their effects – and also through analogy. Only mystics have eyes to see the essence of God's attributes.

Those who attain direct vision of God, do not need the support of theologians and philosophers. Having seen the spiritual beauty of God, they are weary of intellectual knowledge. Vision is greater than knowledge.

When love for God has doubled in your heart, you know without doubt that God loves you. You have never heard one hand clapping without the other.

People of intelligence must be broken, if they are to appear before God; people of love break themselves before God out of choice. People of intellect are like slaves in chains; people of love are sweet and beautiful. People of intellect must be dragged towards God; people who have lost their hearts to God, come willingly.

Rumi: Masnavi 3

The pearl and the stone

The body moves by means of the soul; but you do not see the soul. You can understand the soul by observing the body's movements.

Outwardly the earth is made of dust. But inwardly it consists of the light of God. Its outward form is in conflict with its inward essence; inwardly it is a pearl, and outwardly it is a stone. Its outward form declares: 'I am this, and no more.' Its inward essence says: 'Look carefully at what lies behind and beyond.' Its outward form denies the existence of the inward essence, saying: 'The inward essence is nothing.' The inward essence says: 'Just wait! We shall show you.'

Pass beyond form. Escape from names. Flee from forms and titles, and seek essences.

Since your intelligence puffs you up with pride, become a simpleton; then your soul will remain healthy. Sacrifice your intelligence for the love of God, who is your friend; after all, he gave you your intelligence in the first place. If your intelligence departs from your head in confusion, then every hair on your head will become truly intelligent.

Rumi: Masnavi 4

Two kinds of knowledge

There are two kinds of knowledge. The first kind is acquired from books and teachers; it consists of definitions which you learn by rote, and concepts which you grasp by reflection. This kind of knowledge is a burden; and the more you acquire, the greater the burden becomes. The second kind of knowledge is a gift from God. It springs up from the soul, and flows through the breast; it never becomes stagnant or discoloured.

Hearsay is for those who are absent, not for those who are present. Those who attain vision, have no more need of hearsay. When you sit with your beloved, you send away the go-betweens.

Unbelievers say: 'We see nothing but the outward form of things.' They never reflect that the outward form gives news of the inward essence. Indeed, the value of every outward thing lies hidden in the inward – just as the healing power of a medicine lies hidden.

Rumi: *Masnavi* 4

The oil and the light

The outward form is the oil of the lamp; the essence is the light. It is for this reason that you need to ask questions. If outward form existed for its own sake, there would be no questions to ask. Yet it is absurd to think that the outward form of the heavens exists for its own sake; and it is equally absurd to think that the outward forms of the creatures on earth exist for their own sake.

The fire of hell is a threat to frighten the wicked. But although God has the power to inflict the most severe and terrible punishment, he draws back. Compare the heat of hell with the coolness of his mercy. His desire to show mercy is always stronger than his impulse to punish. His threats are truly awesome; but as you begin to tremble, the threats soften and shrink.

Rumi: Masnavi 4

A basketful of bread

You must turn your face in one direction or another. Saints turn in the direction that has no directions.

The body brings much suffering. The bird of the soul is imprisoned within a bird of a different kind. The soul is a falcon, whereas the body is a crow. Falcons are frequently wounded by crows.

A basket full of bread sits on your head; yet you go from door to door begging for crusts. Attend to your own head. Knock on your heart's door.

People look for the material causes of things; but these are veils over their eyes, preventing them from seeing the craftsmanship of God. You must train your eyes to pierce the veil of material causes, and see the original cause, which is God. When you perceive the original cause of things, you realize that working and trading for material profits are nonsense. Every pleasure and every pain comes from the original cause; material causes count for nothing – they are like ghosts on the road of life, which distract you.

Loving the self leads to a state like drunkenness: it removes coherent thought from the head, and sensitivity from the heart. The intoxication of self-love has lured a hundred thousand generations to their destruction.

Rumi: *Masnavi* 5

An unwritten page

Does anyone write on a page which is already full of writing? No; a sensible person looks for paper untouched by a pen. Does anyone plant a sapling where a tree is already growing? No; a sensible person looks for a place where nothing has been planted. Look within yourself for the unwritten page, the unplanted earth; look for the empty place.

Love cannot be contained in words; it cannot be conveyed through speaking and listening. Love is an ocean whose depths cannot be plumbed. Would you try to count the drops of water that a sea contains? In comparison with the ocean of love, the seven seas are nothing.

Melancholy may enter your soul, and ambush your happiness; but it will prepare you for true joy. Melancholy drives out all other emotions and feelings, so the source of all goodness may occupy the whole house. It shakes the yellow leaves from the tree, allowing fresh leaves to grow. It pulls up old bodily pleasures by the roots, allowing divine spiritual pleasures to be planted. Melancholy takes many things from the soul, in order to bring better things in return.

Rumi: Masnavi 5

The water of life

Human beings are created from the dust of the earth; but do they resemble dust? Grapes come from vines; but do grapes look like vines? Does theft have the same shape as gallows? Does piety resemble eternal life? Nothing resembles its consequences. So the root of pain and torment is not evil.

The prospect of dying in union with you is sweet; but the prospect of eternal separation from you is horribly bitter.

The water of life renews every soul; you, O God, are the water of life. At every moment you cause me to die and rise; through death and resurrection you guide my life. I acknowledge your generosity.

Rumi: *Masnavi* 4

The foam and the wave

God created suffering and heartache, so that joy might be known as their opposite. Hidden things become manifest through their opposites. But God has no opposite; so he remains hidden. Light is known as the opposite of darkness. But God's light has no opposite. Thus we cannot know him through our eyes.

Your actions, motivated by your soul and enacted by your body, will cling to you, as a child clings to the mother's skirt.

How should we seek knowledge? By no longer trying to possess knowledge. How should we seek peace? By no longer trying to possess peace. How should we seek life? By no longer trying to possess life. How should we seek apples? By no longer trying to possess apples.

Love is an attribute of God, who himself has no need of love. Love for any other being derives from the love of God.

How can the foam move without the wave beneath it? How can the dust rise without the wind blowing it? When you look at the dust, see the divine breath. When you look at the foam, see the divine power.

Rumi: *Masnavi* 6

The bird of grace

Spiritual progress depends on the grace of God. But you must exert yourself also; do not merely wait for God's grace. Those who do not exert themselves, are showing disdain for God. Is disdain for God worthy of a spiritual warrior? Young people, do not try to curry favour with God, and do not fear being rejected by him. Simply remember his commands and prohibitions; hold them constantly in view. Then suddenly the bird of divine grace will fly down from its nest; suddenly the dawn of grace will come, and you will be able to put out the candle of exertion.

A just king is a parable of God's justice. Human scholarship is a parable of God's knowledge. Generations come and go, but justice and knowledge remain the same.

In reality God is worshipped by all people, since all people are searching for the road to happiness. But some have turned their faces away from God, and are lost.

My religion is to live in the service of love. When I live in the service of this body, I am ashamed.

Every object in the world, and every event which occurs in the world, is a snare for the fool, but a means of salvation for the wise.

Rumi: *Masnavi* 6

A gift to a thief

A particular Sufi was held in low regard by the people. So a local dignitary went to a Sufi master, and asked his opinion. The Sufi master replied: 'In his outward behaviour I can find no fault. As for any inner defects he may have, I shall not speculate.'

A Sufi was in a mosque, with tears pouring from his eyes. He said: 'Merciful and compassionate God, you know how sinful and ignorant I am. I beg you to forgive me for the feebleness of my service to you. If I were a sinner, I could repent. But as it is, I can only offer you words of praise. Do to me that which is worthy of you, not that which is worthy of me.'

A thief entered a Sufi's house. He searched everywhere, but could find nothing worthy of stealing. He was about to leave in despair, when the Sufi awoke. Seeing the thief's sadness, the Sufi took the mat on which he was lying, and gave it to the thief.

A group of travellers agreed to journey together, sharing their joys and hardships. A Sufi asked to join them, but they refused. The Sufi said: 'People of your eminence have no need to shun lowly people like me; indeed, your eminence is enhanced by offering friendship. Besides, lowly people tend to be physically capable, so they make useful companions on a journey.' One of the travellers replied: 'Do not be upset at our answer. Only a few days ago we were robbed by a thief dressed as a Sufi.'

Sadi: Gulistan 2

Physical and spiritual wounds

A king invited a Sufi to eat at his table. At every meal the Sufi ate less than normal; and at the end of each meal, he prayed to God for longer than normal. He hoped to impress the king with his piety. When the Sufi returned home, he asked his son to prepare a huge meal. His son asked: 'Did you eat nothing at the king's table?' The Sufi replied: 'I ate little and prayed much in order to impress him.' The son said: 'In that case you must first repeat your prayers – since in reality you have not prayed at all.'

A Sufi master addressed a group of worshippers in a mosque. But their hearts were cold, so he made no impression on them; the flame of his ardour could not ignite their green wood. Then a passer-by entered the mosque, and heard the Sufi's words. The passer-by was so enthralled that he applauded. The other people in the mosque applauded in sympathy; and they began to be excited by the Sufi's words. The Sufi exclaimed: 'Praise be to God!'

A Sufi was wounded by a leopard. He tried every kind of medicine to heal his wounds, but none was effective. Yet the Sufi never ceased to give thanks to God. Some people said to him: 'You are suffering greatly, and yet you constantly thank God. How is this?' The Sufi replied: 'I give thanks to God that I am suffering a physical wound caused by an animal, and not a spiritual wound caused by sin.'

Sadi: Gulistan 2

Stealing and taking

A Sufi needed a blanket, and stole one from the house of a friend. He was caught, and the judge ordered his hand to be cut off. The owner of the blanket said to the judge: 'I have forgiven the Sufi. I beg you not to punish him.' The judge replied: 'The lawful punishment must be carried out, regardless of your plea.' The owner said: 'That is true. But a Sufi does not possess anything, and is possessed by nothing. Therefore the blanket was not stolen, but merely taken.' The judge turned to the Sufi, and said: 'Is the world so small that you had to take from the house of a friend?' The Sufi replied: 'It is better to take everything from the house of a friend, than even to knock at the door of an enemy's house.' The judge released the Sufi.

Sadi: Gulistan 2

Kings and Sufis

A man had a dream in which he saw a king in paradise, and a Sufi in hell. When he awoke, he went to a Sufi master and related his dream. Then he asked: 'Surely I should have seen the Sufi in paradise, and the king in hell?' The Sufi master said: 'A king will go to paradise if he is friendly to Sufis. A Sufi will go to hell if he curries the favour of kings.'

A king invited a Sufi to his palace. The Sufi said to himself: 'I shall take a medicine which will make me look emaciated; that will impress the king.' He took too much of the medicine, and died.

A certain Sufi had the habit of eating a vast meal in the evening; then he would recite the Quran in its entirety, before going to sleep. Another Sufi, renowned for his wisdom, was asked about this. The wise Sufi replied: 'It would be better if that Sufi ate a small lump of bread, and then went straight to sleep.

The disciple of a Sufi master was accused by an enemy of acting wrongly in a certain way. The disciple was innocent. So he went to the master, and asked for advice. The Sufi master said: 'Make your enemy blush by the sweetness of your conversation.'

Sadi: Gulistan 2

Pious travelling

A group was travelling from one city to another, and spent the night on the edge of a forest. A Sufi was one of the group. As soon as dawn broke, the Sufi awoke, and started singing and dancing. The other travellers asked why he was behaving in this manner. The Sufi replied: 'The nightingales are singing in the trees; the partridges are calling from the mountains; the frogs are leaping in the water; and the wild beasts are howling in the forest. When all these creatures are engaged in praising God, how can I neglect God by remaining asleep?'

A group of young men, who aspired to be holy, were on a journey. They constantly sang hymns and recited mystical poems. They were joined by a wise old Sufi, who was not impressed by their pious chanting. One evening they arrived at a certain village. A rough, uneducated boy in the village began to sing a hymn in a loud, raucous voice. The pious young men looked at the boy with contempt. Their camels ran off into the desert. The wise old Sufi asked the young men: 'Why does this boy's praises move your camels, yet leave you unmoved?'

Sadi: Gulistan 2

The Sufi becoming king

A king reached the end of his life, with no heir to succeed him. He made a will, stating that the royal crown should be placed on the head of the first person who walked through the city gates after his death. It so happened that the first person entering the city after the king's death was a Sufi. He had spent his entire adult life eating scraps and wearing rags. Now he was crowned king, and owned all the treasures of the kingdom.

The Sufi ruled in a just manner. Then some of the nobles of the kingdom turned against him; and they gained the support of the king of a neighbouring country. The Sufi led his own troops into battle, but was forced to concede part of his kingdom to his enemies. He became very dejected at this.

In the days when he had lived in poverty, the Sufi had shared his house with a close friend, who was also a Sufi. This Sufi had gone on a long journey; and when he returned, he was astonished to find his friend had become king. He went to the palace, and congratulated him on his fortune. The king replied: 'Do not congratulate me; have pity on me. When we lived together, my only worry was finding bread to eat. Now I have all the cares of the world on my shoulders.'

Sadi: Gulistan 2

Ten and a hundred coins

A disciple said to his Sufi master: 'The sun is a source of many blessings. Yet I have never heard anyone referring to the sun as a friend. Why is this?' The Sufi master replied: 'Through most of the year we see the sun every day; it is so familiar that we barely notice it. Only in the dark days of winter, when it is hidden from view, do we truly appreciate it.'

A certain young man led a virtuous life. Then he grew weary of virtue, and became dissolute. Eventually he found himself in gaol. An older man, who had known him in the past, heard of his predicament, and paid ten silver coins for his release. Then he insisted that the young man should marry his daughter, giving him a dowry of a hundred silver coins. The young woman turned out to be very quarrelsome, with a sharp tongue. One day in a fit of temper she said: 'You are the man whom my father ransomed for ten silver coins.' The man replied: 'Yes, he ransomed me with ten coins, and then he purchased me for a hundred.'

A certain man was renowned for his virtue. The king asked him: 'How do you spend your time?' The man replied: 'I spend the nights praying, and I spend the days labouring. I try to regulate my family's expenses, so I can spend as little time as possible labouring, and as much time as possible praying.' The king gave the man enough money to support himself and his family, so that he could pray during the day as well as the night.

Sadi: Gulistan 2

The scholarly and the devout

A Sufi lived in the desert, and ate only the leaves of trees. The king went to visit him, and said: 'I should like to build a house for you in the garden of my palace, where every comfort would be provided. Then you will have no material anxieties to distract you from praying. I and my subjects will benefit from your prayers.' The Sufi agreed to the king's proposal.

When the Sufi had settled in his new house, the king sent a beautiful maiden to live with him. Then he sent a handsome young man to be his servant. Then he sent soft, fine garments for him to wear. And each day he sent the finest food for him to eat. Gradually the Sufi lost his inner tranquillity, and became listless and discontented.

At length the king decided to visit the Sufi. He was pleased to see that the Sufi had grown fat, and his pale complexion had turned red. The king remarked to his courtiers: 'Of all the people in the world, I value two sorts most highly: those who are scholarly, and those who are devout.' Amongst his courtiers was a wise old man, who replied: 'To scholars you should give gold, that they may study more. To the devout you should give nothing, that they may remain devout.'

Sadi: Gulistan 2

Words of truth

A Sufi arrived at the house of a wealthy dignitary after a long journey. The Sufi was tired and hungry; but the dignitary insisted that the Sufi should immediately give a discourse to his friends. When the friends had gathered, the Sufi sat in silence. One them said: 'Please say something to us.' The Sufi replied: 'I have no eloquence and no education. I can speak only one truth to you: I am hungry.' The audience laughed at the Sufi's wit. The host said: 'I shall order my servants to roast some meat for you.' The Sufi said: 'I shall speak a second truth: to a Sufi dry bread is roast meat.'

A disciple said to his Sufi master: 'What shall I do? I am harassed all day by people visiting me; their coming and going disturbs my tranquillity.' The Sufi master replied: 'Make loans to those who are poor; demand loans from those who are rich. Then neither the poor nor the rich will visit you again.'

A band of dissolute young men came up to a Sufi, and hurled foul insults at him. The Sufi was very upset, and went to his master. The master said: 'The patched robe of the Sufi is a garment of resignation. Those who cannot endure insults and hardships with patience, are impostors, and should not wear the Sufi robe.'

A Sufi saw an athlete who was foaming at the mouth with anger. He asked the people nearby: 'What is the matter with this man?' They answered: 'Someone has insulted him.' The Sufi said: 'A man may have the strength to lift ten men, but be unable to support a few unpleasant words.'

Sadi: Gulistan 2

A holy fault

A person of great eminence said to a Sufi master: 'People who become holy, must in the process acquire at least one fault. What is that fault?' The Sufi master replied: 'The worst fault of holy people is that they place greater importance on the wishes of their friends than they do on their own wishes.'

A wealthy lawyer had an extremely ugly daughter. Despite her huge dowry, no one was willing to marry her. Eventually the lawyer found a blind man, who agreed to take her as his wife. Some friends told the lawyer about a doctor living in a distant land who could cure blindness; and they urged him to send his son-in-law there. The lawyer said: 'There are some instances where the inability to see the truth is a blessing.'

A certain king regarded Sufis with contempt. So a group of Sufis came to see him, and said: 'Your majesty, we are certainly inferior to you in military power. But we are happier than you are, even in this world. In death we shall be equal with you. And on the day of resurrection we shall be superior to you.'

Some people asked a Sufi master: 'Which is better, courage or generosity?' The Sufi master replied: 'Those who are generous, have no need for courage.'

Sadi: Gulistan 2

The merchant and the scholar

There were two brothers, who were descendants of Muhammad. One became a Sufi, while the other became a wealthy merchant. The wealthy merchant looked with contempt at his brother, and said: 'I have acquired great wealth, while you have remained in poverty.' The Sufi said: 'I have acquired the true wealth which our ancestor bequeathed; and so I thank the most high God for his generosity.'

Two Sufis, who were close friends, were travelling to a certain city. One was thin from constant fasting; he normally ate only once every two days. The other was fat from excessive eating; he had three large meals each day. When they arrived at their destination, they were arrested on suspicion of being spies; and they were put in prison with no food. After a fortnight facts came to light which showed they were innocent. When the gaoler went to release them, he found the fat Sufi was dead, and the thin one was alive.

A man was lying sick. His friends asked him: 'What would you most desire?' The sick man answered: 'My greatest desire is to desire something.'

Sadi: Gulistan 3

Dying honourably

Two Sufis incurred a debt of a few coins to a butcher. Every day the butcher pressed them to pay the debt; and every day they promised to pay him. As time passed, his words became rougher and more angry. When their master heard of their predicament, he summoned them, and said: 'It is easier to put off the stomach with the promise of food, than to put off a butcher with the promise of payment.'

A brave soldier was badly wounded in war. He returned home disabled and penniless. A neighbour said: 'A merchant in the town has a remedy for wounds. If you ask him, perhaps he will give you a little.' The warrior replied: 'That merchant is notorious for his stinginess. If I ask him for the remedy, he may give it, or he may not. And if he gives it to me, it may help me, or it may not. Thus to ask him for the remedy is deadly poison.'

The warrior's words were reported to a Sufi, who said: 'If water were offered to a man dying of thirst, and the price were honour, it would be better for that man to refuse it. To die honourably is preferable to living in disgrace.'

A man of great wealth supported a Sufi with a small allowance. The Sufi lived simply, and the wealthy man held him in high regard. Then the Sufi asked his patron to increase the allowance. The wealthy man did so; but he ceased to respect the Sufi.

Sadi: Gulistan 3

The paradox of value

A man called Hatim was renowned for his generosity. Someone asked Hatim: 'Have you heard of anyone more generous than you?' Hatim replied: 'One day I met a woodcutter, who had just collected a bundle of twigs. I said to him: "Go to Hatim's house, where you will receive food freely." The woodcutter replied: "Those who earn their bread by their own efforts, should not seek bread from Hatim." That man is more generous than I am.'

A man lost his way in the desert, and wandered aimlessly for several days. He ran out of food, and thought he would die. Then he saw a bag lying in the sand. He opened it, and at first thought it was filled with grains of barley. He was overjoyed. But when he tried to eat them, he discovered they were pearls – and he plunged into despair.

In the same way a traveller lost his way in a vast plain. After several days his food and strength were exhausted; he only had some gold coins left in his belt. He threw the gold coins on the ground in despair. Then he lay down, and died.

Sadi: Gulistan 3

A peasant and a fisherman

A king and his principal officers were out hunting on a winter's day. When night fell, they found themselves in a remote
place. They saw a peasant's house, and the king said: 'Let us
spend the night there, so we do not suffer from the cold.'
One of the officers said: 'It would not be suitable for the dignity of a king to spend the night with a lowly peasant. Let us
pitch our tent here, and kindle a fire.' The peasant overheard
this conversation. He went up to the king, and kissed the
ground. Then he said: 'The dignity of a king cannot be lowered; but the dignity of a peasant can be raised.' The king was
pleased with these words, and stayed with the peasant.

A strong fish was caught in the net of a weak fisherman.
The fisherman could not keep hold of the net; the fish
dragged the net from his hands, and escaped. The other
fishermen mocked him for being defeated by a fish. The weak
fisherman said: 'What could I do? I was not destined to be
lucky today; and the fish was destined to live for many days
more.'

A Sufi, who had been an advisor to the king, went to live
in a cave in order to detach himself entirely from the world.
The king soon forgot about him entirely. But the king of a
neighbouring country heard about him, and sent a message
inviting him to eat at his palace. The Sufi accepted. After the
meal the king apologized for having disturbed his tranquil life
in the cave. The Sufi rose up and embraced the king. Then he
insisted on waiting at the king's table.

Sadi: Gulistan 3

Avoiding malice and disgrace

A Sufi said to another Sufi: 'I have decided to abstain from speaking, because on most occasions speech contains evil as well as good – and the ears of God's enemies hear only the evil.' The other Sufi replied: 'Malice remains quiet as long as the object of its hatred is an ordinary person. But towards a holy person malice is vocal in its anger.'

A merchant lost a thousand silver coins in a transaction. The merchant said to his son: 'You must not tell anyone about this matter.' The son said: 'Father, I shall tell no one, as you command. But what advantage is there in keeping this matter secret?' The merchant replied: 'We should keep it secret to avoid doubling our misfortune. Our first misfortune is to have lost a thousand silver coins. If news of this were to spread, our second misfortune would be to suffer the malicious pleasure of our neighbours.'

There was an intelligent young man, who was well-versed in many subjects, and possessed a fine intellect. Yet when he was in the company of wise and learned people, he never uttered a word. Eventually his father asked: 'Why do you not speak about some of the subjects on which you possess knowledge?' The young man replied: 'I am fearful that others would ask me about something of which I am ignorant; then I should bring disgrace upon myself.'

Sadi: Gulistan 4

Interfering and harsh voices

A Sufi master was considering the purchase of a certain house, but was uncertain. A man came to him, and said: 'I have lived in this neighbourhood for many years. Ask me what is the real value of this house; then you will know whether the seller is asking a fair price. I can assure you the house has no faults.' The master replied: 'I can see the house has no faults – except that you live nearby.'

A Sufi regarded himself as a fine preacher; but he had a very harsh voice, so it was hard to concentrate on the substance of what he was saying. The people of the town, out of respect for his holiness, did not like to tell him of this affliction; and so they quietly endured his sermons. Then a Sufi from a neighbouring town, who disliked the preacher, came and said to him: 'I have had a dream. I hope it has a helpful meaning.' The preacher asked: 'What was your dream?' The visitor said: 'I dreamt that your voice was pleasant, and that people enjoyed listening to your sermons.' The preacher reflected a little, and said: 'Your dream is most helpful, for it has acquainted me with my failings. I now realize that I have a harsh voice, and that people are distressed by my delivery. From now on I shall say nothing, except in a very low voice.'

Sadi: Gulistan 4

The brightness of friendship

A Sufi master had many young disciples who were exceedingly handsome and intelligent. Yet he held in particular affection a disciple who was plain in appearance and mediocre in intelligence. When he was asked to explain this, the master replied: 'Whatever pleases the heart, is beautiful to the eye.

One night a friend arrived at the house of a Sufi. As soon as the Sufi saw the friend, he put out his lamp with the sleeve of his robe. When he had sat down, the friend asked: 'Why did you put out your lamp as soon as you saw me?' The Sufi replied: 'It seemed as though the sun had entered my house.'

A Sufi had a friend whom he had not seen for a long time. When at last they met, the friend said: 'Where have you been? I have longed to see you.' The Sufi replied: 'Longing is better than loathing.'

A Sufi had a friend who was so close that they were like two kernels in a single almond. On one occasion the Sufi had to undertake a long journey, causing him to be away for many months. When at last he returned, the friend reproached him for not sending a messenger during his absence. The Sufi replied: 'I did not want a messenger to be brightened by your beauty, while I was excluded.'

Sadi: Gulistan 5

The carpet of desire

A group of wealthy merchants were making the pilgrimage to Mecca. They were accompanied by a Sufi. One of the merchants was so impressed by the Sufi's wisdom that he gave him a hundred silver coins. Then a group of robbers attacked the group, and took everything of value. The merchants were very distressed, but the Sufi was quite calm. They said to the Sufi: 'Why are you not distressed, as we are? Perhaps the robbers did not take your money.' The Sufi replied: 'Yes, they took my money. But I was not so attached to it, that I should break my heart at losing it.'

A Sufi fell in love with a young man. When the young man was present, the Sufi gazed adoringly at his beauty; when the young man was absent, he thought constantly of his beauty. The young man became the Sufi's main interest in life. Then one day the young man died. The Sufi kept watch for many days and nights at the young man's grave, suffering great anguish. Finally he left the grave, vowing that he would fold up the carpet of desire, and never again make an intimate relationship.

Sadi: Gulistan 5

The table of life

A Sufi master reached a great age. Eventually he realized that he was dying. His disciples gathered at his bedside, and he said to them: 'Life is a table piled with delicious dishes. I have hardly tasted any of them, and now it is time for me to leave.' His disciples asked: 'How do you feel in your present condition.' He replied: 'You have all suffered the agony of a bad tooth; you long for the tooth to be pulled out. That is how I feel.' The disciples said: 'Please dismiss from your mind the idea of death. Even if a disease is terrible, it need not be fatal. Let us send for a physician, who may have remedies to cure you.' The master replied: 'The leeches are in despair, for they will take no more blood from me. The makers of healing oils will provide no more oil for my skin. When the body has lost its poise, no medicines can restore it.'

An old man possessed great riches, and had a handsome son. A Sufi came to stay at the old man's house; and in the evening the old man, the Sufi and the son sat together. The old man said: 'There is a tree in a nearby valley, where people go to pray. I have spent many nights at the foot of that tree, praying to God, and thanking him for granting me this son.' The Sufi heard the son say under his breath: 'If only I knew the location of this tree, I should go there and pray for my father's death.'

Sadi: Gulistan 6

Childhood and adulthood

A certain young man was known for his cheerful and amiable disposition; he had no trace of melancholy, and he was quick to laugh. A Sufi living nearby enjoyed his company. The Sufi had to go on a long journey; and when he returned, he heard that the young man had married, and was now the father of several children. He went to see him, and found that he was sad and anxious. The Sufi asked him why his disposition had changed. The man replied: 'As soon as I had children of my own, I ceased to be a child myself.'

A young man once raised his voice against his mother, in a fit of anger. The mother sat down in a corner and wept. Through her tears she said: 'You have forgotten the innocence of your childhood – that is why you treat me with such rudeness.'

The son of a rich miser fell sick. The miser's friends said to him: 'If you want God to spare your son, you should read the Quran from beginning to end; and you should take your finest sheep, and offer it as a sacrifice to God.' The miser reflected for a moment, and said: 'I shall read the Quran, because I have a copy close at hand. But I shall not sacrifice my finest sheep, because the flock is at some distance.' A Sufi, who was told about the miser's response, said: 'He chose to read the Quran, because the Quran is on the tip of his tongue. But he chose not to sacrifice a valuable sheep, because gold is at the centre of his heart.'

Sadi: Gulistan 6

Intelligence and education

Two types of people labour fruitlessly, exerting themselves to no purpose. There are those who gain wealth, but do not know how to enjoy it. And there are those who acquire knowledge, but do not practise it.

Learned people who fail to restrain their passions, are like blind people carrying torches; they guide others, but not themselves.

Monarchs stand in greater need of the counsel of the wise, than the wise stand in need of the friendship of monarchs.

Three things will not last, unless they are combined with something else. Wealth will not last, unless it is combined with work. Intelligence will not last, unless it is combined with education. And an empire will not last, unless it is combined with justice.

To show compassion to the wicked is to oppress the righteous; to pardon oppressors is to tyrannize the oppressed.

Do not rely on the friendship of kings, nor on the sweet voices of children. The first is changed by caprice, and the second by time.

Do not reveal to friends all the secrets you possess; they may one day become enemies. Do not inflict on enemies every injury in your power; they may one day become friends.

Sadi: Gulistan 8

Enemies and friends

Let the words between two enemies be such that, if they were to become friends, they would not be ashamed.

When you are in doubt about a decision, choose the course which has the least likelihood of causing injury.

Anger that has no limit, causes terror. Kindness that is inappropriate, does away with respect. So do not be so severe with others, as to terrify them; and do not be so lenient with others, as to make them take advantage of you.

The enemy of good order is a king without mercy; the enemy of good religion is a preacher without knowledge.

When you have heard news that will cause pain to another person, do not rush to convey that news; perhaps the news will sound better from someone else.

Those who give advice to the arrogant and proud, are themselves in need of advice.

Do not be ensnared by the schemes of an enemy, nor pleased by the compliments of a flatterer. The one has the hand of hyprocisy, and the other has the mouth of greed.

Those who are greedy are never satisfied, even if they have all they want. To be contented you must be satisfied with a crust.

Sadi: Gulistan 8

Ignorance and wisdom

Life hangs on a single breath; only a single breath stands between this world and the next. Those who barter religion for the pleasures of this world, are asses.

The finest ornament for the ignorant is silence; but if ignorant people knew this, they would not be ignorant.

Those who dispute with the wise, in order to make themselves appear wise, merely reveal their ignorance.

Do not divulge the secrets of others; by disgracing them, you make yourself appear untrustworthy.

Those who have acquired learning, but do not put into practice what they have learnt, are like a man who ploughs, but does not sow seed.

Those who appear graceful, may not possess graceful hearts. Judge people by actions not appearances, because actions come from the heart.

It is not a sign of wisdom to grapple with a lion, or strike a sword with a fist.

Those who do not listen to advice, should anticipate hearing themselves reproached.

Sadi: Gulistan 8

Power and purpose

Wise people delay eating. Devout people do not satisfy their appetites. Hermits take only enough to sustain life. The young eat until the dishes are taken away. The old eat till they sweat.

A wise person who engages in controversy with fools, should not expect to be treated with honour. And if a fool should overpower a sage with eloquence, no one should be surprised; a common stone can break a jewel.

Do not be surprised that the dissolute do not heed the words of the devout; the music of a lute is drowned by the beat of a drum.

A natural talent without training is pitiable; training without a natural talent is wasted.

A wise person is like a tray at a pharmacist – in silence it manifests its own merits. An ignorant person is like the drum of a warrior – loud and useless.

Friendship takes many years to establish; so do not fall out with a friend over a single disagreement.

Reason is captive in the hands of passion – just as a weak man is captive in the hands of an artful woman.

Purpose without power is mere weakness and deception; power without purpose is emptiness and insanity.

Sadi: Gulistan 8

Equality on the spiritual path

On the spiritual path no one has higher or lower status than anyone else.

A Sufi master had a slave called Zairak; and Zairak was exceedingly wise and virtuous. When the master was dying, his disciples asked: 'Who will take your place?' 'Zairak,' the master replied.

The master had four sons. Zairak said to the master: 'Your sons will not allow me to succeed you. They will be constantly angry with me.' The master said: 'Set your heart at ease. If they cause you any trouble, I shall defend you from their evil plots.' When the master died, Zairak succeeded him.

The sons now said to Zairak: 'You are our slave. What right have you to take our father's place?' They harassed him continually. Eventually the harassment grew so intense that Zairak went to the master's grave, and pleaded with him to honour his promise.

A few days later some unbelievers attacked the area, and the inhabitants went out to fight them. The master's four sons joined the fight; and all four were killed. Thereafter Zairak was free of harassment.

Nizam al-Din: Fawa'id al-Fu'ad 1.2

Desiring nothing other than God

Contentment consists in desiring nothing other than God.

A Sufi master was sitting in his house, sewing a patch on his robe. One of his legs was stretched out in front of him. A disciple, who was destined to be his successor, arrived. The master did not move, but invited the disciple to come in. The disciple was offended at the sight of his master's leg, which was uncovered, and said: 'Please fold your legs.' The master ignored him. The disciple repeated the request two or three times.

Later, as the disciple was about to leave, the master clasped his hand, and said: 'While you have been present, I have willingly folded my arms; therefore I do not need to fold my legs. I have never desired, and am not now desiring, anything from you. I grasp nothing; I have folded my arms as a sign of this. I am free not to fold my legs, if I so choose.'

Nizam al-Din: Fawa'id al-Fu'ad 1.6

Foundations for spiritual progress

It is important to lay the foundations for spiritual progress.

A man once came to a Sufi master, and asked to be a disciple. The new disciple expected the master to instruct him on the invocations and prayers he should use. But the master said: 'Whatever you do not wish for yourself, do not wish it for others; and whatever you wish for yourself, wish for others.'

The disciple went away; and after a while he returned. He said to the master: 'When I first came to you, I hoped you would give me prayers and invocations I could repeat; but you gave me nothing. Today I again expect this.' The Sufi master asked: 'When you came before, what instruction did I give you?' The disciple was taken aback, and could not answer. The master smiled, and said: 'On that day I told you that whatever you do not wish for yourself, you should not wish for others; and whatever you wish for yourself, you should wish for others. Yet you have not remembered that instruction. Since you have not learned the first lesson, how can I give you another?'

Nizam al-Din: Fawa'id al-Fu'ad 1.6

Renouncing the world

Renouncing the world means detachment from material possessions.

A Sufi master used to say to his disciples: 'Virtuous deeds, prayers, fasting, and invocations may fill a cauldron; but you need meat to make a stew.' The disciples did not know what this analogy meant; and finally they asked him to explain it. The master said: 'Virtuous deeds, prayers, fasting, and invocations all presuppose that you have renounced the world, and have no attachments to material objects. Whether or not a person prays, fasts and so on, does not really matter; if that person has not renounced the world, prayer and fasting are worthless.'

The master continued: 'If you put oil, pepper, garlic and onion into a cauldron, and merely add water, you have not made a stew. The basis for a stew is meat; the other ingredients are optional. Similarly, spiritual progress depends on detaching yourself from material possessions; other virtuous practices are optional.'

Nizam al-Din: Fawa'id al-Fu'ad 1.6

Sound intention

An essential element in the spiritual life is sound intention.

A certain mosque in a large city possessed a huge endowment. The administrator of that mosque was so powerful that he was like an emperor. Indeed, if the real emperor needed money, he would borrow a portion of the mosque's endowment from the administrator.

One day a man came to the mosque, hoping that one day he would be appointed the administrator. He demonstrated great spiritual devotion, and sought to make himself useful, with the intention of gaining people's respect. But his efforts seemed to go unnoticed.

Then one day he said to God: 'From now on I shall worship you for your sake alone. I shall no longer be concerned with gaining control of the mosque's endowment.' He continued to act outwardly in exactly the same way as before. In due course the leaders of the mosque approached him, and asked if he would become administrator. He refused, saying: 'For a long time I wanted that job, but you did not offer it. Now that I no longer want it, you deem me worthy of it.'

Nizam al-Din: Fawa'id al-Fu'ad 1.24

Grace and mercy

Remember the grace and mercy of the sublime creator.

A king once imprisoned a young man. The young man's mother came to the king, and pleaded with him for the release of her son. The king replied: 'I have given the command that he should be imprisoned. So long as a single member of my family survives, your son will remain in gaol.'

Hearing these words the woman began to weep. She looked up to the sky, and exclaimed: 'The king has given his command. What is your command?' At that moment the king's heart was moved. He issued a command for her son to be released; and he ordered that a fine horse be purchased for him.

Then the king issued a further command. The young man should ride through the streets of the city, led by the king's servants. And the servants should proclaim: 'This young man has been freed by God, against the king's will.'

Nizam al-Din: Fawa'id al-Fu'ad 1.28

Love bringing patience

Love brings patience.

A Sufi master was sitting quietly, when a group of men came to punish him for wrongs he was accused of committing. The men rained blows on the Sufi master, hitting him a thousand times. Yet the Sufi master remained silent, and no sign of pain appeared on his face.

After they had finished beating him, the men took the Sufi master to the court. The judges asked: 'How did you suffer no pain when you were beaten?' The Sufi master replied: 'When the men were raining blows on me, my beloved wife was looking on. Her love made the pain seem easier. Then I thought that, if the loving gaze of a human being can ease pain, the loving gaze of God can eliminate pain altogether.'

Nizam al-Din: *Fawa'id al-Fu'ad* 2.9

Three stages of trust

There are three stages of trust.

The first stage is that of a client to his advocate. The advocate knows the law, and wishes to do well for his client. The client says to himself: 'My advocate knows his business, and looks on me as a friend.' From time to time the client asks the advocate a question, or suggests a method of arguing the case. In the same way, at the first stage Sufis trust God as a knowledgeable friend; they feel free to question God, and even make suggestions to him.

The second stage is that of a baby to its mother. The baby trusts its mother, but does not question her. It does not say: 'Give me milk at such-and-such a time.' When the baby feels hungry, it simply cries. The baby has complete confidence in the mother's compassion. In the same way, at the second stage Sufis have complete confidence in God's compassion.

The third stage is that of a corpse in the hands of a washerwoman. The washerwoman finds the corpse floating in the river. The corpse asks no questions, and does not move on its own. The fate of the corpse depends entirely on what the washerwoman chooses to do. In the same way, at the third stage Sufis depend entirely on God's will.

Nizam al-Din: Fawa'id al-Fu'ad 2.9

ISLAMIC PHILOSOPHY

Islamic philosophers were open to ideas from all sources, most especially ancient Greece; and they in turn helped to re-awaken medieval Europe to classical thought. Often they were also scientists and physicians, regarding all aspects of logical inquiry as essentially the same.

Razi (d. 925), from Raiy near modern Tehran, travelled to Baghdad, where he studied medicine, and then directed a hospital. He wrote a monograph on smallpox and measles, which guided the treatment of those diseases across the world until the nineteenth century. He also turned his mind to 'spiritual medicine', offering guidance on moral and spiritual health.

Ibn Sina (d. 1037), known in the West as Avicenna, was a distinguished physician and astronomer in Isfahan. In his religious writings he sought to apply the philosophical insights of Aristotle to Islam. He was frequently accused of heresy.

Ibn Rushd (d. 1198), known in the West as Averroes, was born in Cordoba; and as a young man moved to Morocco where he advised the ruler. As a thinker his primary concern was to explore the relationship of religion and science.

The value of reason

God the creator gave us the faculty of reason, that we might attain the highest state that our nature allows us to attain, both in this world and the next. Reason is God's greatest blessing to us; and there is nothing surpassing it as a means of gaining pleasure and joy.

By reason human life is sweetened and made beautiful; by reason our deepest desires are fulfilled. By reason we have built ships, and learnt to sail them across the ocean, so we can visit distant lands. By reason we have developed medicines which can cure diseases in every part of the body. By reason we have acquired numerous arts and skills from which we benefit.

By reason we have come to understand many obscure and mysterious matters, which would otherwise be hidden from us. By reason we have learnt the shape of the earth and the sky; we have calculated the dimensions of the sun, the moon, and the stars, and mapped their courses.

By reason we have even achieved some knowledge of almighty God – and that is our most valuable attainment.

Razi: Kitab al-Muluki

Reason over passion

Since reason is our most precious gift from God, we should do nothing to reduce its status or degrade it. Since reason should govern our conduct, we should allow nothing to govern it. Since reason is the sovereign over all human faculties, it should not be made subject to any other faculty.

We should consult reason in every situation and on all matters. We should accord it the highest respect, and trust its conclusions. We should order our affairs in this world as reason dictates; and we should bring any venture to an end, if reason commands.

In particular, we must not give any passion mastery over reason. Passion blemishes reason; it clouds reason, diverting it from its proper path and purpose. Passion prevents people from receiving the right guidance, and thus impedes their salvation.

No; we must learn to control and govern our passion, compelling it to obey the commands of reason. If we succeed in this, our reason will become clear and pure; it will illuminate us with its light, enabling us to attain all that we wish to attain.

Let us rejoice in God's free gift of reason.

Razi: Kitab al-Muluki

The need for a supervisor

You are naturally inclined to love yourself: you approve and admire your own actions, and you look with favour on your own character and conduct. Thus you are unlikely to have a clear view of your own vices and bad habits. Since you are not properly aware of your vices, you find it hard to rid yourself of them.

Therefore you need a person of insight whom you see frequently, and whom you can trust. This person should ask you many questions about yourself, gathering information about your vices. You must answer these questions honestly, indicating that you are grateful for the opportunity to reveal the worst aspects of yourself. You must not be shy, nor should you give trite and easy answers; and you should hold nothing back.

Eventually this supervisor will begin to tell you about yourself. When this happens, you should not show any sorrow or shame. On the contrary, you should seem to rejoice at what you hear, and indicate your eagerness for more. If you think that your supervisor is concealing something about yourself, or is being too moderate in expressing disapproval, you should assert that you wish to hear the whole truth about yourself. Equally, if you feel your supervisor has been excessive in expressing disapproval and disgust, you must on no account fly into a rage.

Razi: Kitab al-Muluki

Deriving benefit from enemies

The task of your personal supervisor is slow and unending. Moreover, vices and evil habits are apt to reassert themselves after they have been suppressed. Thus you must ask your supervisor time and time again to report on your moral and spiritual state. You should also encourage your supervisor to ask neighbours, colleagues and friends about you – what they find in you to praise, and what they find to blame.

If you have such a supervisor, hardly any of your vices will remain hidden from you; even the smallest and most secret vices will be laid bare.

You will now have nothing to fear from enemies who take delight in exposing your weakness and vices. Your enemies will reveal nothing that you do not already know; and so you will not be humiliated. On the contrary, you will be able to assure them that you are already seeking to overcome the vices they have exposed; and you will express gratitude to them for their encouragement in this. Thus you will treat your enemies as additional supervisors, and derive benefit from them.

Razi: Kitab al-Muluki

Conceit

Since you are in love with yourself, you are inclined to over-estimate your own strengths, and underestimate your own weaknesses; equally you are inclined to underestimate the strengths of others, and overestimate their weaknesses. If you allow this attitude to grow freely, without any restraint, it becomes conceit.

The irony of conceit is that it leads to the diminution of the strengths which are the original object of conceit. Conceited people never seek to enhance the strengths about which they are conceited. And their conceit makes them deaf to the advice and guidance of others. Thus, if they are conceited about the quality of their work, they think it cannot be improved. And when they cease trying to enhance their strengths, those strengths diminish – and they become inferior to those of their rivals, whom they disparage.

To overcome conceit you should not judge yourself by those who lack the strengths about which you feel conceited. Instead you should judge yourself by those who excel. In this way you will observe things day by day which reduce your estimate of yourself, and increase your admiration of others.

Razi: Kitab al-Muluki

Envy

Envy consists in taking pleasure in the injuries that befall others, and resenting anything that occurs to their advantage – even though they have done you no harm, nor offended you in any way. Envy is worse than miserliness: misers do not want to give anything of their own to others; envious people do not want others to receive anything, regardless of who owns it.

The first method of repelling envy is to recognize it as a form of malice – which is hated both by God and by human society. God hates malice because he wants the best for all, whereas malicious people want the worst. Human society hates malice because it undermines its very purpose – which is to bring benefits to all its members.

A further method for expunging envy is to consider carefully those who are the objects of envy. If you are gripped by envy, you believe that other people are intensely happy, and enjoy great wealth and luxury; and you think that their happiness and wealth are undeserved. But, if you were to inform yourself more fully about their condition and history, you would probably find that you are quite mistaken. Such happiness as they experience, is probably quite transient and shallow; and such wealth as they have accumulated, causes them as much anxiety as it does comfort – and they have worked hard to get it.

You will then reach the conclusion that modest wealth is most conducive to contentment – and to envy those with more, is to display ignorance.

Razi: Kitab al-Muluki

Anger

Anger is put into animals, including humans, as a stimulus to repel those who threaten injury, or to take revenge on those who have already caused injury. When anger goes beyond its proper bounds, it is liable to cause injury to others disproportionate to the injury they may inflict. You should try and recall incidents when anger has had harmful consequences; and you should picture yourself as the person who is gripped by disproportionate anger.

If you keep such incidents constantly in mind, you will be better able to control your anger. Those who do monstrous things in a state of anger, have allowed anger to overwhelm their reason. Thus, when your anger is aroused, you should do nothing immediately; you should give yourself time to reflect and deliberate – and only if you are convinced that your anger is proportionate, should you act upon it.

Moreover, during the time when you are acting angrily, you should not allow arrogance to fuel your fury. Do not think yourself superior to the person who has enraged you – because that will make it even more difficult to control yourself. If your anger is proportionate, and if it is free of arrogance, you will act justly.

Razi: Kitab al-Muluki

Lying

Many people enjoy authority; and in particular, they enjoy imparting information, because that makes them feel superior to the recipients of the information. Inevitably this pleasure tempts them to tell lies. And telling lies inevitably causes anxiety about potential exposure. Indeed, habitual liars can hardly escape exposure, either because through carelessness or faulty memory they contradict themselves, or because their listeners already know the truth. The enjoyment derived from lying can never equal the disgrace and shame of being exposed; and the prospect of exposure leads to constant worry and regret.

It should be said that some kinds of untruth are justified. If, for example, someone tells some lie to the king, in order to prevent an innocent man being executed, this person should be praised, not blamed. But where the lie is intended to make people admire the teller, or to secure some personal advantage, then it cannot be justified.

The most dangerous liars are those who lie for the pleasure of deceiving others, even when they stand to gain little from their lies. They are capable of telling far greater lies when they are likely to profit from them.

Razi: Kitab al-Muluki

Miserliness

Miserliness has a variety of causes. Some people are miserly out of an excessive fear of poverty; some are miserly because they do not want to be vulnerable to changes in fortune; and some are miserly because they relish their wealth for its own sake. Thus miserliness is based on people's natural disposition. We can see this clearly in children: some children freely give away their possessions to their friends, without thought for the future; while other children are naturally cautious, clasping their possessions closely.

Miserliness should only be opposed if it springs out of passion. This diagnosis can be made by asking miserly people why they hold on to their possessions. If they can offer no coherent reason, but are confused and repetitious in their response, then their miserliness comes from passion – and should be condemned. If, on the other hand, they have a clear and valid explanation for their behaviour, showing that they have thought and reflected deeply about it, then their miserliness comes from reason – and should be praised.

It should be said that when someone is near the end of life, miserliness is always irrational, and can never be justified.

Razi: Kitab al-Muluki

Worry and anxiety

Worry and anxiety, although they can be stimulated by reason, can nevertheless be extremely harmful in excess; they can prevent you from achieving the very things that you are anxious to achieve. Thus, if worry and anxiety are acute, you should strive to relax; and this can be done by engaging in amusing and entertaining activities, which divert your mind from the objects of worry and anxiety. If you fail to relax in this way, your body will grow thinner and weaker, until finally you collapse.

People differ greatly in the amount of anxiety and worry they can stand: some can endure a great deal without being adversely affected, while others soon show signs of strain. You should observe yourself closely, so that you understand your own powers of endurance. By this means you will learn to divert yourself before any harm is done.

You should not indulge excessively in amusing and entertaining activities merely for their own sake; once your body and mind are relaxed, you should resume your proper work.

Razi: Kitab al-Muluki

Grief

Grief clouds thought and reason, and harms both the soul and the body; so you should repel it, or reduce it as much as possible. This can be done in two ways: you can strive to prevent grief from occurring; and you can banish grief when it does occur.

Grief arises from the loss of loved ones. Since it is inevitable that loved ones will die, it follows that those who love the greatest number of people, and whose love is most ardent, will suffer the greatest amount of grief. Equally those who love very few people, and whose love is cool, will suffer little grief. Thus you should reduce the number of people with whom you feel emotionally involved; and you should reduce the emotional strength of your involvement with those who remain.

It could be argued that by avoiding emotional involvement with others, you merely put yourself in a permanent state of grief. But in fact the lack of involvement does not cause grief; the only cause of grief is the loss of someone with whom you have been involved. The person with no children feels no grief at this lack; but the parent who loses a child, feels intense grief.

Insofar as you are attached to particular people, you can diminish the eventual grief of their loss by a simple mental exercise. Day by day you should imagine yourself without them; you should picture yourself after their death. Thus when the calamity finally comes, you will respond with great fortitude.

Razi: Kitab al-Muluki

Gluttony

Gluttony causes both physical and mental pain. The physical pain arises from indigestion, which leads on to all manner of serious illness. The mental pain arises from the mockery and contempt of other people.

Gluttony occurs when the animal soul, in which appetite resides, is not controlled by the rational soul, in which reason resides. When truly gluttonous people have eaten so much that they can eat no more, they become sad and tearful at the thought of the food they are missing. When the rational soul controls the animal soul, a person eats in order to live – whereas the gluttonous person lives in order to eat.

Some people see no harm on spiritual grounds in eating as much food as they want. If you are such a person, you should simply weigh the physical pleasure of food against the physical pain of subsequent illnesses. Moreover, once these illnesses become chronic, the pleasure of food fades – and you are left only with pain.

Gluttony feeds on itself. The more that the appetite is indulged, the stronger it becomes – and the harder it is to control. But if the appetite is restrained, then it soon grows weak and feeble, and finally disappears altogether.

Razi: Kitab al-Muluki

Drunkenness

Habitual drunkenness is one of the most powerful stimuli to passion, and one of the greatest threats to reason. It strengthens the appetites, and enhances the tendency towards anger; it weakens the power of thought, and strengthens the urge to act impetuously. In short, under the influence of alcohol the animal soul can easily dominate the rational soul.

Thus you should beware of drink. If you touch it at all, you should do so only when anxiety and worry overwhelm you. At such times you should not drink for the pleasure of it; on the contrary, you should take only those types of wine which you actually dislike.

Indeed, the avoidance of physical pleasure is more important with regard to alcohol than to any other aspect of life. This is because alcohol is addictive. So drunkards reach the stage when they cannot conceive of living without alcohol; and during rare moments of sobriety they feel oppressed by all manner of imaginary cares. Drunkenness is thus more insatiable than gluttony; and so you should be even more determined not to indulge it.

Alcohol should only be used as a medicine to relieve anxiety and fear. Faced with an event which carries great danger, you may drink some wine to calm your nerves, and give you courage.

Razi: Kitab al-Muluki

Fidgeting

In order to give up fidgeting, all that is required is a firm resolve to do so, combined with a sense of disdain for such a
foolish habit. Let resolve and shame act as strings which restrain restless hands and fingers.

The story is told of a king, a man of intelligence, who
had the habit of twiddling his beard. A courtier frequently
pointed out this habit to the king; but the king said that he
was unaware of doing it, and so could not stop it. This continued for a long time. Then one of his ministers said to him:
'You should make a specific decision to overcome this folly,
as any sensible person would.' The king went red with rage;
but never twiddled with his beard again. The minister's
words, by making him angry, had stimulated his rational soul
to take command of his body.

In the same way, whenever you become aware of a stupid habit or mannerism, you should become angry about it.
This will stimulate your rational soul to overcome it. Unless
you can overcome these trivial things, you will never succeed
in taking control of the more serious passions.

Razi: Kitab al-Muluki

Obsession

Many people become obsessed with cleanliness; washing themselves becomes a ritual which they perform with undue frequency. Cleanliness should be a matter of bodily health and comfort, rather than a mental requirement. If something is not dirty in relation to the needs of the body, then we should regard it as clean.

People sometimes justify their obsession with cleanliness on religious grounds; but true religion is not concerned with outward purity. And if we strive to attain absolute cleanliness,

we are doomed to fail. After all, the water used for cleaning may come from a source which has been polluted by animal droppings, or some other form of filth. God does not require his servants to be perfectly clean; indeed, he never requires his servants to do anything that is impossible.

In truth people become obsessed with cleanliness because they are squeamish about dirt. Squeamishness is a passion; and like any other passion, it must be made subject to reason.

Razi: Kitab al-Muluki

Human beings can only survive and flourish on the basis of co-operation and mutual help. Thus it is your duty, in common with all adults, to undertake some job that will benefit others; and to labour to the best of your ability at that task. You should avoid the two extremes of indolence and overwork: indolence makes you a pauper and a burden on others; and overwork makes you a slave without prospect of freedom.

Do not ask your neighbours to give you anything, without offering something in exchange; to do so would put you in the position of someone prevented by paralysis or injury from earning a living. Equally you should not strain yourself to earn more than you need; if you struggle to make yourself rich, you are ultimately the loser, because the pleasure you gain from your riches will be empty. The object of work is to cover your necessary expenditure, and to accumulate a little capital for accidents and emergencies.

The best possible form of acquisition is a skill, enabling you to do things or make things which other people want. Material property and treasure can never be secure; a skill is the most secure of all assets.

Razi: Kitab al-Muluki

Status

Should you try to move from your present status to a higher status? The purpose for doing so would be to enjoy greater comfort and power.

The only way of raising your status is to drive yourself exceedingly hard. Yet if you have reached maturity without ever holding a position of authority, you would surely be foolish to desire authority. In order to fulfill your ambition, you would have to undergo far greater hardship and suffering than the pleasure you would eventually enjoy. Thus, in forming the ambition in the first place you would have deceived yourself, picturing in your mind its fulfilment, without also seeing the hard road that leads there.

Moreover, the pleasure of success is short-lived. For a brief period you would relish your high status; then you would become accustomed to it, so that you felt no different than before. Actually you would feel worse, because you would now have the burdens of high office weighing heavily upon you. And since the passion of pride would not allow you to give up the high office, you would be trapped. In short you would have gained nothing, and lost much.

The same is true of every aspect of our material circumstances. If you are accustomed to a simple diet and rough clothes, then the pleasure of having fine food and soft clothes soon fades. So long as you have enough, be content with what you have.

Razi: Kitab al-Muluki

Virtue

Virtue may be defined quite simply: it consists in treating all people justly. Thus it implies acting graciously to others, showing self-control, compassion, and benevolence. It also implies striving for the well-being of all people – except for those who themselves act unjustly, oppressing others and undermining social order.

Some religious groups have laws and systems which actually require them to act unjustly, deceiving and betraying others. Other religious groups require their members only to act virtuously towards one another, and to deny help to everyone else – even the hungry and the sick. These groups are dangerous to society as a whole, and ultimately do great harm to their own adherents.

Those who act virtuously, earn the respect of those around them. So be assured that if you stay on the path of virtue, never straying from it, you will rarely quarrel with others, and will be safe from malicious attack. If you add kindness and mercy to virtue, you will earn the love of those around you.

Razi: Kitab al-Muluki

Fear of death

If you believe in the afterlife, and if you believe that the afterlife is preferable to the present life, then you should have no
fear of death. But you may feel uncertain on this matter; and
this may cause you to be frightened of death.

Let us assume that at death the soul dies with the body. It
follows that all pain will be expunged; pain is a sensation,
and sensation is a property of living beings. Life contains a
great deal of pain. Since freedom from pain is obviously
preferable to pain itself, death is therefore preferable to life.

You may argue that life also contains a great deal of pleasure; and that if the pleasure of life outweighs the pain, life
is preferable to death. The response to this argument is a
question. Will you feel pain, or be troubled in any way,
merely because you cannot enjoy any pleasure? The answer is
manifestly negative, since pain and trouble only affect the
living, and cannot affect the dead. Since, therefore, lack of
pleasure will cause you no pain, and since freedom from pain
is preferable to pain itself, we may repeat that death is preferable to life. So there are no grounds for fearing death.

Let us now assume that the soul survives the death of the
body. If you live virtuously, and abide by all the laws of religion, then you can also be sure that death will bring not
only freedom from pain; but also great pleasure. So lead your
life as if religion is true – and whether it is true or not, you
have nothing to fear.

Razi: Kitab al-Muluki

The single necessary being

Every being must either have a cause of its existence, or have no cause. If a being has a cause of its existence, we describe it as contingent. If a being has no cause of its existence, we describe it as necessary. It can readily be proven that a necessary being – a being without a cause – must exist.

The cause of the existence of a contingent being must be either another contingent being, or a necessary being. There cannot, however, be an infinite chain of contingent beings. The chain of contingent beings must end in the necessary being – who is the ultimate cause of all other beings. This ultimate necessary being we call God.

There cannot be more than one necessary being. Let us imagine there are two necessary beings. They must be distinct from one another, otherwise they would not be separate. But they share the same essence, that of being necessary. Therefore, their distinctness must lie in accidental features; and these features must be contingent, in that their cause is the essence. It follows that these features are themselves contingent. We conclude that the essence, which both share, is the single necessary being.

Thus there cannot be many gods; there can only be one God. He is all truth and all unity.

Ibn Sina: al-Risalat al-Arshiya

Knowing, living, willing, speaking, hearing

God has no ultimate cause. The ultimate cause of a being is the ultimate reason why that being exists. Yet God does not exist for the sake of any other being; he exists for the sake of his own perfection, which is both the cause and the consequence of his existence.

It follows that his attributes also have no cause. He is pure benevolence. He is utterly self-sufficient, in that he requires nothing, and nothing disturbs him. If he required something, he would have to bring it into being for all eternity. If something disturbed him, he would have to destroy it for all eternity. Yet it is a contradiction to create something or destroy something for all eternity – since creation and destruction exist in time.

God never needs to act out of expediency or obligation, as some have suggested. If he were to act out of expediency or obligation, he would not merit our gratitude and praise; he would be acting as if he were repaying a debt – and this would be contrary to his pure benevolence.

Therefore, we can with certainty say these things about God: he knows; he lives; he wills; he speaks; and he hears.

Ibn Sina: al-Risalat al-Arshiya

God's knowledge

God has knowledge of his own essence. Knowledge means understanding something in itself, without any material barriers. Material things are subject to change. But God, as the one necessary being, cannot be subject to change. Therefore nothing material can attach to God – and so there can be no material barriers to his knowledge of his own essence.

God is knowledge; he is knowing; and he is being known. Since God has knowledge of his own essence, and since God is one, it follows that the essence of God is knowledge. And knowledge means that he knows himself, and is known by himself.

God knows beings other than himself. If God were not able to know beings other than himself, he would be suffering some disability. And this disability would affect also his knowledge of himself. Therefore, since he knows himself, he must know beings other than himself.

God knows all beings that exist. Since God is the only necessary being, all other beings are caused by him. And since God is knowledge, he must know all that he has caused.

Ibn Sina: al-Risalat al-Arshiya

Good and evil in the world order

A man once asked Muhammad's cousin Ali about predestination. Ali answered: 'Predestination is a deep sea; do not embark on it.' The man asked a second time. Ali answered: 'Predestination is a hard road; do not take it.' The man asked a third time. Ali answered: 'Predestination is a steep mountain; do not climb it.'

The mystery of predestination consists of three propositions. The first is that the world is ordered. There is nothing in the entire world which does not have God as its ultimate cause, which is not known by God, and which God does not move according to his will. On the contrary, all things are caused by God, known by God, and moved according to his will.

This world, which we know, is affected by both good and evil forces; and its inhabitants act sometimes righteously and sometimes wickedly. We conclude, therefore, that good and evil are both part of the world order; without both of them the world order would not be complete. If only pure righteousness prevailed in the world, the world would not be the one which we know; it would be another world. God has ordered the world to include evil as well as good.

Ibn Sina: Kitab al-Najat

Pleasure and pain for the soul

The second proposition concerning predestination is that human actions will be rewarded and punished. As the soul attains a higher degree of purity, it experiences a greater intensity of pleasure; this pleasure is what is meant by reward. As the soul becomes more corrupt, it experiences a greater intensity of pain; this is what is meant by punishment. By corruption of the soul we mean remoteness from God; and by purity of the soul we mean closeness to God. Thus reward is quite simply the blessing that comes from being near to God. And punishment is quite simply the curse that comes from being distant.

The third proposition concerning predestination is that the soul is restored to life after death. When the body has died, the human soul returns to its original world.

If we accept the propositions concerning predestination as valid, we need to add that God does not intend evil. The apparent evils which occur in this world, do not conform to God's purpose for the world. The purpose for which the world exists, is the triumph of good; evil is the frustration of that purpose.

Ibn Sina: Kitab al-Najat

Revenge and sanctions

Some theologians believe that sinners will be bound in heavy chains, and cast into a huge fire; and they will be taken out of the fire from time to time, and snakes and scorpions will be let loose against them. This is what happens on earth when people take revenge on their enemies, paying them back for having attacked them. Yet it is clearly unthinkable that God could be vengeful; indeed, God urges people not to take revenge on their enemies.

God has given humanity sacred laws which permit certain actions and forbid other actions. Without these laws people would be uncertain how to obey God; and out of ignorance they would disobey him. It is right that these laws should be upheld by sanctions, since sanctions prevent people from continuing an evil course of action. Thus the combination of reason and fear of punishment maintains order in human society. If the chains of reason and fear of punishment were loosed, people would behave in ways which were quite intolerable, and human society would be undermined. But God knows better than we do, and is wiser than we are.

Ibn Sina: Kitab al-Najat

The need for a law-giver

Human beings differ from some other animals in that they cannot live happily in isolation; in order to satisfy their needs, human beings need to live in groups. This is partly because human beings have complementary abilities. Thus one person is adept at building, another at baking bread, another at making clothes, and so on. For this reason human beings construct villages, towns and cities.

It follows that human beings must behave like citizens. Merely to survive they must learn to co-operate, transacting business in an honest fashion. This means that they must have a code of law and regulation; and this in turn means they must have a law-giver and regulator. Such an individual must be able to speak to people in ways which they understand; such a person must be a human being, as they are.

It is inconceivable that human beings should have to rely on their own opinions in determining the laws governing human society. If that were the case, there would be constant disagreements, with each family advocating laws that favoured its own interests. The survival of humanity, and the personal fulfilment of individual men and women, requires the existence of a law-giver – far more than the face needs eyelashes and eyebrows, or the foot needs a hollow instep.

Ibn Sina: Kitab al-Najat

The prophet as law-giver

It is inconceivable that God should have designed the human body so perfectly, and yet left human beings without laws to govern their conduct. It is absurd to imagine that God and his angels were so adept in their craftsmanship, and so negligent in ordering society. Indeed, since God has designed human beings in such a way that they need to live together, he must surely have given them laws enabling them to do so.

It follows that a prophet must exist; and that this prophet should be a human being. It also follows that this prophet must have some feature or mark which distinguishes him from other human beings, so that they may recognize him as standing apart from them.

This prophet – wherever and whenever he exists – must prescribe laws governing human affairs, in accordance with God's will and authority. Thus God must inspire him, by sending down his Holy Spirit upon him. The fundamental principle on which the prophet's code of law rests, must be that there is one God; that this one God created the world; that he is omnipotent and omniscient; that his commands must be obeyed; and that he will reward those who obey his commands, and punish those who disobey them.

Ibn Sina: Kitab al-Najat

Parables, symbols and images

The prophet should not trouble people's minds with theology; they simply need to know that God is one, that he is true, and that there is no being like him. Any theological notions beyond this are likely to strain people's minds, and confuse them. Indeed, when people begin to engage in theological speculation, they are apt to stray from the road of righteousness, forming opinions which are quite contrary to good order, and which are inconsistent with sound reason. In short, most people are not mentally equipped to understand metaphysics; and those who are equipped, should not make a show of it. For this reason the prophet should teach by means of symbols and parables.

Similarly, when the prophet speaks of the afterlife, he should use images which come within the range of people's experiences, and hence satisfy their souls. He should compare the bliss of paradise with happy experiences on earth; and he should compare the misery of hell with unhappy experiences on earth. As regards the actual condition of paradise and hell, he should merely say that the human eye and ear cannot conceive it.

The prophet may, however, include in his discourse hints and allusions, to stimulate those who are inclined towards philosophy. The task of philosophers is to understand the value of different forms of religious practice, in relation both to this world and the next.

Ibn Sina: Kitab al-Najat

Reminders of God

A prophet is unlikely to appear in every age; the abilities, as well as the degree of perfection, required for prophecy are exceedingly rare. Thus the prophet must devise means of ensuring that people remember his teaching. He will prescribe certain acts which people should repeat at regular intervals. These intervals should be quite short, so that, if the performance of an act is missed, the next performance should be due while the memory is still fresh.

These acts must, of course, be linked with some means of calling God to mind; thus they must involve reciting appropriate words, or doing certain things which stimulate the imagination. People must also believe these acts are means of winning God's favour, and securing some great and generous reward. In short, these acts should be reminders; and reminders must either be positive or negative. An example of a positive reminder is formal prayer; an example of a negative reminder is fasting. Undertaking a fast jolts the mind and the body, and so compels the faster to reflect on the purpose of the fast – which is to win God's favour.

The prophet should mix these basic acts with other events, which strengthen and broaden people's faith in God. A good example is pilgrimage. The prophet should specify certain places in the world as being particularly suitable for worship, declaring that they belong exclusively to God. And he should stipulate certain rituals that must be done at these places, in order to please God.

Ibn Sina: Kitab al-Najat

The three souls

A human being has an animal soul; thus humans are linked with animals. A human being has a physical soul; thus humans are linked with plants. And a human being has a rational soul; thus humans are linked with angels. Each of these souls has a special sphere, and a particular function to perform.

The function of the physical soul is to eat and drink, and thence maintain the organs of the body; and to cleanse the body of all waste. The purpose of this function is to keep the body in order and the limbs in balance, while supplying strength to the muscles. The proper order of the body is shown by bright skin, sturdy limbs, and robust muscles.

The function of the animal soul is movement and imagination. Its sphere is confined to appetite and anger; anger is a form of appetite, since it seeks to repress and overcome. Its purpose is to preserve the body, and to perpetuate the species. The species is perpetuated by means of sexual activity; and this is stimulated by appetite.

The function of the rational soul is to reflect upon things of art, and to meditate on things of beauty; it looks towards the higher world. It is not concerned with eating and drinking, nor with comfort and sexual pleasure; its function involves waiting for the revelation of divine truth, and reflecting on the mysteries which are revealed.

Ibn Sina: Kitab al-Najat

Death and resurrection

The rational soul functions by means of knowledge and perception; and it is concerned with memory, petition and worship.

Through thought people may attain knowledge of God. Through reason, acting upon knowledge, people may apprehend the essence of God. Through intellect, acting upon reason, people may perceive the goodness of God. Thus people may come to understand the spirit of creation; they see all created things as expressions and reflections of God's glory.

Once people see God's glory all around them, they want to have a personal relationship with God; they passionately desire to be intimate with him. Thus they constantly humble themselves before God, and they meditate upon him with great fervour; they pray ceaselessly, and they fast willingly. And as they draw closer to God, their souls enjoy great happiness. This happiness is the reward which they have been promised; and they know that it will survive the death of the body.

Death is the separation of the soul from the body. Resurrection is the union of the soul with God. Paradise is the joy of that union.

Ibn Sina: Kitab al-Najat

Prayer and knowledge

Prayer is that which enables the soul to realize its divinity. Through prayer human beings worship absolute truth, and seek an eternal reward. Prayer is the foundation-stone of religion; and religion is the means by which the soul is purified of all that pollutes it. Prayer is the worship of the first cause of all things, the supreme ruler of all the world, the source of all strength. Prayer is the adoration of the one whose being is necessary.

Prayer depends on knowledge, and is the means by which knowledge is attained. Through prayer we become aware of God's existence; and through prayer he seizes our hearts. Through prayer he cleanses the soul; through prayer the soul attaches itself to him. The nature of prayer, therefore, is to know God in his uniqueness, as a being whose existence is wholly necessary, whose essence is infinitely exalted, and whose attributes are infinitely holy.

We must be sincere in prayer; by this I mean that we should exclude from our minds any notion of other gods whom we may worship.

Ibn Sina: Kitab al-Najat

Outward and inward prayer

Prayer is divided into two parts: the outward part, which is visible and formal, and which relates to the body; and the inward part, which is true prayer, and which relates to the soul.

The outward part is prescribed by the religious law, and is recognized as a fundamental duty of religion. Our lawgiver has imposed it as an obligation on all people. The number of prayers is specified, and the times precisely laid down. It is connected with the body in that it involves particular postures and movements, such as genuflection and prostration, and also involves recitation of particular words.

The inward part of prayer consists in the contemplation of God with a pure heart – a heart cleansed of all desires. The prophet himself was often engaged in the contemplation of God, such that he ignored or shortened formal prayer. Inward prayer is a secret conversation with the Lord. It does not involve audible words; conversation with words occurs with those who are contained within space and time. God, the supreme being, is neither circumscribed by space, nor touched by time; he cannot be found in a particular direction, and his essence cannot change. The secret conversation is thus entirely spiritual; it is a direct encounter between God and the soul, abstracted from all material constraints.

Ibn Sina: Kitab al-Najat

Prayer for different sorts of people

People vary one from another according to the relative influence of the three souls. Those in whom the physical and animal souls prevail, are passionately attached to the body; they love to keep the body in good order; they feed it well, give it ample to drink, and clothe it in fine robes; they want to secure every comfort for the body, and to ward off all dangers to it. Such people need the discipline of the religious law, which compels them to pray at particular times and in particular ways.

Those in whom the rational soul prevails, have control over their bodily passions. They do not need compulsion in order to worship God; the desire to pray is the strongest desire they possess. And since their souls are free from bodily passions, they are ready for prayer at all times. They need only turn towards God, and his love and joy will swiftly flow over them.

Thus those in whom the physical and animal souls prevail, practise only outward prayer; and they experience only a small portion of God's joy. And those in whom the rational soul prevails, practise inward prayer; and they experience the full measure of God's joy.

Ibn Sina: Kitab al-Najat

The notion of the afterlife

The afterlife is a notion received from religious teaching. There is no way of establishing its truth; it must be accepted on the authority of prophets through the ages. These prophets describe what will occur at the resurrection; and their accounts of the pleasures that will be enjoyed by the righteous, and the torments that will be suffered by the wicked, are too well known to require repetition. Indeed the prophet Muhammad has described in detail the state of happiness and misery awaiting us after death.

Some further support for the idea of the afterlife can be gained through reason and insight. Those who pray inwardly, and who contemplate God closely, actually experience for themselves eternal joy. But we must recognize that the reports of such people do not give a complete picture.

Philosophers, and those with a mystical inclination, have a greater desire for spiritual happiness than for any kind of bodily happiness. Indeed, they are largely indifferent to bodily pleasure; and when they experience any bodily pleasure, they consider it insignificant compared with spiritual happiness. They recognize that spiritual happiness consists in proximity to God; and since God is eternal, they identify this spiritual happiness with the eternal joy promised to the righteous after death.

Ibn Sina: Kitab al-Najat

The process of dying

Let us consider the process of dying, when the soul separates itself from the body.

Already, while still within the body, the soul has become aware of that perfection which is its ultimate purpose; and although it has not attained that perfection, it has yearned for it. Indeed, the soul has known that its preoccupation with the body has acted as an impediment on the path to perfection.

Yet as the moment of death approaches, the soul feels sorrow at the prospect of losing the body, which it has cherished for so long. This sorrow adds greatly to the bodily pain of the final illness. Gradually, however, sorrow and pain are overwhelmed by a strange sensation that is like burning and freezing simultaneously. This sensation acts as a drug, so that all suffering ceases.

This sensation also overwhelms any excitement the soul may feel at the prospect of eternal joy. Thus death itself is like a person eating some delicious food, but being unable to taste it. But once the process of dying is complete, the drug wears off; and great pleasure engulfs the soul.

Ibn Sina: Kitab al-Najat

Science and religion

Science is the study of all that exists, with the purpose of understanding the great artisan who created all that exists. The more closely we study his creation, the deeper our knowledge of him will become. Thus religion requires science.

The method of science is to infer deeper truths from what we can observe – to infer the unknown from the known. Its tool is reason. Thus we are obliged to study all that exists by means of intellectual reasoning. It follows that science is the most perfect form of study, since intellectual reasoning is the highest human faculty.

Ibn Rushd: Kitab Fasl al-Maqal

Different paths to faith

People come to religious faith by different paths. Some come to faith through observation: by observing the glories of creation, they come to believe in the creator. Some come to faith through dialectical argument: they listen to and consider all the arguments against religion, until they realize that these arguments are flawed. Some come to faith through rhetorical argument: they listen to and consider all the arguments in favour of religion, until they are convinced by them.

There are some people who never come to religious faith. The reason is that they do not want the obligations which religious faith imposes; so they are deliberately stubborn and obtuse.

Ibn Rushd: Kitab Fasl al-Maqal

Allegorical interpretation

When science reaches a conclusion about some aspect of creation, that conclusion is either not mentioned or mentioned in the Quran. If it is not mentioned, there can be no contradiction. If it is mentioned, the apparent meaning of the words either accords with science or conflicts with it. If the apparent meaning accords with it, there can be no further argument. If the apparent meaning conflicts with it, then we must conclude that this passage of the Quran should be interpreted allegorically.

The method of allegorical interpretation is to take the literal meaning of a passage, and then interpret it as a metaphor for some profound truth. Allegorical interpretation is traditional in Arabic. There are many instances where an object is called by the name of something resembling it, or of something associated with it in some way. Thus if ordinary people may speak allegorically, religious thinkers may interpret the Quran allegorically.

Ibn Rushd: Kitab Fasl al-Maqal

Three classes of being

Those who study science, agree that there are three classes of being, two extremes and one intermediate class.

One extreme class consists of those beings which are brought into existence by that which is other than themselves; and they are made from something, and come into existence at some point in time. This class includes water, air, earth, animals, plants, and so on.

The other extreme class consists of that being which is not brought into existence by any other being; this being is not made from anything, and exists beyond time; it is sometimes described as pre-eternal. This being is referred to as God.

The intermediate class consists of that which is not made from anything, and exists beyond time; and yet which is brought into being by that which is other than itself. This intermediate class is the universe as a whole. The universe always has existed and always will exist; it is thus beyond time. It is not made from anything apart from itself. And God created it.

Ibn Rushd: Kitab Fasl al-Maqal

True and practical science

The purpose of the Quran is to teach true science and right conduct. True science consists of knowledge of God, and that which he has created; and it consists of knowledge of how to attain happiness and avoid misery, both in this life and the next. Right conduct consists of acting in ways that bring happiness and avoid misery; this may be called practical science.

Practical science has two parts. The first part concerns outward bodily acts – how people should behave in different situations. The second part concerns inward spiritual acts – such as gratitude, patience, and other attitudes of the soul which the Quran encourages.

Ibn Rushd: Kitab Fasl al-Maqal

Symbolizing life after death

All religions agree on the belief that souls experience states of happiness or misery after death. But they differ on the way they symbolize these states, and explain them to their adherents.

In our religion the states of happiness and misery after death are symbolized in very materialistic ways. This is perfect for the majority of men and women, because it provides the greatest incentive for them to behave in a righteous manner in this life – which is the primary purpose of popular religion. Spiritual symbolism is more accurate, but seems to provide less stimulus to good behaviour than material symbolism, because it is less vivid.

Ibn Rushd: Kitab al-Kashf

BIBLIOGRAPHY

There are a number of translations of the works represented in the present volume. These are the most accessible.

Attar, Farid al-Din, *Muslim Saints and Mystics*, tr. A. J. Arberry (London and New York, Viking Penguin, 1990).

Ghazali, *The Faith and Practice of Al-Ghazali*, tr. W. Montgomery Watt (Oxford, Oneworld Publications, 1994).

Ibn Arabi, *Bezels of Wisdom*, tr. R. W. J. Austin (New York, Paulist Press, 1980).

Ibn Ishaq, *The Life of Muhammad*, tr. A. Guillaume (London, Oxford University Press, 1955).

Ibn Rushd, *Averroes*, tr. George F. Hourani (London, Luzac & Co., 1961).

Ibn Sina, *Avicenna on Theology*, tr. A. J. Arberry (London, John Murray, 1951).

Junayd, *The Life, Personality and Writings of al-Junayd*, tr. Ali Hassan Abdel-Kader (London, Luzac & Co., 1962).

Nizam al-Din, *Morals for the Heart*, tr. Bruce B. Lawrence (New York, Paulist Press, 1992).

Quran, *The Koran*, tr. N. J. Dawood (London, Penguin Books, 1956).

Razi, *The Spiritual Physick of Rhazes*, tr. A. J. Arberry (London, John Murray, 1950).

Rumi, *The Sufi Path of Love*, tr. William C. Chittick (Albany, State University of New York Press, 1983).

Sadi, *The Rose Garden*, tr. Edward B. Eastwick (London, The Octagon Press, 1979).

Sells, M. A., *Early Islamic Mysticism*, (New York, Paulist Press, 1996).

The illustrations in this volume have been taken from Gayet A., *L'Art Arabe* (Paris, Librairies-Imprimeries-Reunies, 1893).

INDEX OF WRITERS